THE *Uncommon* COOK BOOK

THE UNCOMMON COOK BOOK

BY RUTH MELLINKOFF
ILLUSTRATED BY THE AUTHOR

THE WARD RITCHIE PRESS
LOS ANGELES

To
David and Daniel

Contents

Introduction

NOT ANOTHER COOKBOOK! Why so many cookbooks? Happily for all of us an endless procession of cookbooks accompanies an endless procession of wonderful concoctions that stream forth from an endless multitude of aromatic kitchens. This is the fascination and the glory of cookery. The infinite possibilities of combining an onion with a mushroom, or preparing an apple in a new way, add to the challenge of creating new elements in your cuisine. In other words—spice is the variety of life. Just when you think you know everything there is to know about a potato, you read that somewhere a potato dances to a different tune, you hear how they do it in Morocco or Timbuktu.

Down with common cookery! Each household, yes, even each person, should evolve an individual repertoire of magnificence. It can be simple; it can be complicated; it should be special and personal; it should be the result of loving care, whether of minutes of preparation or hours. The pleasure of eating good food can only be matched by the pleasure of preparing it. The pleasure of preparing and eating good food can only be enhanced by the pleasure of sharing it with friends. The pleasure of preparing and eating and sharing is vastly increased if one takes a moment to develop the skills of the whole process, so that at the end you sit back comfortably with guests to enjoy it. The cuisine of our household has evolved from just such motives. I love to cook, but I also want to enjoy the delicious moments of good conversation at table. Because it is extremely difficult to be simultaneously chef and hostess, I have tried to evolve better ways of magically preparing all kinds of dishes ahead of time.

The Uncommon Cookbook is therefore for uncommon cooks, those who want to serve something different, delicious, and devastatingly marvelous, but who want their guests to believe that it all came forth with the aid of Aladdin's lamp. This cookbook does not contain a discourse on how to become a so-called "gourmet"; rather, it is an account of one woman's way with culinary operations. It stresses methods which can ease the preparation of great dishes for Olympian occasions as well as for informal moments with family and friends.

To further this goal, I have emphasized clarity in the instructions, with details of beforehand procedure added at the end of each recipe: 1) to prepare ahead of time, and 2) to freeze (deleting this latter category when freezing is not recommended). The recipes themselves are either my variations of traditional dishes, or they are innovations which evolved from planned experiment, or out of necessity and accident. I have also included some of the splendid specialties my friends have shared with me; these are appropriately noted in the book.

To cook well, to eat beautifully, requires that you really care. And you should care, for so many hours are spent at the table. They should be filled with things beautiful and delicious to look at, to touch, to hear, to inhale, and to taste.

Cooking is most delightful when it is surrounded with an aura of great expectations. This cookbook is an account of the culinary experiments which have lived up to those expectations.

Appetizers

Appetizers

NEPTUNE'S TINIEST BAY SHRIMP PATÉ [makes 5 or 6 small crocks]

1 pound tiny bay shrimp, cooked
½ pound (1 cup) butter
1 clove garlic, mashed

¼ teaspoon thyme
½ to ¾ teaspoon salt
pinch of pepper

Melt ¾ cup of the butter, add the garlic, then add *half* of the shrimp. Heat thoroughly but do not cook. Add salt, pepper and thyme. Purée in the blender.

Heat remaining shrimp in the remaining ¼ cup of butter and combine with the puréed mixture. Stir gently until somewhat cooled. Pack in crocks or little dishes, cover with plastic wrap and then with foil.

To prepare ahead of time: This can be made a day ahead and kept refrigerated.

To freeze: This freezes beautifully. Bring paté to room temperature before serving for best possible texture and taste.

HEIMDALL'S SMOKED HAM PATÉ [makes 2 small loaves]

1¼ pounds baked smoked ham
1 onion, medium size
½ cup milk
2 eggs

a little pepper
salt if needed
1 tablespoon dry mustard
1 teaspoon prepared mustard
¼ cup ketchup

Grind ham and onion twice, then combine with remaining ingredients and mix thoroughly. Pack into two small, greased loaf pans (3x5x2). (I use the little foil ones.) Bake at 325° for about 1 hour. Cool, then chill. Serve cold.

To prepare ahead of time: This can be baked a day or two ahead of time. Keep them covered and refrigerated.

To freeze: This freezes too. Defrost, if possible, overnight in the refrigerator.

Note: While this is a delicious appetizer, it is equally effective served as the filling for sandwiches with some lettuce and Dijon mustard added.

BRANDIED AND HERBED VERY SPECIAL CHICKEN LIVER PATÉ [makes about 4 or 5 small crocks]

1 pound fresh chicken livers	½ teaspoon pepper
2 medium-size onions, chopped	1 bay leaf
	⅛ teaspoon thyme
½ cup butter	⅛ teaspoon oregano
1 clove garlic, mashed	⅛ teaspoon tarragon
¼ cup butter	3 tablespoons brandy or
1 tablespoon flour	Cognac
1 teaspoon salt	

Sauté the onions in the ½ cup butter with the garlic until tender, then remove from skillet.

Sauté livers in the additional ¼ cup butter until almost tender. Sprinkle with flour and add the salt, pepper, bay leaf, thyme, oregano, and tarragon. Cover and simmer over low heat for about 1 or 2 minutes or until livers are cooked. Remove bay leaf. Combine with the onions.

Add Cognac or brandy to the mixture and purée in the blender, doing about ¼ of the mixture at a time. If you don't have a blender, put mixture through a meat grinder about three times.

To prepare ahead of time: This can be made a day or two ahead and kept refrigerated. It should be packed in crocks or dishes or foil pans and covered with plastic wrap and then with foil.

To freeze: This freezes magnificently. It must be wrapped very tightly, as for refrigerating.

Note: Don't hesitate to use this for sandwiches—especially good on very thin slices of rye bread. I usually make a double recipe of this paté since it is so popular in our household and because it freezes so well.

A ROCOCO CORAL AND WHITE PATÉ OF THE SEA

[serves 10 to 12]

1 pound fresh salmon about ¾ inch thick (weight after trimming)
½ cup dry Sherry
1 bay leaf
½ teaspoon salt
1 ¼ pounds halibut fillets
¾ cup milk
2 egg yolks

3 medium slices white bread, crusts removed (1 ½ ounces of bread after crusts have been removed)
2 teaspoons salt
¼ teaspoon pepper
¼ cup melted butter
additional salt and pepper

Cut salmon into ¾ inch cubes and marinate in the Sherry, bay leaf and the ½ teaspoon of salt for about half an hour.

Drain off Sherry and use it with the milk to purée the halibut in a blender (do a little at a time). Add bread to blender a slice at a time and blend into crumbs. Combine bread crumbs with the halibut and add the egg yolks, 2 teaspoons salt, pepper, and melted butter. Put through a food mill if possible.

Place half of the salmon cubes in the bottom of a well buttered 2 quart casserole. Add half of the halibut as a layer on top of the salmon. (Salt and pepper the salmon cubes lightly.) Add the remaining salmon cubes and then the rest of the halibut mousse.

Cover tightly and bake at 350° for 45 minutes to an hour. Remove from oven and weight the paté using a plate and something heavy to hold it down. When cooled, place in the refrigerator overnight to chill. Invert the paté before serving and garnish with watercress or parsley. Serve with crackers or buttered rye.

To prepare ahead of time: As mentioned, this really should be chilled overnight. It can be done as much as two days ahead and kept tightly covered and refrigerated.

To freeze: This does freeze. It is not quite as perfect in texture after freezing, but really quite good. Perhaps it is best frozen as a leftover for the family to eat at some later time, rather than a beforehand procedure for a party.

Note: This paté makes an excellent first course for dinner served at the table with an icy cold dilled sour cream or Green Goddess dressing.

KATHARINA MARMOR'S EXOTIC CURRIED APPETIZER [serves 10 to 15]

1 cup finely chopped apples	a little lemon juice
⅓ cup finely chopped peanuts	¼ cup mayonnaise
⅓ cup finely chopped raisins	1 teaspoon curry powder
pinch of salt	small bread rounds

Mix apples, peanuts, raisins, salt, lemon juice, mayonnaise, curry powder together. (Use just enough lemon juice to keep apples from turning brown.)

Toast bread rounds slightly on both sides. Place one heaping teaspoon of mixture on each round. Broil until golden brown and hot.

To prepare ahead of time: The fruit-nut mixture can be prepared in the morning, covered and refrigerated. The bread can also be toasted in the morning. Then, shortly before serving, place mixture on the toast and proceed as in the above recipe.

JUNE MELLINKOFF'S ARTICHOKE AND CAVIAR APPETIZER

cooked artichoke bottoms	black caviar
Well seasoned chopped egg mixture (hard-cooked eggs, salt, mayonnaise, etc.)	

Fill cooked artichoke bottoms with the seasoned chopped egg mixture. Top each one with some of the black caviar. Serve whole, or each one cut in half, with colorful hors d'oeuvres picks.

HOT BUT NOT HASTY HAM AND
CHEESE CANAPÉS
[makes about 4 dozen]

Sliced bread, cut in crescents, ovals, rounds, or rectangles, then buttered and toasted in the oven

Ham mixture (recipe follows)
Cheese mixture (recipe follows)

Ham mixture:

½ small onion, finely chopped
2 tablespoons butter
1 tablespoon flour
3 cups ground cooked ham

2 tablespoons prepared mustard
⅓ cup sour cream
½ cup milk

Sauté onion in the butter until lightly browned and tender. Stir in the flour, then the ham and mustard. Add sour cream and milk and stir constantly until mixture begins to boil. Remove from heat and taste for seasoning, adding salt and pepper if necessary. Chill.

Cheese mixture:

1 ½ cups grated Cheddar (at room temperature)
2 tablespoons butter (at room temperature)
¼ cup cream or milk
¼ teaspoon salt

½ teaspoon dry mustard
¼ teaspoon paprika
1 teaspoon Worcestershire sauce
1 egg

Cream the cheese and butter together using an electric beater. Add cream, salt, dry mustard, paprika, and Worcestershire and beat again. Add egg and beat until fluffy. Set aside until ready to use.

To assemble: Spread ham mixture on buttered toasts, then top with a teaspoon of the cheese mixture. Bake at 450° for 8 to 10 minutes.

To prepare ahead of time: These can be prepared in the morning. Cover them with plastic wrap and keep refrigerated until ready to bake.

To freeze: These can be successfully frozen. Place canapés on large cookie sheets and freeze. Then remove them and package in layers or in plastic bags. It is not necessary to defrost these ahead of time. They can go directly from freezer into the hot oven. Allow more time for them to bake, and finish them by browning them under a broiler.

HOT AND THRIFTY PARMESAN CHEESE TOASTS

day old French bread   grated Parmesan cheese
softened butter

Slice French bread, butter the slices, then sprinkle them with Parmesan cheese. Cut slices in halves or quarters and place them on large cookie sheets. Bake for 10 to 20 minutes in the top third of a 450° oven until crisp and brown. Serve hot or at room temperature.

To prepare ahead of time: These can be made in the morning and baked just before serving. These can be made and baked in the morning and reheated in the evening. These can be made and baked the day before and reheated the following evening—a bit crunchier and quite delicious this way. A marvelous way to use not-so-fresh bread —and just as good made with rye bread, etc.

Note: When you have tired of reheating the Parmesan cheese toasts try dicing them and adding them to a tossed green salad.

HOT TOASTED TORTILLAS WITH JACK CHEESE

corn tortillas   Jack cheese
softened butter

Cut tortillas into smaller circles. (If this seems to be just too much waste, try using the tortillas in halves or quarters.) Butter the tortilla and put a small finger of Jack cheese on the buttered side. Roll up and fasten with toothpicks.

Barbecue directly on the grill of a barbecue, turning often until cheese melts. (Remove toothpicks after tortillas begin to heat.)

Or bake in a very hot oven until cheese melts.

To prepare ahead of time: Tortillas can be filled, rolled and toothpicked, and kept refrigerated before barbecuing or baking—at least as early as the morning of the party. I haven't tried doing them any further ahead than that for fear that the tortillas would dry out too much.

8

HOT OR COLD CURRIED CHEESE WITH CHOPPED RIPE OLIVES

2 cups grated, aged Cheddar cheese (¾ pound)
1 cup chopped ripe olives (about 2 small 4 oz. cans, drained)
½ cup mayonnaise
1 teaspoon curry powder
½ cup finely chopped green onions
salt to taste

Grate cheese and place in a bowl. Let it reach room temperature and then beat like crazy with an electric beater. Gradually beat in the mayonnaise until mixture is light and fluffy. Beat in the curry powder. Fold in the drained olives and the chopped green onions. Taste, then add salt if needed.

To serve hot: Spread on toasted bread: rounds, squares, or as a luncheon sandwich, on slices of bread. Place under broiler and watch—when browned and bubbly, serve.

This can also be served at room temperature or chilled. Serve with crisp, unsalted crackers.

To prepare ahead of time: This mixture will keep about 3 to 4 weeks in the refrigerator.

To freeze: It should keep at least 6 months in the freezer.

RED RADISH AND ROQUEFORT RAGE   [serves 6 to 8]

1 3-ounce package cream cheese
¼ pound butter
¼ pound Roquefort cheese
⅔ cup finely chopped red radishes
salt to taste

Whip cream cheese, butter and Roquefort together. Stir in most of the chopped radishes, but save a little for decoration. Stir in salt to taste. Place in a small bowl and top with the reserved chopped radishes. Serve with crackers or croutons.

To prepare ahead of time: This can be prepared one or two days ahead of time and kept refrigerated.

To freeze: If you want to freeze this, eliminate the radishes—add them after you have defrosted the cheese mixture.

PIMENTO-GREEN PEPPER-CHEDDAR CHEESE SPREAD

[makes about 2 cups]

1 tablespoon butter
1 clove garlic, mashed
2 teaspoons flour
½ teaspoon salt
½ teaspoon paprika
1 teaspoon dry mustard
1 cup milk

½ cup chopped pimento
½ green pepper, finely
    chopped
dash cayenne
1 pound Cheddar cheese,
    grated
2 egg yolks

Melt butter, add garlic and sauté gently for one minute. Stir in flour, paprika, salt and dry mustard. Add milk gradually and stir constantly until mixture comes to a boil. Add pimento, green pepper, and cayenne. Now, add cheese and stir over low heat until cheese has melted.

Beat egg yolks slightly. Remove cheese mixture from heat and stir in the egg yolks. Cool and chill until an hour or so before using. Bring spread to room temperature before serving.

To prepare ahead of time: This, of course, can be prepared ahead of time—at least several weeks or more. Keep tightly covered in the refrigerator when not in use.

To freeze: This can be kept frozen for several months.

MEXICAN CHEESE BALLS ROLLED IN PLENTY OF PIÑONS

[enough for 25]

3 cups cream cheese
    (3 8-ounce packages)
3 tablespoons chopped
    green pepper
2 tablespoons chopped
    pimento

2 tablespoons chopped
    onion
1 teaspoon salt
cream to moisten
piñon nuts

Cream the cheese. Add green pepper, pimento, onion, salt, and enough cream to soften only slightly. Form into bite-sized balls and roll each in piñon nuts. Set aside to chill. Arrange cheese balls on a decorative platter and garnish with fresh mint leaves, or parsley. Serve cold.

To prepare ahead of time: You can prepare these the day before or the morning of the party. Keep them covered in the refrigerator until time to serve.

To freeze: You can freeze these but I prefer rolling them in the piñon nuts after they have been defrosted.

WALNUT AND CREAM CHEESE SPREAD FOR WEARY WOMEN [serves 10 to 12]

3 3-ounce packages cream cheese
¾ cup walnuts, finely chopped
1 green pepper, finely chopped

1 teaspoon Worcestershire sauce
½ teaspoon onion powder
salt and pepper to taste

Whip cream cheese until light and fluffy, adding a little cream if necessary to moisten slightly. Add remaining ingredients and chill.

Serve cold with water crackers or any other kind of unsalted cracker.

To prepare ahead of time: This can be prepared several days ahead of time and kept refrigerated until ready to serve.

To freeze: Yes, this does freeze. Defrost overnight in the refrigerator if possible.

EASIEST AND PRETTIEST CAVIAR AND CREAM CHEESE HORS D'OEUVRE [enough for 8 to 10]

1 8-ounce package cream cheese
a little cream
salt to taste

2 teaspoons grated onion
1 2- or 3-ounce jar of black caviar

Whip cream cheese together with salt to taste, grated onion, and a little cream.

Place mixture in a pastry bag (or use a spoon to shape) and form a "nest" on a serving dish. Fill the "nest" with the caviar. Serve with crackers or rye melba toast.

To prepare ahead of time: The cheese mixture can be prepared a day or two ahead, or in the morning. Form the "nest" and fill with caviar several hours ahead of serving time.

LILLIE MAE HENDRICK'S BEST OF ALL POSSIBLE CRABMEAT DIPS [serves 10 to 16]

2 cans (7-ounce size) crabmeat
1 8-ounce package cream cheese
1 cup mayonnaise
½ cup sour cream
few drops soy sauce
1 tablespoon Worcestershire sauce
¼ teaspoon Tabasco sauce
dash of cayenne pepper
salt to taste
2 large cloves of garlic, mashed

Soften the cream cheese and mix until smooth with the mayonnaise, sour cream, Worcestershire, soy sauce, Tabasco, cayenne, salt, and garlic. Stir in the crabmeat. Taste for seasoning. This should be made at least several hours ahead.

Serve with potato chips, tostadas, toasts, crackers, or whatever you prefer.

To prepare ahead of time: I really prefer this made the day before so that all of the seasonings, particularly the garlic, have a chance to mellow.

A NON-WORRISOME WATERCRESS DIP WITH CUCUMBER STRIPS [serves 10 to 12]

¾ cup watercress (pack it down to measure)
1 cup mayonnaise
2 tablespoons chopped parsley
1 clove garlic, mashed
¼ teaspoon salt, or to taste
¼ cup water
3 cucumbers, cut into strips

Combine all ingredients except the cucumbers and place in a blender. Blend until smooth. Pour into a serving bowl and surround with the cucumber strips which are used by your guests for dipping instead of crackers.

To prepare ahead of time: This can be prepared the day before using.

CAPONATA—AN UNAUTHENTIC BUT PLEASANT VERSION [serves 10 to 16]

1 medium size eggplant
   (do not peel)
2 cups thinly sliced celery
½ cup olive oil (don't
   substitute)
2 tablespoons additional
   olive oil
1 large onion, finely
   chopped
1 green or red pepper, finely
   chopped

⅓ cup vinegar
2 teaspoons sugar
salt and pepper to taste
1 clove garlic, mashed
3 tablespoons tomato paste
   mixed with ½ cup water
1 tablespoon chopped parsley
½ cup sliced pimento-
   stuffed olives
⅓ cup capers

Dice eggplant into cubes about ½ inch thick. Sauté them in the ½ cup olive oil for 10 to 15 minutes. Stir frequently. Remove eggplant, add remaining 2 tablespoons olive oil, and sauté the chopped onion for several minutes. Add the sliced celery and the chopped green or red pepper, and sauté for 4 or 5 minutes. Add remaining ingredients, stir thoroughly, cover, and simmer over very low heat for about ten minutes. Season to taste with salt and pepper. Serve chilled with sesame crackers or thinly sliced French bread.

To prepare ahead of time: This can be prepared several days ahead of time. Keep refrigerated until ready to use.

To freeze: This can be frozen. Stir gently, but thoroughly, before using.

PINEAPPLE OR MELON WITH A SEAFOOD SURPRISE

[enough for 4 or 5 as a first course]

1 large pineapple
1 large apple, peeled and
    diced (about 1 cup)
¾ cup diced cooked lobster
    (about a 7 or 8 ounce
    cooked lobster tail)

¾ cup diced cooked shrimp
    (about ¼ pound cooked
    shrimp)

Cut off the top of the pineapple, but save it. Remove the insides and dice the pineapple, carefully retaining the shell of the pineapple.

Place 1 cup of the diced pineapple in a bowl. Add the remaining ingredients and toss lightly. (The remaining pineapple can be saved and used for some other meal.) Prepare the following sauce:

Sauce:

¼ cup mayonnaise
¼ cup ketchup
1 tablespoon Port
1 tablespoon Curaçao
1 tablespoon chopped parsley

1 teaspoon chopped fresh
    tarragon (or ¼ tea-
    spoon dried)
pinch of salt

Combine ingredients.

To assemble and serve: Pour as much of the sauce as you like over the fruit-seafood mixture. Stuff pineapple with this just before serving, top with the sliced-off pineapple top and bring to the table. Remove to serve the "surprise" to delighted guests.

To prepare ahead of time: The seafood can be cooked the day before. The fruit can be prepared and mixed with the seafood in the morning. But combine fruit and seafood and sauce not more than 3 or 4 hours before serving, and stuff pineapple shortly before bringing it to the table.

Note: The pineapple can be replaced by 1 large, or 2 medium-size melons (cantaloupe, crenshaw, etc.). Cut off a slice from the top of the melon (or melons) and proceed as directed above, substituting melon for pineapple. Replace top to serve as a surprise.

GIANT PRUNES WITH MACADAMIAS AND BACON

very large, if possible
"giant" size, prunes
macadamia nuts, in halves
or pieces

slices of bacon, cut
in halves

Cook prunes a day or so ahead of time. Pit prunes and stuff cavities with macadamia nuts. Wrap each prune with a half a slice of bacon and fasten with a toothpick. Broil slowly until crisp and serve hot.

To prepare ahead of time: The prunes, of course, can be cooked several days ahead of time. This appetizer can be fully prepared in the morning. Don't overcook. After broiling, set aside at room temperature lightly covered. Reheat in a very hot oven shortly before serving.

ARTICHOKES STUFFED WITH CRABMEAT   [serves 10 as a first course]

10 fresh artichokes
juice of 1 lemon
1 can crabmeat (about 1 cup)
3 green onions, finely chopped
½ teaspoon dry mustard
½ green pepper, finely
   chopped

salt and pepper to taste
mayonnaise to moisten
20 pitted ripe olives
20 tiny raw carrot sticks
watercress

Cut about 1½ inches off the top of each artichoke. Cook artichokes in salted water to which lemon juice has been added until tender. Remove, drain, and cool. Carefully remove the choke and undesirable leaves of the center of each artichoke.

Combine crabmeat with the green onions, dry mustard, green pepper, and mayonnaise. Season to taste with salt and pepper. Chill.

Put a tiny carrot stick through the center of each of the pitted ripe olives.

Put some of the crabmeat mixture in the hollowed out center of each artichoke. Place each stuffed artichoke on an individual salad plate and garnish each with watercress and two of the carrot-stuffed olives. Serve very cold.

To prepare ahead of time: The artichokes can be cooked the day before. The crabmeat mixture can be combined the day before. Don't stuff the artichokes until the afternoon of the party, then cover with plastic wrap and keep cold until ready to serve.

EASY, CHEESY STUFFED MUSHROOMS

36 large mushrooms	1 cup grated Cheddar cheese
1 onion, finely chopped	additional grated Cheddar
¼ cup butter	cheese
salt and pepper	additional butter

Clean mushrooms and separate caps and stems. Chop or grind the stems.

Sauté the chopped onion in the butter until tender but not browned. Add chopped mushroom stems and sauté for about 2 minutes, adding more butter if necessary. Season with salt and pepper. Stir in the 1 cup of grated cheese and remove from the heat.

Sauté caps briefly in some additional butter. Stuff caps with the mixture previously prepared and top them with additional grated cheese. Bake at 400° until cheese begins to melt and brown. If necessary, place under broiler briefly.

To prepare ahead of time: These can be stuffed and refrigerated the day before using. If they are cold it may be neecssary to bake them a little longer.

MUSHROOMS STUFFED WITH CRABMEAT

18 to 24 large mushrooms
¼ onion, finely chopped
(or 1 tablespoon de-
hydrated chopped onion
soaked in 2 tablespoons
water)
½ green pepper, finely
chopped
⅛ teaspoon garlic powder
3 tablespoons butter
2 tablespoons flour
1½ teaspoons dry mustard

¾ cup cream or milk
1 teaspoon Worcestershire
sauce
salt and pepper to taste
1 small can crabmeat
(about 7 or 8 ounces)
2 egg yolks
1 teaspoon chopped parsley
1 green onion, finely
chopped
grated Parmesan cheese

Clean and dry the mushrooms. Remove stems and put them through a meat grinder or chop them finely. Sauté these stems in the 3 tablespoons of butter, together with the onion, for several minutes. Add the green pepper and cook a little longer. Sprinkle over the flour and dry mustard and stir. Take off heat and stir in the cream or milk. Return to heat and cook, stirring constantly, until mixture comes to a boil. Simmer for a few minutes. Add seasonings and Worcestershire sauce. Stir in crabmeat and taste for seasoning. Beat egg yolks and stir a little of the hot mixture into them, then return to saucepan and stir over very low heat for about 1 minute. Remove from heat and stir in the parsley and chopped green onion. Cool, then chill.

Sauté mushroom caps quickly in some butter. Season lightly, then stuff with the crabmeat mixture. Sprinkle with Parmesan cheese and place in a 425° oven until hot and puffy.

To prepare ahead of time: The stuffing is better made ahead of time and chilled before filling the caps. They can be stuffed the day before and kept refrigerated until shortly before serving time. Just heat a little longer, and perhaps run under the broiler before serving.

To freeze: These freeze satisfactorily, but not magnificently. I suggest freezing them as leftovers, not as a beforehand procedure.

Note: These make a perfectly elegant luncheon or first course placed on hot buttered croustades, then heated and served under glass bells. Glass bells can be purchased inexpensively at any restaurant supply house.

GRAPE LEAVES PATIENTLY STUFFED WITH RICE, DILL, AND PIÑONS [makes 36 to 48]

Will need: 36 to 48 pickled grape leaves

Stuffing:

3 onions, finely chopped
½ cup olive oil
1 cup uncooked rice
½ cup fresh chopped dill
8 green onions, finely
    chopped
juice of one lemon

6 tablespoons piñons
1 ½ to 2 teaspoons salt
½ teaspoon black pepper
½ cup finely chopped
    parsley
½ cup water

To cook them in:

1 cup water
½ cup olive oil

juice of 1 lemon
½ cup water

Sauté chopped onions in the ½ cup olive oil until tender and golden. Add rice and mix over low heat, cooking for about 5 or 10 minutes. Add dill, green onions, juice of lemon, piñons, salt, pepper, and the ½ cup water. Cover and simmer for 10 minutes, then stir in the chopped parsley and remove from heat. Cool.

To assemble: Rinse the grape leaves thoroughly in warm water, drain, and cut off the stems. Place grape leaves on a board or table with the smooth side down. Place about a teaspoon of the stuffing in the center of each leaf. Fold the sides of the leaves into the center, then roll them up tightly, starting from the stem end. Arrange the rolls in a very large skillet and pour over the 1 cup of water, ½ cup olive oil and the juice of the other lemon. Put a plate on top of them to weight them down. Bring to a boil over moderately high heat and cook rapidly for 5 minutes. Add the additional ½ cup water, reduce heat and simmer for about 25 minutes uncovered. Remove plate, cover skillet and simmer gently an additional 20 minutes. Chill and serve cold or at room temperature.

To prepare ahead of time: These can be made easily as much as 4 or 5 days ahead of time and kept closely covered in the refrigerator.

EGGS STUFFED WITH LIVER PATÉ

12 hard cooked eggs	⅓ cup liver paté
2 tablespoons softened butter	(preferably homemade chicken liver paté)
2 tablespoons mayonnaise	salt and pepper to taste
	chopped fresh parsley

Cut peeled eggs lengthwise. Mash the yolks or put them through a food mill. Whip the mashed yolks with the butter, mayonnaise, liver paté, and salt and pepper. If possible use an electric beater for this job.

Fill the egg whites with the mixture, using a pastry bag if possible. Top with a bit of the parsley. Chill.

To prepare ahead of time: The stuffing can be prepared a day ahead, but don't fill them until the following morning. Then fill them and cover them tightly with plastic wrap and keep chilled until ready to serve.

CUCUMBER AND ONION QUICK CANAPÉS, MERYL MATHES' WAY

melba toast rounds	grated onion
softened butter	mayonnaise
very thinly sliced cucumbers	salt

Spread melba rounds with butter. On each round place the following: slice of cucumber, dab of grated onion, ½ teaspoon of mayonnaise. Sprinkle lightly with salt. Broil until lightly browned, then serve at once.

To prepare ahead of time: These can be prepared in the morning, refrigerated, and then broiled just before serving. The butter will prevent the toast rounds from getting soggy.

Note: I use the commercially packaged melba toast rounds, however there is nothing to stop one from making one's own.

PROPERLY PUFFED UP CREAM CHEESE PASTRY TURNOVERS WITH A MUSHROOM FILLING

Cream cheese pastry:

3 3-ounce packages cream cheese	½ cup butter
	1 ½ cups sifted flour

Mix cream cheese and butter together. Add the flour and work it with your hands or with a pastry blender. Form into a flattened ball and wrap in waxed paper. Chill for at least an hour.

Mushroom filling:

¼ pound fresh mushrooms, finely chopped	¼ teaspoon salt
2 tablespoons butter	⅛ teaspoon pepper
½ onion, finely chopped	1 ½ tablespoons flour
⅛ teaspoon thyme	½ cup sour cream

Melt butter and sauté the chopped onion until just lightly browned. Add the chopped mushrooms, thyme, salt, pepper, and cook for about 5 minutes, stirring frequently. Sprinkle with the flour and stir. Reduce heat and stir in the sour cream. Cook, stirring constantly, until thickened. Cool, then chill.

To assemble: Roll out pastry to about ⅛ inch thickness. Cut into 3-inch rounds. Place about ½ teaspoon of filling on each round, wet the edges, fold over, and press edges with a fork. Prick the top crusts with a fork. Chill, then bake in a 450° oven for about 15 minutes, longer if they have been frozen.

To prepare ahead of time: The filling and the pastry can be prepared several days ahead of time. The turnovers can be prepared ahead of time as well and kept covered in the refrigerator until ready to bake.

To freeze: I freeze these unbaked, packed in a box or tin with layers of waxed paper in between. Defrost for 15 or 20 minutes before baking, then proceed as above. These are certainly among the most successfully frozen appetizers, if anything, freezing perhaps improves them!

EGG MOUNTAIN HIDDEN UNDER A CAVIAR FROSTING

[serves 8 to 10]

8 hard cooked eggs
mayonnaise
salt and pepper

onion powder
1 small jar of caviar

Mash the eggs. Add mayonnaise, salt, pepper, and onion powder to taste. Mound this mixture on a serving dish. Chill thoroughly, then frost with the caviar, covering the egg mixture completely. Chill again. Serve with thinly sliced pumpernickel or with crackers.

To prepare ahead of time: The egg mixture can be prepared the day before, however, don't frost it until several hours before serving.

MOUTHFUL MUSHROOM TOASTS

thinly sliced white bread, crusts removed

Mushroom filling:

4 tablespoons butter
1 onion, finely chopped
½ pound fresh mushrooms,
    finely chopped
¼ teaspoon thyme

½ teaspoon salt
¼ teaspoon pepper
3 tablespoons flour
1 cup sour cream

Melt butter and sauté the chopped onion until lightly browned. Add the chopped mushrooms, thyme, salt, pepper, and then cook for about 5 or 6 minutes, stirring frequently. Sprinkle with the flour and stir. Reduce heat and add the sour cream. Stir constantly until mixture is thickened. Cool, then chill.

To assemble: Make mushroom sandwiches by covering one slice of the bread with a fairly generous amount of the filling and then topping with another slice of bread. Cut these sandwiches into 4 or 6 portions and place them on cookie sheets. Bake in the upper third of a 450° oven until the bread is toasted, turning if necessary.

To prepare ahead of time: These can be completely prepared in the morning, then baked shortly before serving. The filling itself can be made and kept refrigerated 3 or 4 days ahead.

To freeze: The mushroom filling freezes beautifully. Defrost, then stir gently before using.

Note: These can be done as larger sandwiches and served for lunch or late supper.

WING-DRUMSTICKS SESAME, TWO WAYS   [serves 10 as an appetizer]

First Way:

1½ pounds chicken wings, disjoint and make two drumsticks out of each wing, removing a little bone in the flat part, then pushing the flesh down to form a kind of a drumstick

melted butter
salt and pepper
½ cup flour mixed with 1 teaspoon of salt
sesame seeds

Melt butter in the pan to be used for cooking. Season chicken lightly, roll in the melted butter, then coat with the flour and place in the baking pan. Sprinkle with sesame seeds. Bake at 400° for about 20 minutes, turn, sprinkle with more seeds, and bake another 15 to 20 minutes, basting occasionally. Serve hot with plenty of paper napkins.

Second Way:

1½ pounds chicken wings, prepared as above
salt and pepper
flour

1 egg beaten with 1 tablespoon water
sesame seeds
shortening

Season chicken with salt and pepper, then roll in flour. Dip each in the beaten egg, then roll them in sesame seeds. Cook in hot shortening until well browned and tender, then serve.

To prepare ahead of time: Both of these ways of preparation lend themselves to morning cooking. Cover them lightly after they are cooked and leave them at room temperature. Reheat before serving in a 400° oven for about 8 or 10 minutes.

Note: If it seems to be too difficult to make 2 drumsticks out of each wing, then just use the one (of course you'll need 3 pounds instead) and leave the "wing" part for stewing later. These methods of preparation lend themselves equally to "real" drumsticks to be used for a main course.

SMOKED SALMON ROLLS STUFFED WITH EGGS AND TOPPED WITH SHRIMP [serves 10 or 12]

10 or 12 slices smoked
    salmon (about 3" x 5")
4 hard cooked eggs
mayonnaise
salt and pepper
½ teaspoon dry mustard
1 green onion, finely
    chopped

½ teaspoon Worcestershire
    sauce
dash of Tabasco
10 or 12 whole cooked shrimp
finely chopped parsley

Mash eggs, then add mayonnaise, salt, pepper, dry mustard, green onion, Worcestershire sauce, and Tabasco. Taste for seasoning.

Place a spoonful of the egg mixture on each salmon slice and roll them up. Top each roll with one of the cooked shrimp and garnish with the chopped parsley. Chill and serve very cold.

To prepare ahead of time: These can be prepared in the morning, covered with plastic wrap, and kept refrigerated until ready to serve. The egg mixture can be prepared the day before.

SUMIKO BILLER'S LOMI-LOMI [serves 6 to 10 as an appetizer or a first course]

½ pound smoked salmon,
    sliced thin
4 tomatoes, peeled, seeded,
    then chopped

6 green onions, finely
    chopped
juice of half a lemon

Cut salmon in pieces about ½ inch in width. Combine them with the other ingredients, cover and chill until ready to serve. Serve with small plates, forks, and crackers on the side.

To prepare ahead of time: This can easily be prepared in the morning.

TINY FRENCH PANCAKES STUFFED WITH MUSHROOMS [serves 10 to 16]

French pancakes:

6 eggs
2 cups milk
1½ cups sifted flour
¼ teaspoon salt

6 tablespoons melted butter
additional butter for cooking
pancackes

Beat eggs slightly. Add flour and milk alternately to the eggs. Add salt and melted butter and let batter stand for at least 1 hour. Batter should be the consistency of rich cream, so if it is too thick, add more milk.

Heat a Danish skillet, the kind with 7 shallow indentations, and put a little butter in each one. Cook thin pancakes in this and stack them as they are cooked with melted butter in between each one. Failing a skillet of this kind, just use a large skillet or griddle and drop the batter by means of a tablespoon to form small pancakes about 3 inches in diameter.

Mushroom filling:

1 pound fresh mushrooms,
    finely chopped or put
    through a grinder
3 tablespoons butter

2 tablespoons flour
1 cup cream or milk
salt and pepper to taste

Melt butter and sauté mushrooms for 3 or 4 minutes. Sprinkle with flour and stir. Add milk or cream gradually and stir constantly until mixture comes to a boil. Season with salt and pepper. Remove from heat and cool.

To assemble: Spread some of the mushroom filling on each pancake —about 1 teaspoon—and roll up. Place these in a chafing dish or a casserole. When ready to serve, cover tightly and heat very slowly either in a chafing dish over hot water, or in the oven. Serve hot.

To prepare ahead of time: These lend themselves to beforehand preparation. They can be made and filled the day before or the morning of the party, covered, and kept refrigerated until time to heat. Or the pancakes can be cooked and stacked with melted butter, covered and refrigerated one or two days ahead and the filling done the same way. Assemble them the day of the party.

To freeze: These freeze beautifully. The pancakes can be cooked and stacked about 14 to a package with melted butter in between— the filling frozen separately. Alternately, they can be frozen in casseroles already assembled. Defrost before heating them.

TINY FRENCH PANCAKES STUFFED WITH CLAMS
[serves 6 to 12]

French pancakes:

3 eggs	3 tablespoons melted butter
1 cup milk	additional butter for
¾ cup sifted flour	cooking pancakes
pinch of salt	

Beat eggs slightly. Add flour and milk alternately to the eggs. Add salt and melted butter and let batter stand for at least 1 hour. Batter should be the consistency of rich cream, so if it is too thick, add more milk.

Heat a Danish skillet, the kind with 7 shallow indentations, and put a little butter in each one. Cook thin pancakes in this and stack them as they are cooked with melted butter in between each one. Failing a skillet of this kind, just use a large skillet or griddle and drop the batter by means of a tablespoon to form small pancakes about 3 inches in diameter.

Clam filling:

1 8-ounce package of	salt and pepper
cream cheese	garlic powder
1 small can clams	finely chopped green onions
(8-ounce), drained	finely chopped parsley
a little cream or sour cream	

Whip cream cheese until fluffy with a little cream or sour cream. Add the clams and the remaining ingredients, seasoning it to your taste.

To assemble: Spread a little of the filling on each of the pancakes, roll up, and place them in a large shallow casserole. Brush with melted butter. Cover with foil and heat in a 400° oven until very hot. Serve on small plates as hors d'oeuvres or as a first course.

To prepare ahead of time: These can be made and filled the day before or the morning of the party and kept refrigerated. Or the pancakes can be cooked and stacked with melted butter, covered tightly and kept refrigerated one or two days ahead and the filling done the same way. Then assemble them the day of the party.

To freeze: The pancakes can be cooked and stacked about 14 to a package with melted butter in between—and the filling frozen separately. Alternately, these can be frozen in the casserole already assembled. Defrost before heatng them.

Fish and Shellfish

Fish and Shellfish

VIRGINIA'S SOLE [VIRGINIA MORRIS]

[serves 6 as a main course]

salt and pepper
1 shallot
butter about ½ cube
½ cup white wine
½ cup water
6 fillets of sole
2 large cooked lobster
    tails (cut in half for
    4 shells)

3 tablespoons butter
4 tablespoons flour
¾ cup milk
2 egg yolks
½ cup heavy cream
4 to 6 tablespoons
    lobster butter
    (recipe follows)

Lobster butter:

Pound thoroughly, or put small bits in the blender, the shell from a 1-pound cooked lobster, and any of the creamy part of the lobster that clings to it, and the coral, if available. (Perhaps your fish man will save a shell for you so that you can use the lobster tail shells for a later garnish.) If pounding the shell, pound in ½ *cup butter*, but if using the blender, do not add butter until the blender has done its job. Remove lobster shell bits to a bowl, then add the butter and blend thoroughly. Melt the mixture slowly in top of a double boiler, strain it through cheesecloth and cool. Any small particles of shell will sink to the bottom and the creamy pink butter can be spooned off the top.

To prepare: Sprinkle the shallot, finely chopped in a buttered flame-proof dish. Add the fillets, folded lengthwise, and dot them with the ½ cube of butter. Season lightly. Add the wine and water. Bring liquid to a simmering point, cover pan with buttered paper or foil, and bake at 350° for 8 to 10 minutes, or until fish flakes readily. Remove fish to a heatproof platter or shallow casserole, reserving the broth for the sauce. Arrange the cooked lobster, sliced, on top of the fiillets. Cover dish with foil and set aside.

Melt the 3 tablespoons butter, stir in the 4 tablespoons flour, and gradually add the hot broth which you have previously strained. Stir constantly until mixture comes to a boil, then add the ¾ cup milk and simmer. Season. Beat the egg yolks together lightly with the ½ cup cream, then stir in the hot sauce. Return to heat and stir until very hot but not boiling. Gradually beat in the lobster butter.

While preparing the sauce, keep fish hot in low oven (300°). Then spoon hot sauce around the fish, garnish with the lobster shells and serve.

To prepare ahead of time: The fish and the sauce can be prepared in the morning. The fish (and lobster slices) can be covered lightly with foil and reheated in a 300° oven before serving. The sauce can be reheated either over very low heat, stirring often, or in the top of a double boiler. Then proceed as in the above recipe.

To freeze: Only the lobster butter can be frozen. The other part of this recipe is best done on the day it is to be served.

Note: Virginia's sole is for good souls only because it is so heavenly!

FILLETS OF SOLE, APOLLO   [serves 6]

| 12 medium fillets of sole (about 2 pounds) | 3 tablespoons melted butter |
| salt and pepper | 1 cup dry Vermouth |

For the sauce:

¼ pound mushrooms, put through a grinder, or very finely chopped	2 cups liquid (use stock left after poaching fish, plus milk)
4 tablespoons butter	salt (about ½ teaspoon)
3 tablespoons flour	pepper (about ¼ teaspoon)
	freshly chopped parsley

Season fish with salt and pepper, then fold in half lengthwise. Place in a baking casserole with the 3 tablespoons of butter and the Vermouth. Bake at 400° for 15 to 20 minutes. Baste once or twice. Do not overcook. Remove from oven and drain off the juices to use for the sauce.

Sauté the mushrooms in the 4 tablespoons of butter, stirring until lightly browned. Reduce heat and sprinkle the flour on the mushrooms. Add the 2 cups of liquid and stir constantly until it boils. Reduce heat and simmer for 5 or 6 minutes. Taste for seasoning. Place fish in a heat-proof dish, or in individual casseroles, and spoon on the sauce. Reheat in a 375° oven until very hot but don't overdo the cooking. Sprinkle with parsley and serve.

To prepare ahead of time: This can be prepared in the morning or the day before. Remove from the refrigerator at least one hour, cover with foil and heat at 375° for 15 to 20 minutes or until very hot.

To freeze: This freezes very nicely. Defrost it overnight in the refrigerator, if possible. Otherwise, defrost at room temperature, cover with foil and heat in a 375° oven until very hot, but not overcooked.

FILLETS OF SOLE WITH DUCHESSE POTATOES AND A WHITE WINE SAUCE [serves 12]

12 *very large* fillets of sole	Duchesse potatoes (see
1 cup melted butter	recipe below)
3 cups fish stock (see	white wine sauce (see
recipe below)	recipe below)

Season fish with salt and pepper. Place them folded lengthwise in one or two large baking pans. Cover with the melted butter and bake at 450° for about 10 minutes, basting once. Add the 3 cups fish stock and return to the oven for another 10 minutes but at a reduced temperature of 350° Remove from oven and drain juices to make the sauce.

Fish stock:

2 pounds of fish bones	pinch of thyme
4 cups dry white wine	a little salt
4 cups water	2 onions, chopped

Cook, uncovered, for about 30 minutes. Strain and use as needed.

Wine sauce:

6 tablespoons butter	1 cup heavy cream
6 tablespoons flour	6 egg yolks
3½ cups liquid (juices from poaching the fish)	salt and pepper to taste

Melt butter, stir in flour and add the juices. Bring to a boil, stirring constantly. Simmer over low heat for 5 to 10 minutes. Add cream and simmer again for 5 minutes. Taste for seasoning. Beat egg yolks slightly. Add some of hot liquid to the yolks, then return all to the saucepan and beat with a whisk for a minute or two.

Duchesse potatoes: Add one or two egg yolks to ordinary mashed potatoes. Season with salt and pepper. You can even use instant mashed potatoes, with the egg yolks added.

To assemble: If possible provide individual casseroles for each person, otherwise place fish fillets in one or two large shallow casseroles and spoon over them the prepared wine sauce. Top with small mounds of Duchesse potatoes (nicely done with a pastry bag and decorative tube). Heat in a 450° oven until bubbly and brown. Use broiler if necessary.

To prepare ahead of time: This can be mostly done in the morning or the day before. Pour sauce over the fish and cover and refrigerate. Take out of refrigerator an hour before heating time. Add the potatoes, then proceed with the heating as in the above recipe.

To freeze: This can be frozen, but should be frozen without the potatoes. It is best defrosted slowly in the refrigerator overnight, but it is not absolutely essential. Bring to room temperature, add potatoes, then proceed with the heating as in the above recipe.

FILLETS OF SOLE ON A COMFORTABLE
BED OF MUSHROOMS [serves 6]

6 large fillets of sole
salt and pepper
1 cup dry white wine
2 tablespoons butter
2 tablespoons flour
½ cup cream (or milk)
½ cup Hollandaise sauce
  (recipe follows)

½ pound fresh mushrooms,
  sliced
½ small onion, finely
  chopped
2 tablespoons butter
salt and pepper

Season fillets with salt and pepper. Fold in half lengthwise, place in a large shallow casserole, and pour over the wine. Cover lightly and poach in a 375° oven for 15 to 20 minutes. Do not overcook. Remove from oven and drain juices to use for the sauce.

> *Hollandaise:* (This makes more than you will need for this quantity of fish. Refrigerate the rest and use for vegetables, or freeze it and use later.)

4 egg yolks
1 or 2 tablespoons lemon
  juice
¼ cup water

¼ teaspoon salt
⅛ teaspoon paprika
½ cup softened butter

Place egg yolks, salt and paprika in the top of a double boiler and beat slightly. Bring water and lemon juice to a boil in a small saucepan, then pour it over the egg yolks, beating vigorously. Place over simmering water and stir constantly with a spoon or whisk until mixture begins to thicken. Gradually add the butter and continue to stir. When the mixture reaches the desired consistency, remove from heat and cool, stirring occasionally. To reheat, place over warm water and stir constantly.

Sauce:
Melt 2 tablespoons of butter and stir in the flour. Add remaining fish juices (should be 1 cup—if more, reduce—if less, add a little milk or cream). Add the ½ cup cream (or milk) and stir over heat constantly until mixture comes to a boil. Reduce heat and simmer for 5 or 10 minutes. Taste for seasoning.

Mushrooms:

Sauté the finely chopped onion in the 2 tablespoons of butter for a few minutes, add sliced mushrooms and continue cooking for 3 or 4 minutes. Season with salt and pepper.

To assemble: Place the sautéed mushrooms in a large ovenproof casserole. Place the poached sole on top of these mushrooms. Add the Hollandaise sauce to the prepared sauce and then pour this evenly over the fillets. Place in a 375° oven until very hot, then run under the broiler quickly just to brown.

To prepare ahead of time: This can be completely prepared ahead of time, either the day before or in the morning. Refrigerate until 1 or 2 hours before heating time, bring to room temperature, then proceed as in the above recipe.

To freeze: This can be prepared and frozen. Defrost completely, bring the fish to room temperature if possible, then proceed as in the above recipe.

BUBBLY AND BROWN FILLETS OF SOLE BONNE FEMME
[serves 4]

4 large fillets of sole
salt and pepper
1 cup fish stock (see
   recipe below)
2 tablespoons butter
2 tablespoons flour

½ cup cream (or milk)
8 large mushroom caps,
   sautéed briefly in butter
½ cup Hollandaise sauce
  (see recipe below)

Fish stock:

1 pound of fish bones
2 cups dry white wine
2 cups water

pinch of thyme
a little salt
1 onion, chopped

Cook uncovered for about 30 minutes. Strain and use as needed.

Hollandaise:

2 egg yolks
1 tablespoon lemon juice
2 tablespoons water

pinch of salt and paprika
¼ cup softened butter

34

Place egg yolks, salt and paprika in the top of a double boiler and beat slightly. Bring water and lemon juice to a boil in a small saucepan, then pour it over the egg yolks, beating vigorously. Place over simmering water and stir constantly with a spoon, or preferably with a whisk, until mixture begins to thicken. Gradually add the butter and continue to stir. When mixture reaches desired consistency, remove from heat and cool, stirring occasionally. To reheat, place over warm water and stir constantly.

To prepare and assemble: Season fillets with salt and pepper and fold them in half lengthwise. Place them in a large shallow casserole. Pour fish stock over them, cover lightly with foil and poach in a 350° oven for about 25 minutes. Drain off liquid to make a sauce:

Melt the 2 tablespoons of butter, stir in flour, then add liquid from the fish which should be about 1 to 1¼ cups. Cook, stirring constantly, until mixture boils. Add cream (or milk) and simmer for about 5 minutes. Taste for seasoning.

Spoon 2 or 3 tablespoons of this sauce over each fillet. Top each fiillet with two of the sautéed mushroom caps. Add the Hollandaise sauce to the remaining prepared sauce and then spoon it over the fillets. Place uncovered in the top part of a 450° oven until bubbly and brown, placing under a broiler for a minute if necessary to brown.

To prepare ahead of time: This can be prepared ahead of time, either the day before or in the morning. Refrigerate until 1 or 2 hours before heating time, bring to room temperature. Reheat briefly at a lower temperature—about 350°, then proceed with the heating and browning at 450°.

To freeze: This can be frozen. Defrost completely, bring to room temperature, then heat briefly at a lower temperature—about 350°, then proceed with the heating and browning at 450°.

FISH FILLETS OF YOUR CHOICE WITH BROCCOLI
AND A MUSHROOM SAUCE [serves 4]

2 pounds of fish fillets
  (try ling cod)
½ onion, sliced
salt and pepper
1 cup dry white wine
¾ pound fresh mushrooms,
  remove and reserve 8
  whole caps
½ onion, finely chopped

2 tablespoons butter
1 ½ tablespoons flour
1 cup liquid (juices left from
  poaching fish)
½ cup cream
2 egg yolks
8 large cooked shrimp
Broccoli purée (recipe
  follows)

Broccoli purée:

1 package frozen chopped
  broccoli
1 tablespoon butter
1 tablespoon flour

¼ teaspoon garlic powder
salt and pepper
½ cup sour cream

Put broccoli through a meat grinder, even though it is already chopped. Melt butter, stir in flour. Add seasonings and sour cream. Cook, stirring constantly, until mixture comes to a boil. Add broccoli and cook a few minutes. Taste for seasoning.

To prepare: Place fish in a casserole with the sliced onion, wine, salt, pepper, and cover lightly with foil. Bake at 400° for 15 to 20 minutes. Remove and drain off the juices for making the sauce.

Slice mushrooms after reserving 8 very nice caps for later garnish. Sauté the mushrooms and the chopped onion in the 2 tablespoons of butter until lightly browned. Sprinkle with the 1 ½ tablespoons of flour and stir. Add the 1 cup fish juices and cook over low heat, stirring constantly, until sauce comes to a boil. Beat cream and egg yolks together lightly and add to the mixture. Stir over low heat for 1 or 2 minutes.

In one casserole (or in individual ones) place the broccoli purée. Put the poached fillets on the broccoli. Spoon on the sauce, then top each serving with 2 shrimp and 2 sautéed mushrooms. Return to oven at 350 or 375° until very hot.

To prepare ahead of time: This can be done in the morning or the day before. Keep refrigerated but bring to room temperature before heating as in the above recipe.

To freeze: This can be frozen. Bring to room temperature before heating as in the above recipe.

WINED AND SAUCED WHITEFISH [serves 8]

2 whole whitefish (each
  weighing about 2
  pounds, with heads)
5 tablespoons melted butter
salt and pepper
1 small onion, chopped
pinch of thyme
parsley

2 cups dry white wine
3 tablespoons butter
2 tablespoons flour
1 ½ cups liquid (left
  from baking the fish)
½ cup cream
2 egg yolks

Remove fish heads and combine with the onion, thyme, parsley, and white wine. Simmer for about 15 minutes, then strain.

Season fish with salt and pepper. Place in a large shallow casserole and cover with the melted butter. Bake at 450° for about 15 minutes. Pour strained fish stock over fish and return to a 375° oven for about 30 minutes. Baste occasionally. Remove from oven and prepare the sauce:

Melt the 3 tablespoons of butter and stir in the flour. Add 1 ½ cups of juice left from baking the fish and stir over heat until mixture boils. Beat egg yolks with the cream, then add, beating, to the hot mixture. Heat and stir until very hot but do not boil. Pour over the fish. Garnish with parsley.

To prepare ahead of time: This can be prepared the day before or in the morning. Refrigerate, but bring to room temperature before heating.

To freeze: This can be frozen. Bring to room terperature before heating.

RED SNAPPER IN ANCIENT SAUCE [serves 4]

2 pounds red snapper fillets
1 onion, sliced
a few sprigs of parsley
1 teaspoon salt

¼ teaspoon pepper
2 tablespoons tarragon
  vinegar
1 cup dry white wine

Place onion, parsley, salt, pepper, vinegar, and white wine in a large skillet. Bring to a boil, then reduce heat and simmer 10 minutes. Add fish fillets, cover tightly and poach over low heat for 10 to 12 minutes. Remove fish from the pan with a skimmer and place fillets in a shallow casserole. Strain juices for use in the sauce.

Ancient sauce:

2 tablespoons butter
2 tablespoons flour
1 ½ cups fish stock
(juices strained from
cooking fish)
½ cup cream
1 small can sliced mushrooms

1 tablespoon capers
2 tablespoons finely
chopped sweet pickle
salt and pepper to taste
¼ cup grated Parmesan
cheese

Melt butter, stir in flour and cook, stirring for a minute, add fish stock and cream and stir constantly until sauce comes to a boil. Reduce heat and add mushrooms, capers, sweet pickle and salt and pepper. Taste for seasoning.

Pour sauce over the fish fillets. Sprinkle with the grated Parmesan and place in a 350° oven until hot.

To prepare ahead of time: Yes, you can prepare this in the morning or the day before. Remove from refrigerator an hour or two before heating, then reheat at 350°.

To freeze: This can be frozen. Defrost and bring to room temperature, then heat at 350°.

A FIERCELY FANCY FLOUNDER, STUFFED WITH A MIRACULOUS MOUSSE AND COVERED WITH A SILKEN SAUCE

1 very large flounder
(5 pounds), boned, but
fins and tail left on
Halibut mousse (recipe
follows)
Fish stock (recipe follows)

Wine sauce (recipe follows)
½ cup white wine
lemon
sliced black truffles or
black olives

First, ask your fish man to bone the flounder so that you can stuff it, but ask him for the large bone that he removes so that you can prepare the following stock:

Fish stock:

bone of the fish	1 carrot, coarsely chopped
1 onion, sliced	2 cups of water
½ teaspoon salt	sprig of parsley
3 peppercorns	¼ teaspoon thyme
2 tablespoons vinegar or	½ bay leaf
lemon juice	

Combine these ingredients and cook slowly for about 30 minutes. Strain and set aside. You should have about 2 cups of liquid.

Halibut mousse:

¾ pound halibut fillets	2 egg whites, unbeaten
1 teaspoon salt	1 ¼ cups heavy cream
¼ teaspoon pepper	

Put halibut through the finest blade of a grinder about 4 or 5 times. Place in a chilled bowl and add the egg whites, beating with a wooden spoon. Now gradually beat in the cream and seasonings. Set aside until ready to use.

Alternate procedure: Purée the halibut with the cream (a little at a time) in a blender, then add egg whites and seasonings.

Now, season the flounder inside and out with salt and pepper and rub lightly with a bit of lemon. Open and stuff the flounder with the halibut mousse. Press sides together firmly. If you think it is necessary fasten gently with a few long skewers. Place the flounder in a large shallow casserole, preferably one you can also serve it in. Pour the strained fish stock over the fish and the ½ cup dry white wine. Cover tightly with foil and bake at 400° for about 40 or 45 minutes. Remove from oven and spoon out the juices or drain them off.

Wine sauce:

3 tablespoons butter	2 or 2 ½ cups fish juices
4 tablespoons flour	(previously strained)
½ cup cream	2 egg yolks

Melt butter, stir in flour, add liquid gradually, stirring constantly, until it boils. Remove from heat. Beat egg yolks slightly and add a little of the hot mixture to the yolks, then return all to the sauce and stir vigorously over very low heat for a minute or two. Taste for seasoning and remove from heat.

To assemble: Remove top skin from the flounder. Spoon sauce over and around the flounder. Garnish with sliced black truffles or a few sliced black olives. Reheat at 350° only until piping hot.

To prepare ahead of time: This can be prepared in the morning or the day before and kept refrigerated. Bring to room temperature, then heat as in the above directions.

To freeze: This freezes. Bring to room temperature, then heat as in the above directions.

TROUT STUFFED "IN THE MANNER OF" LA PYRAMIDE

[serves 4]

4 trout	2 cups fish stock
1 carrot, chopped	(recipe follows)
1 onion, chopped	Vegetable stuffing
salt and pepper	(recipe follows)
pinch of thyme	Sauce (recipe follows)
½ cup Port	

Fish stock: Combine about 1 pound of fish bones with 2 cups dry white wine, 2 cups water, pinch of thyme, 1 sliced onion and a little salt and cook uncovered for about 30 minutes. Strain and use as needed.

Vegetable stuffing:

2 carrots, finely chopped (about 1 cup)	4 tablespoons butter
	4 tablespoons flour
2 celery stalks, finely chopped (about ¾ cup)	salt and pepper
	4 egg yolks
4 or 5 large mushrooms, finely chopped	½ cup milk

Sauté the carrots gently in the 4 tablespoons of butter with the skillet covered, over low heat for about 10 minutes. Add chopped celery and mushrooms and cook an additional 10 minutes. Season to taste with salt and pepper. Sprinkle the flour over the vegetables and stir. Combine egg yolks and milk and add to the vegetables, stirring vigorously, until mixture is very thick. Remove from heat and cool. Chill.

To prepare: Season trout with salt and pepper and stuff with the chilled vegetable stuffing. Sew or skewer the sides of the fish together. Place trout in one or two casseroles and add the chopped carrot and onion, salt, pepper, thyme, fish stock (2 cups), and Port. Cover with foil and bake at 350° for about 30 minutes (longer if the fish is very cold). Remove from oven, transfer fish to a heatproof dish or dishes, and strain remaining juices to use in the sauce:

Sauce and Garnish:

2 tablespoons butter	¼ cup Port
2 tablespoons flour	squeeze of lemon
salt and pepper	2 egg yolks
1 cup strained juices	12 small cooked shrimp
½ cup cream	12 sautéed mushroom caps

Melt butter, stir in flour, then add strained juices and cook over low heat, stirring constantly until mixture comes to a boil. Add Port and lemon. Beat egg yolks slightly with the ½ cup cream and add to the sauce, beating constantly. Season to taste.

Pour sauce over the fish and garnish each with 3 shrimp and 3 sautéed mushroom caps. Reheat only if necessary. Garnish with parsley.

To prepare ahead of time: This can be done ahead in the morning, just pour a little of the sauce on the fish, cover and set aside—or in the refrigerator—until before serving. Reheat the fish covered in the oven. Remove from oven and pour remaining sauce (which you have warmed and stirred over low heat) over the fish. Garnish as in above recipe.

SHERRIED HALIBUT FOR HARRIED HOUSEWIVES

[serves 6 to 10]

4 or 5 pounds of halibut
fillets or slices, cut
about 1 inch thick
salt and pepper
1 can frozen shrimp soup,
undiluted

1 can cream of mushroom
soup, undiluted
⅓ to ½ cup Sherry
tiny cooked bay shrimp
(optional)

Season fish with salt and pepper and place in a large casserole, with the pieces side by side. Combine the soups and heat, stir in Sherry and pour over the fish. Bake for about 40 minutes at 375°, uncovered. Fish is done when it flakes easily. Garnish with the shrimp.

To prepare ahead of time: This can be prepared in the morning or the day before. Do the baking just before serving.

To freeze: This does freeze, however, the preparation is so very simple that it hardly seems worthwhile.

TRITON'S TRICK, AN EASY BUT SPLENDID WAY WITH HALIBUT

[serves 4]

1 pound poached halibut
fillets
1 cup mayonnaise
¾ cup sour cream
1 teaspoon salt (about)
¼ teaspoon pepper

3 or 4 green onions, finely
chopped
1 generous tablespoon lemon
juice
dash of Tabasco
Duchesse potatoes for piping
on the casseroles

Combine the mayonnaise, sour cream, salt, pepper, chopped green onions, lemon juice and Tabasco. Cut halibut in largish squares, then combine with the sauce. Place in four individual, buttered casseroles. Pipe on the potatoes around the outside rim of the halibut (or put on in dabs using a teaspoon). Bake in a 375° oven for about 35 minutes. Turn on broiler if needed to make the potatoes extra brown—but not until the very end of the baking time.

For the Duchesse potatoes: Add one or two egg yolks to ordinary mashed potatoes. Season with salt and pepper. You can even use instant mashed potatoes, with the egg yolks added.

To prepare ahead of time: This can be prepared the day before or in the morning. Don't add the potatoes until shortly before time to put the casseroles in the oven.

To freeze: Yes, freeze it, but not with the potatoes.

Note: This is an excellent way to use any leftover poached or broiled fish such as sole, salmon, etc. To simplify further, one can do these casseroles without the potatoes. Leftover cooked seafood can be used as part of the quantity of the fish for an interesting variation.

A WHOLE FISH, POACHED AND CHILLED WITH GUACAMOLE [serves 12]

1 ling cod, or similar fish, about 7 or 8 pounds
2 large onions, sliced
salt and pepper

1 bay leaf
½ teaspoon thyme
juice of 2 lemons
2 quarts water

For the guacamole:

4 large ripe avocados
juice of 1 lemon
salt to taste

dash of Tabasco
2 teaspoons onion powder

Garnishes:

sliced pimento olives
pearl onions

strips of canned green chilies, or strips of green pepper

Simmer together the sliced onions, salt, pepper, bay leaf, thyme, lemon juice, and the 2 quarts of water for 15 or 20 minutes. Set aside until ready to poach the fish.

Ask your fish man to clean and bone your fish, but to leave it whole—if possible keeping head and tail on. Season the fish, then wrap it in cheese cloth and place in a large roasting pan. Pour over the seasoned court bouillon which you have just prepared. Cover the roasting pan and place in a 375° oven and bake for about 1 hour or just until the fish will flake easily. Remove from oven and let fish cool in its broth. If possible, place fish in its broth in the refrigerator overnight. Next morning lift fish out on to a large platter, remove cheesecloth, skin carefully, and let fish drain. Pour off the moisture as it accumulates. If necessary, some of it can be soaked up with paper towels.

Mash avocados and combine with the lemon juice, salt, Tabasco, and onion powder.

Cover the fish with a thick layer of the guacamole. Decorate with the sliced olives (using them to indicate scales), and with the pearl onions and strips of peppers (using the latter to indicate tail, fins, etc.). Cover tightly with plastic wrap and refrigerate until ready to serve, then add parsley as a final garnish.

To prepare ahead of time: The fish should be cooked the day before, but the guacamole sauce should not be prepared or added to the fish until the day of the party.

BETTE CHASE'S SHRIMP DE RUSO   [serves 4]

large green shrimp (about 2 pounds)
3 quarts water
½ cup salt
2 large onions, coarsely chopped
2 teaspoons cayenne pepper
1 lemon, squeeze juice into brine, then drop in peel
1 cup vinegar
3 or 4 garlic cloves, drop in whole
1 medium celery heart, including tops, sliced in large pieces
1 teaspoon Worcestershire sauce
1 teaspoon fine herbs (I use thyme, parsley, tarragon, and sweet basil)
2 bay leaves

Put all ingredients—except shrimp into the water and boil for about ½ hour. Strain off the brine and discard vegetables. When ready to serve, bring brine to a boil, add shrimp and cook until they turn

44

nicely pink. Do not overcook. Serve in shells in a large bowl with individual ramekins of about ¼ lemon juice and ¾ butter.

To prepare ahead of time: The brine can be prepared a day or so before or in the morning; bring to a boil before adding the shrimp, then proceed as in above recipe.

Note: Bette says: "You do not devein the shrimp for this dish. If anybody is delicate about this they can do it as they eat them at table."

"Serve with liberal stacks of large paper napkins and even bibs if you wish, and with hot steaming towels to finish off with."

"Our guests have nearly always liked this so much that they become embarrassed about the piles of empty shells growing on their plates. . . . once they get over the idea of being served an entree in such an unorthodox manner."

UNBELIEVABLY GOOD GUMBO WITH SHRIMP, OYSTERS AND CRAB [serves 6]

2 10-ounce packages frozen baby okra
2 large onions, finely chopped
½ cup butter
2 tablespoons flour
1 large can tomatoes (3 cups)
5 cups strong chicken broth
salt and pepper
dash of cayenne
2 pounds raw shrimp (I use jumbos)
1½ pints oysters
2 whole crabs, well cracked (crabs should weigh at least 1½ pounds each)

Peel and devein the shrimp while they are raw and set aside.

Chop the okra and sauté in about 6 tablespoons of the butter. Do this in a large heavy pan. Keep cooking, stirring often, until very well browned, and until all of the white strings have completely disappeared. This takes at least 15 minutes. Remove okra from the pan. In the same skillet add remaining 2 tablespoons of butter and sauté the chopped onions until well browned. Sprinkle with the flour, stir, then add the tomatoes and cook, stirring constantly until mixture comes to a boil. Add the chicken broth and okra, season, cover and simmer, stirring occasionally, for 2½ to 3 hours. Taste for seasoning. To be a true gumbo it should be a little on the peppery side.

45

Before serving, bring the above sauce to a simmer and add the raw peeled shrimp and cook for 2 minutes. Now add the oysters and cook for another few minutes. Add the cracked crab and cook only until the mixture comes to a very gentle boil. Do not let this boil hard after adding the seafood or the fish will toughen. To reheat, be sure to bring to a boil very gently.

Serve the gumbo in large soup bowls with a small spoonful of boiled rice in the center.

To prepare ahead of time: The sauce for the gumbo can be prepared 2 or 3 days ahead of time and kept refrigerated until ready to use. It is really easier and better to add the seafood the day of the party, however, I have reheated the whole thing the following day and found it very good.

To freeze: It would be impractical to freeze the whole thing, but the sauce, which is the time consuming part, freezes magnificently.

MARY CULLINS' OYSTER LOAVES   [makes 6]

6 individual French rolls
1 pint of frying oysters
salt and pepper

flour
cornmeal

For the sauce:

1 onion, chopped
1 green pepper, chopped
1 cup tomato ketchup
dash of Tabasco

1 teaspoon Worcestershire
    sauce
juice of half a lemon

Cut a top off each of the French rolls and scoop out some of the soft part of the roll.

Make the sauce: Combine the onion, green pepper, ketchup, Tabasco, Worcestershire, and lemon juice and bring it to a boil. Simmer for a few minutes, then set aside.

Season oysters with salt and pepper, then roll them in a mixture of half flour and half cornmeal. Fry them in oil until brown and crisp. Drain on paper towels.

Fill each scooped out roll with some of the fried oysters. Spoon sauce over the oysters. Place top of roll back on, then put in a 450° oven for about 10 minutes.

To prepare ahead of time: Yes, these can be easily prepared ahead of time, the day before or in the morning. Wrap each one in foil and refrigerate. To heat: First heat for 10 minutes in the foil, then remove foil and heat for 15 minutes as in the above recipe.

To freeze: Yes, do freeze them. Wrap each one in foil and freeze. If frozen, start heating them at about 450° in foil for 15 or 20 minutes, then unwrap and continue heating for about 10 minutes.

OYSTERS "RUTH-E-FELLER" [serves 4 persons, 3 large oysters per person]

½ cup finely chopped spinach (can use fresh or frozen, but put through a grinder to make certain it is finely chopped)
⅔ cup fresh bread crumbs (not the dry kind)
¼ cup butter
1 tablespoon finely chopped parsley

½ teaspoon salt
¼ teaspoon pepper
¼ teaspoon dried tarragon
¼ teaspoon thyme
2 tablespoons Port
¼ cup softened butter (preferably sweet butter)
12 large oysters in their shells
rock salt

Sauté the bread crumbs in the ¼ cup butter until just lightly browned. Remove from heat and add the spinach, parsley, salt, pepper, tarragon, thyme, and Port. Stir until blended and taste for seasoning. Whip in the softened butter, then set aside until ready to use.

Place oysters in their shell on a bed of rock salt in an ovenproof pan. Place in a preheated 400° oven for about 5 minutes. Remove from oven and top each oyster with a spoonful of the prepared mixture and return to the oven for another 5 to 7 minutes. Serve oysters at once.

To prepare ahead of time: The spinach mixture can be prepared the day before or in the morning.

SHRIMP WITH GRAPES EN COQUILLE   [serves 6 to 8]

1 pound raw peeled shrimp, weight after peeled
1½ tablespoons butter
2 tablespoons very finely chopped onion
salt and pepper to taste
1 teaspoon A-1 steak sauce
few drops of Worcestershire sauce
few drops of Tabasco
½ teaspoon Accent
½ cup dry white wine

1 cup heavy cream
2 tablespoons lemon juice
2 tablespoons melted butter mixed with 2 tablespoons flour
green seedless grapes for garnishing
½ cup Hollandaise sauce (recipe follows)
¼ cup whipping cream, whipped

Hollandaise:

2 egg yolks
1 tablespoon lemon juice
2 tablespoons water

pinch of salt and paprika
¼ cup softened butter

Place egg yolks, salt, and paprika in the top of a double boiler and beat slightly. Bring water and lemon juice to a boil in a small saucepan, then pour it over the egg yolks, beating vigorously. Place over simmering water and stir constantly with a spoon, or preferably with a whisk, until mixture begins to thicken. Gradually add the butter and continue to stir. When mixture reaches desired consistency, remove from heat and cool, stirring occasionally. To reheat, place over warm water and stir constantly.

Sauté the raw shrimp, cut into halves or thirds, gently in the 1½ tablespoons of butter for about 2 minutes. Remove and set aside while making the sauce. Add the onion to the skillet and cook for a few minutes. Add salt, pepper, A-1 sauce, Worcestershire, Tabasco, Accent, white wine, 1 cup heavy cream, and lemon juice and bring to a gentle boil. Stir in the butter-flour mixture and bring to a boil again, reduce heat and simmer for 2 or 3 minutes. Remove from heat and stir in the shrimp.

Divide the shrimp and sauce into 6 individual shells (coquilles) and heat for a few minutes in a 375° oven. When they are hot, remove from oven. Combine Hollandaise and whipped cream. Arrange about 6 or 8 grapes per serving on the shells, then top each with about 2 tablespoons of the Hollandaise-cream mixture. Broil about 5 inches from the heat for just one or two minutes—just until brown. Watch so it doesn't burn. Serve at once.

To prepare ahead of time: These can be prepared ahead of time up to the part where the final broiling is done. In other words, fill the shells, refrigerate them covered, then the next day heat them in a 350° oven until hot, then proceed with the adding of the grapes, the Hollandaise-cream mixture, and the broiling.

To freeze: These can be frozen with the same reservation as noted under ahead of time preparation. Defrost the filled shells before heating, heat, then add the grapes, Hollandaise-cream mixture, and broil.

SHRIMP AND SALMON SO PRETTY NEWBURG

[serves 4 to 6]

4 tablespoons butter
4 tablespoons flour
3 cups light cream
salt and pepper to taste
1 teaspoon dry mustard
1 teaspoon paprika
¼ cup grated Parmesan
 cheese

4 egg yolks
2 tablespoons Sherry
1 tablespoon Cognac
3 cups cooked fresh salmon,
 cut into large pieces
 (don't use canned salmon
 for this)
2 cups cooked shrimp

Melt butter, stir in flour and cook without browning for a few minutes. Add cream and stir over low heat until mixture comes to a boil. Add salt, pepper, mustard, and paprika and simmer for about 5 or 6 minutes, stirring occasionally. Beat egg yolks in a bowl and gradually add hot mixture to the yolks, beating constantly. Return this to the saucepan and add the Sherry, Cognac, salmon, Parmesan cheese and shrimp. Heat and stir gently until all is very hot. Do this over very low heat so that the egg yolks don't curdle.

Serve with hot boiled rice.

To prepare ahead of time: One can prepare this the day before or in the morning. Do exercise caution in reheating this. If possible reheat over simmering water, stirring occasionally but very gently.

To freeze: You can freeze this. If possible, defrost in the refrigerator overnight, then reheat slowly and carefully as directed above.

HAPPY WARRIOR SCAMPI [serves 4 to 6]

18 jumbo shrimp, deveined
but leaving tails and
shells attached
salt, pepper and a little
paprika
1 large shallot, finely
chopped
¼ cup butter

½ cup dry white wine
½ cup brown sauce (see
recipe below)
¼ cup butter
juice of half a lemon
1 tablespoon finely chopped
parsley
1 clove garlic, mashed

Brown sauce: Melt 1 tablespoon of butter, stir in 1 tablespoon of flour, then add ½ cup undiluted canned beef bouillon and bring to a boil, stirring constantly. Add one tablespoon of Sherry.

Cut shrimp open (butterfly) but not all the way through, then flatten the shrimp and place them on an ovenproof platter or shallow casserole with the flesh side up. Season with salt, pepper, and a little paprika.

Sauté shallots briefly (about 1 minute) in the ¼ cup butter, add wine and reduce this to ⅓ of the original volume. Stir in the brown sauce and bring to a boil. Remove from heat, then add the additional ¼ cup butter, lemon juice, and parsley.

Use about ¾ of this mixture and spoon it evenly over the shrimp. Add the garlic to the remaining ¼ of the sauce and set it aside.

Broil shrimp about 6 to 8 inches from broiler for about 5 minutes. Remove and drain off, or spoon off, the juices, adding them to the garlic sauce. Now—baste the shrimp with this mixture. Broil again for one or two minutes and serve very hot.

To prepare ahead of time: The basting sauce can be prepared ahead of time.

WORTHY OF YOUR TIME SHRIMP NANTUA

[serves 4 as a main course]

1 large onion, finely
    chopped
2 carrots, finely chopped
3 or 4 celery stalks, finely
    chopped
¼ cup butter
½ teaspoon salt
¼ teaspoon pepper
1 ½ pounds peeled, deveined,
    raw shrimp
¼ teaspoon thyme
1 bay leaf

¼ cup Cognac
¾ cup dry French
    Vermouth
1 tomato, seeded, then
    chopped
sprig of parsley
Shrimp butter (see recipe
    below)
Special sauce (see recipe
    below)
Bread Croustades (see
    recipe below)

Slowly sauté the onion, carrots and celery in the ¼ cup of butter, stirring occasionally. This will take anywhere from 10 to 20 minutes. The vegetables should be very tender and lightly browned. Add the shrimp and stir over high heat for about a minute. Add the salt, pepper, thyme, bay leaf, and then add Cognac and flame. Add Vermouth, parsley, and tomatoes, reduce heat and cover. Simmer very gently for about 3 or 4 minutes. Do not overcook. Remove from heat and cool the shrimp in the liquid. This can be done the day before and refrigerated.

Shrimp butter:

¼ cup cooked shrimp
    (from the above amount)

¼ cup hot melted butter

Whirl together in a blender which has been previously warmed by pouring in hot water, then dumping it out. Chill.

Special sauce:

2 tablespoons butter
2 tablespoons flour
1 cup liquid: Remove
    cooked shrimp to an-
    other dish. Cook the
    remaining mixture for
    about 15 minutes, then
    strain. Should have 1
    cup, if more, reduce to
    1 cup.

¼ cup cream
1 egg yolk
salt and pepper, to taste

Melt butter, stir in flour and cook and stir over low heat for 2 or 3 minutes. Stir in the 1 cup of shrimp liquid and cook, stirring, until it boils. Beat egg yolk in another bowl with the cream, then beat in the hot mixture. Return to saucepan and taste for seasoning. Stir in shrimp. Set aside until ready to serve.

Bread croustades: Cut solid bread into 3-inch square blocks. Remove all crusts. Scoop out part of the center of each block, brush with melted butter and bake for 5 to 10 minutes in the top third of the oven at 450°. These can be reheated before serving.

To serve: Slowly reheat the shrimp in the sauce, stirring often. Just before serving, stir in about 2 tablespoons of the shrimp butter. (The rest of the shrimp butter can be frozen.) Serve hot over the hot, buttered croustades and top with a sprinkling of parsley.

To prepare ahead of time: This can be prepared the day before or in the morning. Reheat slowly and stir in the shrimp butter just before serving.

To freeze: This can be frozen. Freeze shrimp in their sauce separately from the shrimp butter. Before serving, reheat shrimp slowly, then stir in the shrimp butter and proceed as in the above recipe. The bread croustades can be frozen too. Reheat to use.

A SIMPLE SHRIMP MARENGO [serves 4]

¼ pound bacon, diced
1 small onion, finely chopped
½ cup chopped celery
1 clove garlic, mashed
½ pound mushrooms, sliced
1½ teaspoons salt
¼ teaspoon pepper
½ teaspoon Accent
¾ teaspoon dried rosemary
1 bay leaf, crushed

¾ teaspoon dried sweet basil
1 teaspoon sugar
1 one-pound can of tomatoes
1 six-ounce can tomato paste
1 or 2 drops Tabasco
2 pounds raw shrimp, peeled and deveined
1 large green pepper, cut in fairly large dice

Sauté bacon until crisp, remove and save. Add onion to the bacon drippings and sauté until tender, then add celery and garlic and sauté for 3 to 5 minutes. Add sliced mushrooms and cook an additional minute or two. Add seasonings and return bacon to the pan. Add canned tomatoes and tomato paste and Tabasco. Simmer covered for about 10 minutes, then simmer uncovered for another 15 minutes. Add shrimp and green peppers and simmer only until shrimp are tender—about 5 to 10 minutes. Taste for seasoning and serve hot in small casseroles.

I like to serve this with Parmesan-garlic toasted bread.

To prepare ahead of time: This can be done the day before or in the morning. Reheat gently but don't overcook the shrimp.

To freeze: This freezes. Defrost and reheat gently but do not overcook the shrimp.

CASSANDRA'S LOBSTER AND MUSHROOMS [serves 6]

4 small lobster tails (the 8- or 10-ounce size), cooked and sliced
6 tablespoons butter
½ onion, finely chopped
½ pound fresh mushrooms, sliced
4 tablespoons flour
½ cup chicken stock
1 cup cream (or milk)

2 egg yolks
¼ cup cream
salt, pepper, and paprika
1 teaspoon Worcestershire sauce
dash Tabasco
2 tablespoons grated Parmesan cheese
2 tablespoons Sherry
2 cups cooked rice

Tomato garnish:
6 thick slices of tomato
2 tablespoons of softened butter mixed with
1 generous teaspoon of anchovy paste

Sauté onion in the 6 tablespoons of butter for 3 or 4 minutes, then add the mushrooms and continue cooking for about another 3 minutes. Sprinkle flour over, stir, then add the chicken stock and the 1 cup of cream. Stir constantly until the mixture comes to a boil. Sim-

53

mer gently for 5 to 7 minutes. Beat egg yolks lightly with the ¼ cup of cream and then add to the sauce. Stir over low heat for about one minute. Season with salt, pepper, dash of paprika, Worcestershire, Sherry, Tabasco, Parmesan, and add the lobster slices. Continue stirring gently until well blended, then remove from heat.

Divide the cooked rice into 6 small casseroles and then place the lobster-mushroom mixture on top of the rice. Place in a 350° oven just long enough to get hot. Remove and top each casserole with a slice .of tomato and each slice of tomato with a dab of the butter-anchovy mixture. Place under the broiler for a few minutes, garnish with chopped chives and serve hot.

To prepare ahead of time: This can be prepared in the morning or the day before, but add the tomato garnish just before serving.

To freeze: This freezes. Defrost, heat, and at the very last, add tomato garnish.

HOMARD A L'AMERICAINE   [serves 6 to 8]

4 pounds frozen small
    lobster tails
1 medium onion, finely
    chopped
⅓ cup finely chopped
    carrots
¼ cup butter
salt and pepper
1 teaspoon finely chopped
    shallots
1 clove garlic, mashed
⅓ cup Cognac
1 can of tomatoes (1 pound)
2 or 3 tablespoons tomato
    paste
½ teaspoon dried tarragon

1 cup fish stock (made from
    cooking some white fish
    bones with a little
    onion, thyme, parsley
    and dry white wine,
    then strained)
¾ cup dry Vermouth
¾ cup dry white wine
1 generous teaspoon meat
    concentrate such as
    Bovril or Wilson's BV
2 tablespoons softened butter
    mixed with 2 table-
    spoons flour
chopped parsley

Defrost and wash the lobster tails. Remove the heavy membrane, but leave the shells. Chop lobster into fairly large pieces.

Heat the butter and sauté the onion and carrots for 5 minutes or longer, until lightly browned and tender. Add lobster and sauté until shells turn red. Season with salt and pepper. Add remaining ingredients *except the butter-flour mixture*. Simmer over very low heat for 15 to 20 minutes. Remove lobster pieces to another casserole. Thicken the sauce with the butter-flour mixture by adding it and cooking, stirring constantly, until sauce comes to a boil. Pour over the lobster and keep warm but do not boil. Sprinkle with chopped parsley. Serve with white rice and with crusty French bread and a lively green salad.

To prepare ahead of time: This can be done the day before or in the morning. Reheat slowly just to the simmering point.

To freeze: This can be frozen. Defrost, then reheat just to the simmering point.

CRABMEAT EGG FOO YUNG [serves 4]

3 tablespoons oil
½ onion, finely chopped
½ green pepper, finely chopped
½ cup canned sliced mushrooms
1 cup fresh bean sprouts

½ to 1 teaspoon finely chopped fresh ginger
1 cup crabmeat (6½- to 7-ounce can)
salt and pepper
6 eggs
oil for sautéing

For the sauce:

1½ cups soup stock (can use canned, undiluted bouillon)

1 or 2 tablespoons soy sauce
1 tablespoon cornstarch
¼ cup cold water

Sauté the chopped onion in the 3 tablespoons of oil very quickly, and then add the green pepper and mushrooms and ginger and bean sprouts. Stir-fry for about 1 minute. Add crabmeat, salt, and pepper and stir-fry for another minute. Remove from heat and spoon into another bowl.

Beat eggs lightly and then add the vegetable mixture. Set aside.

Prepare the sauce: Heat the bouillon, soy sauce, and cornstarch dissolved in the cold water, stirring, until mixture boils. Remove from heat and rewarm before using.

Heat additional oil or butter in a large skillet. Add the vegetable-crabmeat-egg mixture and cook over medium heat until eggs are firm and brown underneath. Divide into desired portions and turn over and brown other side. Remove to a warm platter and pour over the warm prepared sauce. Keep warm if necessary in a low oven.

To prepare ahead of time: The vegetable-crabmeat-egg mixture can be prepared in the morning, but cook shortly before serving. If necessary this can be reheated but it is not quite as good.

JOYFULLY EASY CRABMEAT CAKES WITH REMOULADE SAUCE [serves 4]

1 pound crabmeat
1 small onion, finely
    chopped
½ green pepper, finely
    chopped
3 tablespoons butter
¾ to 1 teaspoon salt
¼ teaspoon pepper
¼ teaspoon thyme

1 egg, beaten
1 ½ cups soft bread crumbs
3 tablespoons mayonnaise
dash of Tabasco
1 tablespoon finely chopped
    parsley
(dry bread crumbs for
    rolling cakes in)

Sauté chopped onion and green pepper in the butter until lightly browned and tender. Add crabmeat and stir over heat for about a minute. Remove from heat, add remaining ingredients and mix thoroughly. Chill for at least one hour. Form into 8 balls. Roll in the dry bread crumbs and chill again. Fry in deep fat for a few minutes, or until a rich brown on the outside. Serve with the Remoulade sauce.

Remoulade Sauce:

1 cup mayonnaise
½ cup sour cream
2 teaspoons prepared
    mustard (the Dijon
    type)
1 tablespoon chopped capers

1 tablespoon chopped sweet
    gherkins
2 teaspoons chopped parsley
¼ teaspoon basil
⅛ teaspoon tarragon
1 or 2 tablespoons lemon
    juice

Combine and chill.

To prepare ahead of time: The crabmeat balls can be made the day before or in the morning and kept refrigerated until ready to deep fry them. The Remoulade Sauce can be made several days ahead of time.

To freeze: The crabmeat balls can be frozen. Defrost for about an hour or so, then roll in more dry bread crumbs and proceed with the frying.

Note: This crabmeat mixture can be formed into flat cakes and sautéed in butter.

Poultry

Poultry

LUCIFEROUS CHICKEN WITH A BARBECUE SAUCE
[serves 4]

2 broiler-fryer chickens,
    cut in halves
salt and pepper
melted butter or oil
1 cup ketchup
1 cup water
¼ cup lemon juice
2 tablespoons vinegar
2 tablespoons brown sugar

2 tablespoons Worcester-
    shire sauce
2 teaspoons salt
1 teaspoon prepared mustard
¼ teaspoon pepper
few drops of Tabasco
½ cup finely chopped celery
1 medium onion, finely
    chopped

Season the chicken halves with salt and pepper. Brush with the melted butter or oil and broil on both sides only until nicely browned. While chicken is broiling prepare the sauce: Combine remaining ingredients and simmer them for about 10 minutes.

Place the browned chicken one layer deep in a roasting pan and pour the prepared sauce over the chicken. Bake uncovered at 350° until tender, about 45 minutes, basting occasionally with the sauce in the pan. Add a small amount of water if the sauce becomes too thick.

To prepare ahead of time: This can be done the day before or on the morning of the party. Reheat, covered for a very short time, then continue with the baking as in the above recipe. Perhaps one should reduce the original baking time somewhat if planning to reheat the chicken later.

To freeze: Yes, you can freeze this. Defrost and bring to room temperature. Reheat first covered, then uncovered. If you are planning to freeze the chicken, reduce the baking time somewhat before freezing the chicken in the sauce.

MONTE ALBAN CHICKEN EN PAPILLOTE [serves 8]

4 whole chicken breasts
    split in half (8 pieces)
salt and pepper
flour

¼ cup butter
Monte Alban Sauce
    (recipe follows)

Remove skin from chicken breasts. Season with salt and pepper, then roll in flour and sauté in the butter until browned and tender. Set aside. Either while browning the chicken or earlier (even a day or two earlier), prepare the Monte Alban Sauce.

Monte Alban Sauce:

2 tablespoons butter or oil
3 cloves garlic, mashed
1 onion, finely chopped
1 one-pound can of good
    quality tomatoes
1 tablespoon dried oregano

1 tablespoon dried ground
    cumin seed
½ teaspoon salt
1 teaspoon chili powder
½ cup cold butter

Sauté the garlic and onion in the butter or oil for 3 or 4 minutes, then add the tomatoes, mashing them up well. Simmer for about 5 minutes, then add the oregano, ground cumin, salt and chili powder. Simmer covered for 15 minutes; uncover and simmer an additional 5 minutes.

Place sauce in the blender a little at a time, adding a little of the cold butter each time and spin until smooth. Set aside until ready to use.

To assemble: Take 8 parchment sheets, about 12″ by 18″ and fold each in half, then cut in a heart shape and open up. Place a chicken breast in the center of one side of the heart, cover with about ¼ cup of the sauce, fold up and seal, then place chicken packages on a baking pan. Bake in a 350° oven for about 20 minutes if at room temperature. If at refrigerator temperature, bake 30 to 40 minutes, or until very hot. Let each guest open his own papillote, providing a spoon for each to scoop out the juices, and an extra plate or bowl for the discarded parchment.

To prepare ahead of time: These can be done the day before or the morning of the party. Do the baking before serving.

To freeze: Yes, these can be frozen. Wrap them tightly in foil, or better yet, place the packages in plastic bags. Defrost before baking them.

CHICKEN MINERVA EN PAPILLOTE [serves 10]

5 large chicken breasts, boned, skinned and split
salt and pepper
flour

¼ cup butter
10 slices of ham (boiled or baked), about 3" by 5"
Mushroom sauce (recipe follows)

Mushroom sauce:

1 onion, finely chopped
¾ pound mushrooms (set aside 10 of the caps, then grind or chop the remaining mushrooms
¼ cup butter
⅓ cup flour

2 cups chicken stock
¼ cup cream
salt and pepper to taste
¼ cup Sherry
1 tablespoon chopped parsley

Sauté the onion in the butter, then add the chopped or ground mushrooms and cook slowly, stirring occasionally. When tender and lightly browned, sprinkle over the flour and stir. Add chicken stock and bring to a boil, stirring constantly. Add cream, seasonings and Sherry and simmer for a few minutes. Taste for seasoning. Remove from heat and add parsley.

To prepare: Season chicken breasts with salt and pepper. Roll lightly in flour and sauté in the butter until browned on both sides and tender.

Sauté mushroom caps briefly in some butter.

To assemble: Take 10 parchment sheets, about 12" by 18" and fold each in half, then cut in a heart shape and open up. Place a chicken breast in the center of one side after spooning some of the sauce underneath. Add some sauce on top of the breast, then add the ham slice then more sauce, then the mushroom cap. Seal tightly. Bake at 350° for 20 to 40 minutes, or until very hot. (You can use foil instead of the parchment papers, but they are not as attractive that way.)

To prepare ahead of time: These can be prepared the day before or in the morning, but reserve the final baking until shortly before serving. If they are cold they will need to bake longer.

To freeze: Yes, these can be frozen. Defrost, then bake until very hot. Keep these well sealed in the freezer either in additional foil or in plastic bags.

SUZANNE MELLINKOFF'S COQ AU VIN [serves 3 or 4]

1 2½ pound disjointed
   chicken
salt, freshly ground pepper
   and nutmeg
flour
¼ cup butter (2 ounces)
1 slice of bacon
1 thinly sliced onion

1 clove garlic, crushed
¼ teaspoon thyme
1 tablespoon chopped
   parsley
1 bay leaf
leaves from 1 stalk of celery
¼ cup Brandy (2 ounces)
2 cups dry red wine

Dry the chicken pieces, then season with salt, pepper, nutmeg. Roll in flour.

Brown bacon in a skillet, then set it aside. Add 1 ounce of the butter to the skillet and sauté the onions until they are limp, but not browned. Transfer them to a casserole. Add remaining butter to the skillet and brown the chicken on all sides. Add chicken to the onions in the casserole, cover and simmer for 3 minutes. Add the Brandy, then ignite. When the flames have burned out, add the red wine, garlic, thyme, bay leaf, parsley, celery leaves and the slice of bacon, crumbled. Cover casserole, bring to a simmer on top of stove, then transfer to a 300° oven and bake for about 1 hour.

To prepare ahead of time: You may cook this earlier, but remove chicken from sauce. Shortly before serving, bring sauce to a boil, add chicken, cover and return to oven only until hot.

Note: Suzanne serves this with roasted potatoes, tossed green salad and French bread.

PROPHETIC CHICKEN IN PORT FOR PROPITIOUS MOMENTS [serves 8 to 10]

8 pounds of roasting
   chicken, cut up into
   pieces (about
   2 roasters)
½ cup butter
salt and pepper
2 carrots, finely chopped

1 very large onion,
   finely chopped
1½ cups Port
1 cup rich chicken stock
cornstarch dissolved in a
   little cold water to
   thicken the sauce

Sauté the onion and carrots in the butter and place in a very large roasting pan that has a cover. Season the chicken and place on top of the vegetables. Place in a 400° oven uncovered and bake, basting frequently and turning occasionally, until chicken has browned. This takes from 30 to 45 minutes. Add Port and chicken stock, cover tightly and place back in oven at a reduced temperature (325°) for 40 to 45 minutes, or just until the chicken is tender. Remove from oven and remove chicken pieces from the roaster, placing them in a serving, heatproof casserole. Thicken the remaining juices to your taste with a mixture made of cornstarch and cold water. Pour this sauce over the chicken, cover and return to oven just long enough to make certain that all is very hot.

To prepare ahead of time: This can be cooked in the morning or the day before. Do not overcook, for it will cook a little more in the reheating.

To freeze: This can be frozen. Do not overcook. Defrost, then heat slowly in the oven until tender and very hot.

AN UNLIKELY BUT SURPRISINGLY DELICIOUS MARRIAGE OF CHICKEN AND KNOCKWURST

[serves 6 to 8]

12 serving pieces of chicken	1 cup dry white wine
salt and pepper	⅓ cup Marsala
flour	1 large knockwurst which
¼ cup butter	has been cooked, then cut
1 onion, finely chopped	in strips (julienne)—
3 tablespoons butter	more knockwurst can
2 tablespoons flour	be used if desired

Sauté the chicken in the ¼ cup butter after seasoning it with salt and pepper and rolling it lightly in flour. When browned place it in a casserole which has a tight-fitting cover.

Sauté the onion in the 3 tablespoons of butter until lightly browned, stir in flour, then add white wine and bring to a boil, stirring constantly. Add Marsala and taste for seasoning. Add the julienned knockwurst and then pour over the browned chicken pieces. Cover casserole and bake at 325° for 40 to 50 minutes, or until tender.

To prepare ahead of time: This can be done the day ahead or in the morning. Do not overcook. Reheat until tender and hot.

To freeze: This freezes, just don't overcook. Reheat in oven after defrosting, baking until tender and very hot.

TERIYAKI CHICKEN   [serves 4]

    2 broilers, split

Marinade:

½ cup soy sauce
¼ cup oil
2 tablespoons sugar
2 tablespoons white wine
    vinegar

1 clove garlic, mashed
1 generous tablespoon
    finely chopped fresh
    ginger

Combine ingredients for the marinade, then marinate the chicken for 1 or 2 hours.

Place chicken in a large shallow roasting pan and bake at 325° for about 1½ hours or longer, basting every fifteen minutes with some of the marinade.

To prepare ahead of time: This can be completed in the morning, left at room temperature, then reheated before serving. (It is very good cold the second day.)

CHICKEN WITH GREEN PEPPERS
IN THE ROMAN STYLE   [serves 6 to 8]

4 pounds chicken parts:
    breasts and thighs
¼ cup butter
¼ cup olive oil
1 medium onion, finely
    chopped
1 clove garlic, mashed

a pinch of sweet basil
4 tomatoes, peeled, seeded,
    and diced
4 to 6 green peppers, seeded,
    then cut into eighths
⅓ cup dry white wine
salt and pepper to taste

Brown the chicken in the butter until golden brown on all sides. Remove to a casserole. Sauté the onions in the olive oil until tender,

66

then add the garlic and cook another minute or so. Add remaining ingredients, cover and simmer for 2 or 3 minutes. Pour over chicken, cover tightly and place in a 325° oven and bake for 35 to 40 minutes or until chicken is tender.

To prepare ahead of time: This can be done the day before or in the morning. Do not overcook. Heat in a 325° oven until tender and hot.

To freeze: This freeezes, but do not overcook the chicken. Defrost, then reheat in a 325° oven until tender and hot.

THE QUEEN'S CHICKEN À LA KING [serves 4]

4 tablespoons butter
¼ pound fresh mushrooms, sliced
½ green pepper, finely chopped
3 tablespoons flour
1 cup chicken stock (can use a powdered base or canned)
¾ cup heavy cream
½ teaspoon onion powder
¼ cup chopped pimento
salt and pepper to taste
2 cups diced cooked chicken (can use boiled, roasted or fried)
1 egg yolk
¼ cup Sherry
finely chopped parsley

Sauté mushrooms and green pepper in the butter until just barely tender, then stir in the flour. Add stock and cream and bring to a boil, stirring constantly. Reduce heat and add onion powder, salt, pepper, and simmer for a few minutes. Add pimento and chicken and heat slowly. Beat egg yolk lightly with the Sherry and add to the mixture, stirring off heat. Keep this all warm, but do not let it boil after adding the egg yolk mixture.

To serve: If you have a French-fry potato basket gadget, use it to make nests for this chicken à la king. If not, serve it in buttered croustades or with whatever starch you prefer. Garnish with chopped parsley.

To prepare ahead of time: This can be made in the morning or the day before. Reheat very slowly and gently, either over simmering water or on very low heat, stirring occasionally.

To freeze: This freezes. Defrost, then reheat very slowly and gently over simmering water, or on very low heat. Stir occasionally.

SUMPTUOUS SESAME CHICKEN

chicken pieces for frying	beaten eggs
salt and pepper	a large quantity of sesame
flour	seeds

Season chicken with salt and pepper, then roll in flour. Dip in beaten egg, then roll in sesame seeds so that all of chicken is thoroughly covered with the sesame seeds. Brown the chicken slowly in oil or vegetable shortening as you would for "fried" chicken—cover the skillet at first, then turn pieces and sauté uncovered. Do all of this over moderate heat until very nicely browned and tender.

To prepare ahead of time: This can be done in the morning. Leave at room temperature, then reheat in one layer in a large pan at 400° for 10 to 15 minutes, or just until very hot.

CHICKEN BREASTS SMETANA   [serves 10]

5 whole chicken breasts split in half	1 pound fresh mushrooms, sliced
salt and pepper	1 cup sour cream
flour	1 tablespoon cornstarch
¼ cup butter	mixed with ¼ cup
2 cups rich chicken stock	cold water

Season chicken with salt and pepper, roll in flour, then sauté in butter until golden brown on both sides. Add chicken stock, cover and bake at 325° for about 45 minutes, or just until tender. Meanwhile sauté the sliced mushrooms in a little additional butter. Remove chicken from oven and pour all of the juices over the mushrooms. Stir over low heat. Add the dissolved cornstarch and continue to cook over low heat, stirring constantly, until sauce comes to a boil. Turn heat down, add sour cream, stir well and pour all over the chicken. Return chicken and sauce to the oven only long enough to heat through.

To prepare ahead of time: This can be prepared the day before or in the morning. Reheat gently before serving.

To freeze: This can be frozen. Defrost and bring to room temperature, then reheat gently in the oven.

CHICKEN BREASTS WITH SEEDLESS GRAPES

[serves 12]

6 whole chicken breasts,
   split
½ cup butter
salt and pepper
5 tablespoons flour
1 ¼ cups dry white wine

1 cup chicken stock
½ teaspoon onion powder
¼ teaspoon dried tarragon
1 cup heavy cream
2 cups seedless grapes

Season chicken with salt and pepper. Sauté in the butter until browned on both sides and remove from skillet. Drain off all but 5 tablespoons of the butter. Add flour and stir. Add white wine, cook and stir over low heat. Add the chicken stock, onion powder and tarragon, continue cooking over low heat, stirring until sauce comes to a boil. Put chicken breasts in a casserole or roasting pan with a cover, then pour this sauce over them. Cover tightly and bake in a 325° or 350° oven for 35 to 45 minutes, or just until tender. Remove from oven and place chicken on a warm platter or in another casserole. Add cream to the remaining sauce and heat over low heat. Pour over chicken and scatter the grapes over the top. Serve at once.

To prepare ahead of time: This can be prepared the day before or in the morning, but leave the addition of the cream until after you have reheated the chicken, then proceed as in the above recipe .

To freeze: This freezes, but leave the addition of the cream until after the chicken has been defrosted and reheated, then proceed as in the above recipe.

CHICKEN BREASTS WITH PINEAPPLE AND BANANAS

[serves 12]

6 whole chicken breasts,
   split in halves
salt and pepper
butter or oil for sautéing
1 clove garlic, mashed
6 tablespoons butter
6 tablespoons flour
3 cups chicken stock

1 cup sour cream
¼ teaspoon rosemary
¼ cup Cognac
½ teaspoon curry powder
12 slices fresh pineapple
4 bananas, cut into 3 pieces
   each

69

Season chicken breasts with salt and pepper. Sauté them in butter or oil until brown on both sides. Remove from pan and set aside. Melt the 6 tablespoons of butter, add the garlic, cook one minute and then stir in the flour. Add the chicken stock and cook, stirring constantly, until the mixture boils. Turn down the heat and add the sour cream. Add Cognac, rosemary, and curry powder. Add salt and pepper to taste. Place chicken in a casserole or large roasting pan that has a cover and pour the sauce over the chicken. Place in a 350° oven and bake for 45 minutes or until chicken is tender.

Shortly before serving sauté the pineapple slices for a minute or two in some butter. Remove, add more butter and then briefly brown the banana pieces. Place chicken on a large platter and surround with the pineapple and bananas, then garnish with watercress.

To prepare ahead of time: This can be prepared the day before or in the morning, except for the fruit. Reheat the chicken in the oven, saute the fruit, then serve as in the above recipe.

To freeze: This can be frozen but be sure not to overbake the chicken. It will cook further in the reheating. Do not freeze the fruit. After defrosting the chicken, reheat slowly in the oven, sauté the fruit, then serve as in the above recipe.

CHICKEN BREASTS WITH A MAGIC
MUSHROOM SAUCE   [serves 10]

5 whole chicken breasts, skinned, boned and split
salt and pepper
flour
¼ cup butter
½ pound fresh mushrooms, very finely chopped (or put through a meat grinder)

¼ cup butter
3 green onions, finely chopped
4 tablespoons flour
pinch of tarragon
2 cups rich chicken stock
1 cup sour cream
3 tablespoons Cognac

Season chicken with salt and pepper. Roll in flour, then sauté the chicken breasts gently in the ¼ cup butter until lightly browned. Remove from pan. Add the additional butter and sauté the minced mushrooms over high heat for about 2 or 3 minutes. Add the green onions, sprinkle with the flour and stir until blended. Add the tarragon and the chicken stock and stir constantly until sauce comes to a boil. Remove from heat.

Place chicken and sauce in a casserole, cover and bake at 325° or 350° for 30 to 45 minutes, or until tender. Remove from oven. Take out chicken. Add sour cream, Cognac and heat, stirring until sauce is hot but not boiling. Place chicken in a heatproof serving dish or casserole and pour sauce over all. Return to oven long enough to make certain it is very hot. Garnish with finely chopped parsley.

To prepare ahead of time: This lends itself beautifully to preparation ahead of time, either the day before or in the morning. Reheat, covered, in the oven.

To freeze: This freezes. Defrost, then reheat gently in the oven.

MEXICAN CHICKEN DRUNKEN STYLE [serves 10]

5 whole chicken breasts
   split in half
½ cup shortening
salt and pepper
flour
1 ½ cups canned tomatoes
1 teaspoon chopped parsley
1 onion, finely chopped

¾ cup chopped cooked ham
   (optional)
1 cup dry Sherry
¼ teaspoon cloves
¼ teaspoon cinnamon
¼ teaspoon pepper
⅛ teaspoon nutmeg
¼ cup raisins
½ cup blanched almonds

Season chicken with salt and pepper, then roll in flour. Sauté in the shortening until lightly browned on both sides—remove from skillet. In the same skillet sauté the finely chopped onion until just tender. Add parsley and tomatoes and simmer for 10 minutes. Add wine, ham, spices, seasonings, and raisins, and simmer for a few minutes. Meanwhile grind ¼ cup of the almonds (use a blender), and coarsely chop the remaining ¼ cup of almonds. Add these to the skillet and simmer two minutes. Place the chicken in a casserole and pour the contents of the skillet over the chicken. Cover and bake for about 40 minutes at 325°.

To prepare ahead of time: This can be made a day ahead or in the morning, just reheat before serving.

To freeze: Yes, this freezes. Defrost, then reheat before serving.

STUFFED CHICKEN BREASTS, WODAN   [serves 6]

6 *whole* chicken breasts,
    boned but skin left on

salt and pepper
¼ cup butter, melted

For the stuffing:

1 onion, finely chopped
¾ cup finely chopped
    celery
¾ cup butter
salt and pepper to taste

4 cups *fresh* bread crumbs,
    half white and half
    whole wheat
1½ teaspoons poultry
    seasoning

For the sauce:

¼ pound mushrooms, sliced
¼ cup fat drippings left
    from roasting pan
squeeze of lemon juice
1 cup chicken stock

1 tablespoon cornstarch
    dissolved in 2 table-
    spoons cold water
⅓ cup Marsala (can substi-
    tute Sherry)

Make the stuffing: Sauté the chopped onion and celery in the ¾ cup butter slowly until tender. Add bread crumbs and seasonings to taste. Set aside.

Stuff chicken breasts: Open up chicken breasts and season with salt and pepper. Place a good spoonful of the stuffing on one side and then skewer the chicken breasts closed. Place them in a roasting pan and pour the melted butter over the chicken. Bake at 350°, basting frequently, for about an hour. Remove skewers.

Make the sauce: Remove ¼ cup of fat drippings from the roasting pan and sauté the sliced mushrooms in it. Add salt, pepper and lemon juice. Add chicken stock and then thicken, stirring constantly, with the dissolved cornstarch. Add Marsala. Taste for seasoning and set aside. (Reheat later if necessary.)

When ready to serve: Reheat chicken breasts (if necessary) with a foil covering in a 350° oven. Uncover and heat an additional 15 minutes at 350°, basting once or twice. This assumes that the chicken was prepared earlier. Spoon the prepared warm mushroom sauce over each serving and give each guest a whole stuffed chicken breast garnished with watercress.

To prepare ahead of time: The stuffing can be prepared a day or two ahead of time and kept refrigerated. The chicken breasts can be stuffed and baked in the morning, left at room temperature, then reheated as in the above directions.

To freeze: Only the stuffing should be frozen. Defrost completely before using.

DIVINE CHICKEN DIVAN   [serves 10]

5 whole chicken breasts, split
1 large bunch of broccoli (fresh)
½ cup butter
½ cup flour
4 cups chicken stock
3 egg yolks

1 cup whipping cream, whipped
6 tablespoons Sherry
salt and pepper
½ cup grated Parmesan cheese (or more if you like)

Cook or gently sauté the chicken breasts until tender. Remove and bone.

Cook and season lightly the broccoli, then drain and set aside.

Melt the butter, stir in flour and then add the chicken stock. Cook, stirring constantly, until mixture comes to a boil. Simmer gently for about 5 minutes. Cool slightly, then beat in the egg yolks. Whip the cream (not too stiff), and then fold it in with the Sherry. Taste for seasoning.

Place the broccoli in the bottom of an ovenproof dish (or use individual casseroles if you have them). Cover the broccoli with half the sauce. Then cover that with the grated Parmesan. Arrange the chicken over this, then top with the remaining sauce and additional cheese if desired. Place in a 350° oven for 20 minutes or so—just until

73

very hot. If desired you can put this under the broiler for a minute to brown at the very end of the heating period.

To prepare ahead of time: This can be done in the morning or the day before. Bring to room temperature, cover for a short time while reheating in the oven, then uncover and proceed as above.

To freeze: This can be frozen. Defrost and bring to room temperature if possible. Cover with foil for a short time while reheating in the oven, then uncover and proceed as in the above recipe.

CLEVER CASSEROLES OF CONTENTED TURKEY

[serves 4 to 6]

4 or 5 cups of diced cooked turkey
3 tablespoons butter
1 green pepper, chopped
3 tablespoons flour
1 ½ cups chicken stock (or turkey)

1 4-ounce can sliced mushrooms with their liquid
¼ cup cream
1 teaspoon onion powder
salt and pepper to taste
grated Parmesan cheese

Melt butter and sauté the green pepper for a few minutes. Sprinkle with the flour, stir, then gradually add the chicken stock, stirring constantly until mixture boils. Reduce heat and simmer for 1 or 2 minutes. Add mushrooms, mushroom liquid, cream, onion powder, salt and pepper. Stir and simmer for about 5 minutes. Stir in the diced turkey.

Spoon turkey and sauce into small casseroles. Sprinkle generously with grated Parmesan cheese. Place in a 400° oven until very hot. You can brown the top under the broiler if you like.

To prepare ahead of time: These can easily be done the day before or in the morning.

To freeze: These freeze without any problem. If they are cold when ready to bake them, heat first covered, then finish the process uncovered.

Note: This is a good way to use any leftover poultry.

74

TURKEY MORNAY ON SPINACH [serves 8]

8 very large slices of cooked
　　turkey breast
2 packages of frozen,
　　chopped spinach

salt and pepper
butter
Mornay sauce (recipe
　　follows)

Mornay sauce:

2 tablespoons flour
2 tablespoons butter
1 cup turkey stock
1 cup cream (or milk)

salt and pepper to taste
¾ cup grated Parmesan
　　cheese

Melt butter, add flour and stir. Add turkey stock and cook stirring constantly until mixture comes to a boil. Add cream and salt and pepper and simmer gently for 5 to 10 minutes. Stir in the cheese over very low heat and if the sauce seems too thick for your taste, add more cream or turkey stock. Set aside.

To prepare: Cook spinach briefly, then drain thoroughly, squeezing out all of the excess liquid. Season with salt, pepper and butter.

Place the cooked spinach in the bottom of a casserole. Top with the turkey slices, then cover with the sauce. Heat in a 375° oven until hot, then brown under the broiler.

To prepare ahead of time: This can be done the day before or in the morning.

To freeze: This can be frozen.

SIMPLICITY TURKEY CREOLE [serves 4 to 6]

1 medium-size onion,
　　finely chopped
1 green pepper, chopped
4 tablespoons of olive oil
　　(or butter)
½ cup stock or gravy

¼ teaspoon oregano
1 ½ cups canned tomatoes
½ can tomato paste
2 ½ to 3 cups diced
　　cooked turkey
salt and pepper

Sauté onion and green pepper in the oil until tender. Add the stock (or gravy), tomatoes, tomato paste, salt, pepper, and oregano. Simmer slowly for 45 minutes to an hour. Add turkey and heat slowly. Serve with hot white rice.

To prepare ahead of time: Yes, this can be done a day ahead or in the morning, just reheat slowly, stirring gently.

To freeze: This freezes. Defrost, then reheat slowly, stirring gently.

Note: Another good way with that leftover holiday bird.

CORNISH GAME HENS STUFFED WITH RICE, CHICKEN LIVERS, AND MUSHROOMS   [serves 8]

8 Cornish game hens
salt and pepper
1 cup dry white wine
¼ cup Sherry
1 carrot, chopped
1 onion, chopped
1 cup chicken stock
¼ cup melted butter

1 tablespoon cornstarch
  dissolved in ¼ cup
  cold water
Rice, chicken liver and
  mushroom stuffing
  (recipe follows)
watercress

Marinate the game hens in the white wine and Sherry for 2 to 4 hours. While this is being done, make the stuffing:

Rice, chicken liver and mushroom stuffing:

1 onion, finely chopped
1 clove garlic, mashed
¼ cup butter
½ pound chicken livers,
  coarsely chopped
¼ pound fresh mushrooms,
  finely chopped
1½ cups cooked rice

¼ teaspoon oregano
¼ teaspoon sweet basil
¼ teaspoon thyme
1 tablespoon freshly
  chopped parsley
salt and pepper
¼ cup Marsala (or Sherry)

Sauté the onion and garlic in the butter until tender. Add chicken livers and sauté until almost done, then add mushrooms and cook a few minutes longer. Add remaining ingredients, taste for seasoning, remove and cool.

To prepare: Remove game hens from marinade and dry thoroughly, then season with salt and pepper. Stuff each one with the stuffing you have prepared and skewer closed. Place chopped carrot and onion in a large roasting pan and then place the hens on top. Pour melted butter over the hens and bake in a 400° oven for 20 minutes. Reduce temperature to 350° and add the marinade. Baste every 15 minutes for about 40 minutes to 1 hour, or until hens are browned and tender. Remove hens from roaster and make the sauce:

Add chicken stock to the juices remaining in the pan. Add the dissolved cornstarch and cook slowly—stirring constantly—until slightly thickened and transparent. Strain sauce and pour on and around hens. Garnish with watercress.

To prepare ahead of time: The stuffing can be made the day before and refrigerated. The hens can be roasted in the morning, left at room temperature covered, then reheated in a 350° oven before serving. Reheat covered for part of the time. Glaze with a little sauce, then finish reheating uncovered.

To freeze: The stuffing can be made any time and frozen. Defrost completely to use.

SQUABS IN SOY, HONEY, AND GINGER [serves 6]

6 jumbo squabs
½ cup soy sauce
¼ cup honey
1 clove garlic, mashed

1 tablespoon grated fresh
  ginger
¼ cup melted butter or oil

Heat the soy sauce, honey, ginger, garlic, and the butter or oil together.

Season the squabs lightly with salt and pepper, rub with a little oil and place in a 400° oven for 15 minutes. Remove from oven and baste with the sauce. Return to a 350° oven and baste every so often with the sauce until the squabs are tender—45 minutes or longer. Split each squab in half and serve two halves per person.

To prepare ahead of time: These can be done in the morning, covered lightly, and left at room temperature. Reheat in the oven before serving, part of the time covered and the last part of the reheating time, uncovered. These are delicious cold the following day.

77

SQUABS STUFFED WITH APPLES [serves 6]

6 jumbo squabs
salt and pepper

¼ cup melted butter
¼ cup dry red wine

For the stuffing:

4 large or 5 small apples,
  peeled, cored and cut
  into eighths
¼ cup butter

2 to 6 tablespoons sugar
½ cup bread crumbs
1 egg

Make the stuffing: Cook the apples slowly in the butter until just barely tender. Add sugar and stir. Remove from heat and add the bread crumbs. Beat the egg slightly and mix with the apples. Set aside until cool.

Season the squabs with salt and pepper. Stuff with the apple mixture. Close openings with skewers and truss the squabs so that they retain a nice shape. Rub them with the melted butter and place them in a roasting pan. Roast at 425° for 15 minutes. Reduce heat to 325° and add the wine to the pan. Continue to roast, basting occasionally, for about 1 hour, or until squabs are nicely browned and tender.

Remove squabs to a hot platter. Thicken juices if desired, and pour over squabs. Garnish with watercress.

To prepare ahead of time: The stuffing can be prepared a day ahead and kept refrigerated until ready to stuff the squabs. The squabs can be stuffed and roasted in the morning, left at room temperature, then reheated before serving.

To freeze: The stuffing can be frozen. Defrost completely before using.

FIVE NUT STUFFINGS FOR NON-NUTS

1. Sausage and pecan stuffing

2. Gertie Lee Short's pecan and shredded wheat stuffing

3. Just plain pecan stuffing

4. Rice and walnut stuffing

5. Pistachio stuffing for royal purple people

1. SAUSAGE AND PECAN STUFFING
[enough for the largest turkey]

4 onions, finely chopped
2 cups finely chopped celery
1 pound butter
1 pound fresh pork sausage
8 cups fresh bread cubes
3 cups toasted bread cubes

6 cups packaged stuffing
2 cups toasted pecans,
   coarsely chopped
salt and pepper
1 to 3 teaspoons poultry
   seasoning

Sauté chopped onions and celery in part of the butter for 5 to 10 minutes. Add the pork sausage in bits and cook until well done. Add remaining ingredients. Taste for seasoning.

2. GERTIE LEE SHORT'S PECAN AND SHREDDED WHEAT STUFFING
[enough plus some for a large turkey]

4 onions, finely chopped
4 cups finely chopped celery
¾ pound butter
1 loaf 100% whole wheat
   bread
½ loaf white bread
salt and pepper

6 large shredded wheat
   biscuits
1 pound pecans, toasted and
   chopped
about 3 teaspoons poultry
   seasoning

Sauté onions and celery in butter until lightly browned. Place bread in an electric blender one slice at a time and blend into crumbs. Crumble the shredded wheat. Add all of the ingredients to the sautéed vegetables and toss until well combined. Taste for seasoning.

3. JUST PLAIN PECAN STUFFING [enough for 2 five-pound chickens or about 6 game hens or one 10-pound turkey]

2 onions, finely chopped
2 cups finely chopped celery
½ cup butter
3 cups fresh bread crumbs
salt and pepper

1 cup toasted pecans, chopped
½ teaspoon oregano
1 or more teaspoons poultry seasoning

Sauté onion and celery in butter until tender. Stir in remaining ingredients. Taste for seasoning.

4. RICE AND WALNUT STUFFING [enough stuffing for a 10-pound turkey]

2 large onions finely chopped
½ cup butter
2 cup walnuts, coarsely chopped

5 cups cooked rice
1½ cups coconut
salt and pepper
1 cup cooked peas

Sauté onions in the butter until lightly browned. Add walnuts and sauté a few more minutes. Place in a large bowl and add remaining ingredients. Toss well with two forks until all ingredients are blended. Use as needed.

5. PISTACHIO STUFFING [enough for 10 to 12 game hens]

2 onions, finely chopped
2 celery stalks, finely chopped
1½ cups shelled pistachios
1 cup butter
1 clove garlic, mashed

salt and pepper
2 teaspoons poultry seasoning
7 cups fresh bread crumbs

Sauté onions and celery in the butter until tender. Stir in the pistachios and sauté a little longer. Mix all together with the additional ingredients. Cool. Stuff as needed.

To prepare ahead of time: All of these stuffings lend themselves to day ahead preparation. Keep refrigerated.

To freeze: All of these stuffings can be frozen. Defrost completely, then use as needed.

Meat

Meat

SIX VARIATIONS ON A THEME OF STEAK FOR TWO PERSONS

1. Steak Zeus

2. Steak au Poivre

3. Steak Diane

4. Steak Vesuvius

5. Steak Quien Sabe?

6. Steak Smetana

1. STEAK ZEUS

2 New York sirloin steaks,
    cut ½ inch thick and
    flattened to ⅓ inch thick
2 tablespoons butter
salt
1 tablespoon toasted almonds
1 teaspoon finely chopped
    shallots

¼ cup dry red wine
1 round teaspoon of Chicken
    liver paté (see p. 4)
    or buy a good quality
    one
Cognac
freshly chopped parsley

Flatten the steaks, then remove every bit of fat and gristle. Season lightly with salt. Melt butter in a skillet and stir in the shallots for a few seconds, then add the steaks. Cook over moderately high heat for about a minute. Add the almonds around the steaks, turn steaks over and cook about another minute. Add wine and let it bubble up, spread with paté, add a little Cognac and flame. Serve garnished with chopped parsley. The steaks should cook about 1½ minutes on each side, but you have to judge this as you go along.

2. STEAK AU POIVRE

2 New York sirloin steaks,
    cut ½ inch thick, then
    flattened to ⅓ inch thick
freshly cracked black pepper

salt
¼ cup butter
2 tablespoons heavy cream
Cognac

Remove every bit of fat and gristle from the steaks, then press the pepper with palm of the hand into both sides of the steaks. Salt lightly. Heat butter in a skillet and cook steaks for about 1½ minutes on each side—or to your taste. Add cream and cook for a few seconds. Flame with Cognac and serve.

3. STEAK DIANE

2 New York sirloin steaks,
    cut ½ inch thick, all
    fat and gristle removed

salt and pepper
2 tablespoons butter

For the sauce:

2 tablespoons chopped
    green onions
1 tablespoon finely chopped
    parsley
2 tablespoons melted butter

1 tablespoon Worcestershire
    sauce
1 tablespoon A-1 sauce
2 tablespoons Sherry
Cognac

Combine the green onions, parsley, 2 tablespoons melted butter, Worcestershire sauce, A-1 sauce and Sherry and heat gently for about half a minute. Set aside to be used later.

Season steaks with salt and pepper and place in a hot skillet in which you have melted about 2 tablespoons butter. Cook quickly on both sides, add sauce and heat until bubbling, then add a little Cognac, flame and spoon mixture over the meat, then serve immediately. (Steaks should cook about 1½ minutes on each side, or to your taste.)

4. STEAK VESUVIUS

2 New York sirloin steaks,
cut ½ inch thick and
flattened to ⅓ inch thick

salt

¼ cup butter

Cognac

¾ cup finely sliced
mushrooms

additional chopped parsley
and chopped green
onions

For the sauce:

2 tablespoons butter

2 tablespoons chopped
green onions

1 tablespoon finely chopped
parsley

1 tablespoon Worcestershire
sauce

1 tablespoon A-1 sauce

2 tablespoons Sherry

Make the sauce by combining the ingredients and heating them gently for about half a minute. Set aside.

Melt the ¼ cup butter in a skillet. Add steaks and salt very lightly. Add the mushrooms and stir them around a bit. Turn the steak, then add the sauce, simmer for a few seconds, flame with Cognac and garnish with the additional parsley and chopped green onions. (Steaks should cook about 1½ minutes on each side, or to your taste.)

5. STEAK QUIEN SABE?

2 New York sirloin steaks,
cut ½ inch thick and
flattened to ⅓ inch thick,
all fat and gristle
removed

2 tablespoons butter

salt

2 tablespoons toasted
piñon nuts

2 tablespoons raisins which
have been soaked in
Port

2 tablespoons Sherry

2 tablespoons chopped
fresh tomato

Cognac

chopped parsley

For the sauce:

2 tablespoons butter

2 tablespoons chopped
green onions

1 tablespoon finely
chopped parsley

1 tablespoon Worcestershire
sauce

1 tablespoon A-1 sauce

2 tablespoons Sherry

Make the sauce by combining its ingredients and heating them gently for about half a minute. Set aside.

Melt the 2 tablespoons butter in a skillet. Add steaks and salt them lightly. Add the piñon nuts, then the raisins. Turn the steaks and cook briefly, then add the Sauce, the Sherry and then flame them with a little of the Cognac. Stir in the tomato and serve garnished with the chopped parsley. Steaks should cook approximately 1½ minutes on each side—or to your taste.

6. STEAK SMETANA

2 New York sirloin steaks, cut ½ inch thick and flattened to ⅓ inch thick	¾ cup finely sliced mushrooms
salt and pepper	¼ cup red wine
¼ cup butter	½ cup sour cream

Remove every bit of fat and gristle from the steaks. Season lightly with salt and pepper. Heat the ¼ cup butter in a skillet. Add steaks and cook quickly, adding the sliced mushrooms around the sides. Turn steaks and cook briefly, add red wine and reduce it quickly, then add and stir in the sour cream. Serve at once. Steaks should cook approximately 1½ minutes on each side—or to your taste.

PLANKED STEAKS FOR FOUR

4 New York sirloin steaks,
   cut 1¼ to 1½ inches
   thick
salt and pepper
4 tomatoes
8 large mushroom caps

¼ cup grated Parmesan
   cheese
Béarnaise sauce (recipe
   follows)
Duchesse Potatoes (recipe
   follows)

Béarnaise sauce:

½ cup white wine vinegar
½ cup dry white wine
2 teaspoons chopped shallots
¼ teaspoon salt
4 whole peppercorns
pinch of thyme
1 bay leaf
4 egg yolks

2 tablespoons cream
½ pound butter, softened
2 teaspoons chopped fresh
   tarragon or ½ teaspoon
   dried
½ teaspoon chopped fresh
   parsley

Combine vinegar, wine, shallots, salt, peppercorns, thyme, and bay leaf in a saucepan, then reduce to about ¼ cup. Strain into the egg yolks which have been beaten slightly with the cream. Place in top of a double boiler over simmering water and beat with a whisk until mixture begins to thicken. Gradually beat in the softened butter and beat over the hot water until mixture reaches desired consistency. Stir in the tarragon and parsley.

Note: This can be made several days ahead and refrigerated. It freezes too. Defrost overnight in the refrigerator. Reheat over hot water, whisking all of the time so the mixture does not curdle or separate.

Duchesse potatoes:
Add one or more egg yolks to well seasoned mashed potatoes—or to instant mashed potatoes, then set aside until ready to use.

To prepare: Core the tomatoes, then season with salt and pepper. Place 1 tablespoon of the grated Parmesan on top of each tomato, then bake in a 350° oven for about 5 or 6 minutes. Remove and set aside.

Season steaks, then broil until medium rare (or rare) on both sides. Meanwhile, season and sauté the mushroom caps. Oil a large wood plank and around the edge place the mushroom caps alternately with the tomatoes. Place the steaks which have been broiled in the center, then using a pastry bag pipe on the Duchesse potatoes. Place in a 500° oven until potatoes are brown, or place under the broiler). Remove from oven and spoon a little of the Béarnaise sauce into each of the mushroom caps. Decorate the plank with tiny sprigs of parsley and then serve all very hot.

ROAST TENDERLOIN OF BEEF MADEIRA [serves 6 to 8]

1 whole beef tenderloin, trimmed, weighing about 5 pounds	2 tomatoes, peeled and chopped
oil	2 cups beef stock
garlic	½ to ¾ cup Madeira
salt and pepper	1 or 2 tablespoons cornstarch dissolved in ¼ cup cold water
1 onion, finely chopped	
1 large carrot, finely chopped	watercress
½ cup dry red wine	

Season beef with oil, garlic, salt and pepper. Place in a roasting pan with the chopped onion and carrot. Roast in a 400° oven for about 30 minutes to an hour depending upon the size, weight, and temperature of the meat. Baste once or twice. Remove meat from the pan. Deglaze the roasting pan by adding the red wine and the beef stock and the tomatoes. Cook until somewhat reduced and then strain into a saucepan. Add the Madeira and simmer for a few more minutes. Thicken with the cornstarch and water mixture, then cook slowly a few minutes longer.

Garnish the roast with watercress. Slice the tenderloin and spoon some of the sauce on each serving.

To prepare ahead of time: This can be prepared in the morning or early afternoon. Under-roast the beef for it will cook more in the reheating. Make the sauce and leave both beef tenderloin and the sauce at room temperature. Reheat tenderloin, basting once or twice in a hot oven (400°) for about 15 or 20 minutes. Reheat the sauce gently, then proceed as in the above recipe.

ROAST TENDERLOIN OF BEEF WITH DIANE SAUCE

[serves 6 to 8]

1 whole beef tenderloin,
    trimmed, weighing
    about 5 pounds

olive oil
salt and pepper
½ cup dry white wine

For the sauce:

½ cup butter, melted
4 to 6 green onions,
    finely chopped
⅓ cup Cognac

2 teaspoons Dijon-type
    mustard
1 teaspoon Worcestershire
    sauce

Combine ingredients for the sauce, heat gently, then set aside. Season the beef with olive oil, salt and pepper. Roast in a 400° oven for about 30 minutes to 1 hour, depending upon the size, weight, and the temperature of the meat. Baste with the white wine the last 10 minutes.

Place meat on a large platter. Pour the prepared sauce into the roasting pan and heat, stirring together with the remaining pan juices. Pour over the roast. Carve, serving some of the sauce with each portion.

Note: There is really no point in trying to do this ahead of time since it is such a simple operation.

ROAST TENDERLOIN OF BEEF VISIGOTHIC

[serves 6 to 8]

1 whole beef tenderloin,
    trimmed, weighing
    about 5 pounds
oil
salt and pepper
1 large onion, sliced

1 cup chili sauce
¼ cup A-1 sauce
1 teaspoon Worcestershire
    sauce
1 cup dry red wine

Season beef with oil, salt and pepper. Place in an uncovered roasting pan and roast in a 450° oven for 15 minutes. Remove and add the sliced onion. Return to oven for an additional 15 minutes, then remove and pour the chili sauce, A-1 sauce, and Worcestershire sauce over the top of the roast. Return to the oven for another 15 minutes, adding half the wine toward the very end of the roasting period.

Remove meat from pan and place on a platter. Add remaining wine to the sauce in the roaster and stir over heat, scraping pan to get all of the good brown parts. When sauce begins to boil, remove and pour over and around the roast. Carve at the table, giving each person some of the sauce with a slice of meat.

To prepare ahead of time: This can be prepared in the morning or early afternoon. Undercook the beef, and be sure to leave it and the sauce at room temperature. Reheat the beef, basting once or twice, in a 400° oven for about 15 or 20 minutes. Reheat the onion sauce and proceed as in above recipe.

SIRLOIN STRIPPER [serves 12]

a 12-pound sirloin stripper salt and pepper
(also known as the New watercress
York cut sirloin)

Place meat in a large shallow baking pan and season well with salt and pepper. Place in a 450° oven for 15 minutes, reduce temperature to 325° and cook about 1 additional hour. (Meat should be at room temperature.) The fat will baste the roast automatically.

Remove meat to a large platter, slice about ½ inch thick and give each person some of the watercress garnish.

Note: Since this cooks such a relatively short time, and because there is no basting or watching, it would be foolish to do this ahead of time. It can wait for ten minutes in the oven with the oven turned off, and then it can wait on the serving platter an additional 15 minutes, so very close timing isn't really crucial.

STROGANOFF IN THE MELLINKOFF MANNER

[serves 6 to 8]

¾ pound mushrooms, sliced
1 small onion, finely chopped
3 tablespoons butter
salt and pepper to taste
½ cup Sherry
½ teaspoon Accent
¾ teaspoon paprika
2 cups sour cream
2 to 4 tablespoons lemon juice
2 tablespoons butter

2 tablespoons flour
½ cup beef bouillon (can
    use canned, undiluted)
2½ pounds beef tenderloin
    (weight after trimming
    off all fat and gristle)
clarified butter or oil
¼ cup Sherry
1 generous tablespoon
    tomato paste

Sauté sliced mushrooms and chopped onion in the 3 tablespoons of butter, then season with salt and pepper. Cook 2 to 3 minutes. Add the ½ cup Sherry and stir. Slowly whip in the sour cream using a wire whisk. Add the paprika, Accent, and some of the lemon juice and set aside.

In a small saucepan make a thick sauce by melting the 2 tablespoons of butter with the 2 tablespoons flour. Add the beef bouillon over low heat and stir constantly until the sauce is very thick and bubbling. Whip this into the sour cream mixture.

Cut the tenderloin into slices approximately 2″ by ¼″ and then season with salt and pepper. Sauté them quickly in the butter or oil just until browned on both sides, then remove from pan. Don't do too many slices at a time. I do about half of the beef at one time. Drain fat from the skillet and discard after removing beef from the skillet. Add the ¼ cup Sherry to the pan and deglaze.

Stir in the tomato paste, then combine with the sour cream mixture. Stir in the meat. Taste and add more salt, lemon juice, pepper, or paprika, as needed. Set aside. Reheat slowly before serving, but *do not boil.*

To prepare ahead of time: This can be made the day before or in the morning. Reheat slowly, but do not boil.

To freeze: This can be frozen. Defrost completely, then reheat slowly, but do not boil.

BEDEVILED SLICES OF BEEF TENDERLOIN

[serves 8]

1 onion, finely chopped
4 tablespoons butter
1 clove garlic, mashed
5 tablespoons flour
salt and pepper
1½ cups undiluted canned
bouillon
½ cup dry red wine
2½ pounds beef tenderloin
(weight after removing
all fat and gristle)

2 tablespoons oil (or
more if needed)
¾ pound fresh mushrooms,
sliced
½ cup dry red wine
⅔ cup Sherry
2 tablespoons tomato paste
2 tablespoons steak sauce
such as Sauce Robert
or A-1
2 tablespoons prepared
mustard

Sauté onion in the butter until tender, add garlic and cook a minute longer. Stir in flour, season and then add the bouillon. Add the ½ cup red wine and cook, stirring constantly, until the mixture boils, then simmer for about 5 minutes and set aside.

Heat 2 tablespoons oil in skillet. Cut beef into slices ¼ inch thick. Season them, then sauté quickly just until browned. (Do about half the slices at a time, using more oil if necessary.) Remove beef from skillet, then sauté the mushroom slices in same skillet using more butter or oil as needed. Add the other ½ cup red wine and the Sherry, then the tomato paste, steak sauce, and mustard. Stir and simmer gently for a minute or two. Add the meat slices and the onion mixture and heat together, but do not boil.

To prepare ahead of time: This can be prepared the day before or in the morning. Reheat gently without boiling.

To freeze: This freezes. Defrost completely, then reheat without boiling.

SWISS STEAK CHEDDARED [serves 6 to 8]

4 pounds Swiss steak (or
  round steak) cut about
  1 ¼ to 1 ½ inches thick
2 medium onions, sliced
¼ cup oil

flour
salt and pepper
2 cups canned tomatoes
1 cup (or more) grated
  Cheddar cheese

Season steaks with salt and pepper, then pound flour into the meat
on both sides. Shake off the excess. Brown the meat in the oil, then
remove and set aside. Add the sliced onions to the skillet and sauté
slowly for 5 or 6 minutes, stirring occasionally. Layer the meat and
onions in a casserole, adding a little more salt and pepper if desired.
Top with the tomatoes, cover and bake at 275° or 300° for 2 or 3
hours, or until tender. (This is best done the day before, then refrigerated, then reheated before serving.)

Before serving, place meat in a large shallow casserole and spoon the
sauce over. Heat thoroughly. Cover with the grated cheese and
return to oven long enough to melt the cheese.

To prepare ahead of time: This is best in flavor and in texture if
done a day ahead (except for the cheese topping) and reheated the
following day.

To freeze: Yes, by all means, this freezes, but don't add the cheese
topping. Add that just before serving.

SO VERY EASILY STUFFED GREEN PEPPERS
[serves 4 to 6]

4 to 6 green peppers
  (depends on size)
1 pound lean ground beef
1 onion, finely chopped
1 ¾ cups cooked rice
½ cup tomato ketchup

1 tablespoon Worcestershire
  sauce
1 teaspoon salt
2 tablespoons butter
1 cup canned tomatoes

For the sauce:

1 can condensed tomato
  soup, undiluted
1 cup canned tomatoes

½ teaspoon onion powder
salt and pepper to taste

Cut a slice off the top of each pepper and reserve the slices which should be chopped and added to the filling. Remove core and seeds and white membrane. Cover peppers with boiling water and cook for 2 or 3 minutes. Drain and set aside.

Sauté the chopped onion in the butter. Add the chopped pepper slices and sauté for a minute or so. Add the ground beef and sauté until browned. Add the rice, ketchup, Worcestershire, tomatoes and seasonings and cook for a minute or two. Remove from the heat and stuff the green peppers. Shortly before serving, bake them in a 350° oven until very hot—15 to 20 minutes if peppers are at room temperature, longer if they are cold. Serve hot with the following sauce:

Combine ingredients for the sauce and stir until it boils. Turn down heat and simmer for 10 minutes.

To prepare ahead of time: These can be prepared the day before or in the morning. Refrigerate and then heat in the oven until hot. Heat sauce separately.

To freeze: These can be frozen. The sauce can be frozen separately too, but its preparation is so simple that it would seem a foolish procedure.

Note: In the final baking of the stuffed peppers they can be topped with grated cheese for a pleasant variation.

SPICY, SAUCY MEATBALLS [serves 4]

1 pound ground round
1 teaspoon salt
2 tablespoons bread crumbs

a little pepper
⅓ cup tomato juice
butter or oil

For the sauce:

1 small onion, coarsely chopped
1 tablespoon cornstarch
grated rind of one lemon
juice of one lemon
juice of one orange
⅛ teaspoon powdered cloves
¼ teaspoon dry mustard

⅛ teaspoon powdered cinnamon
½ teaspoon fine herbs
1½ cups water
3 tablespoons brown sugar
2 tablespoons butter
½ cup currants
¼ cup rum (optional)

94

Combine the ground round, salt, bread crumbs, pepper and tomato juice and shape into small meatballs. Sauté quickly in oil or butter until browned, then add to the previously prepared sauce.

Sauce preparation: Combine the chopped onion, cornstarch, lemon rind, lemon juice, orange juice, cloves, cinnamon, mustard, fine herbs in a blender and spin until smooth. Heat the water, brown sugar and butter together, adding the currants after mixture is hot. Add sauce from the blender and cook, stirring constantly, until sauce boils. Turn heat down and simmer very slowly for about 10 minutes. Add rum if desired.

To prepare ahead of time: These can be done ahead of time, either the day before or in the morning. Keep them refrigerated in the sauce, then reheat gently.

To freeze: These can be frozen. Freeze in the sauce.

Note: These make a delicious appetizer. Make the meatballs small, place them in a chafing dish with the sauce and let guests help themselves.

JOE'S SPECIAL: BEEF AND SPINACH
SAN FRANCISCO STYLE   [serves 4 to 6]

1 pound lean ground beef
1 onion, finely chopped
1 package frozen chopped
   spinach, cooked and
   drained

¼ pound fresh mushrooms,
   finely sliced
salt, pepper, and garlic salt
4 or 5 tablespoons butter
6 beaten eggs

Sauté sliced mushrooms and onions in the butter until lightly browned, then add beef and cook until it has browned. Stir in the spinach and seasonings. Pour in the eggs and stir until lightly set. Turn over once with a spatula and cook a minute or so longer. Serve very hot with sour dough bread and butter.

To prepare ahead of time: The spinach-beef mixture can be done ahead of time, in the morning or early afternoon. Reheat, then add eggs and proceed with the cooking.

SALISBURY STEAKS WITH SATAN'S
BEST MUSHROOM SAUCE   [serves 4 generously]

1 ¼ pounds ground round
    or chuck
1 teaspoon salt
¼ teaspoon garlic salt
¼ teaspoon pepper
¼ teaspoon thyme
¼ cup water

3 green onions, finely
    chopped
½ green pepper, finely
    chopped
1 tablespoon finely
    chopped parsley

Combine thoroughly and form into 4 oval patties about ½ inch thick. Broil or barbecue to taste. Serve with the following sauce:

Satan's best mushroom sauce:

¼ pound fresh mushrooms,
    sliced
¼ cup butter
salt and pepper
1 tablespoon flour
¾ cup beef stock
¾ cup dry red wine

⅓ cup tomato ketchup
1 teaspoon prepared
    mustard
1 teaspoon Worcestershire
    sauce
2 tablespoons Sherry

Sauté mushrooms in butter, season, then stir in flour. Add beef stock and wine and stir until mixture comes to a boil. Stir in remaining ingredients and then simmer for a few minutes. Serve very hot over the broiled Salisbury steaks.

To prepare ahead of time: The mushroom sauce can be prepared the day before or in the morning. The Salisbury steaks can be made into patties and refrigerated either the day before or in the morning.

To freeze: The Salisbury steaks can be made into patties and frozen. The best way to defrost them is overnight in the refrigerator, but if that is impossible, defrost at room temperature for no more than 3 hours. The sauce can be frozen. Reheat gently, then serve as in above recipe.

SWEET RED PEPPER AND SHORT RIBS   [serves 4 to 6]

3 pounds beef short ribs,
    as lean as possible
2 tablespoons oil
salt and pepper
flour
½ pound fresh mushrooms
12 small boiling onions

2 cups strong beef stock
1 bay leaf
¼ teaspoon marjoram
1 clove garlic, mashed
1 sweet red pepper, peeled
    and cut in 1-inch pieces
½ can tomato paste

Trim excess fat off the short ribs, season with salt and pepper and then roll in flour. Sauté in oil until browned on all sides and remove to a casserole with a tight fitting cover. Place mushrooms and onions in skillet used for browning the meat and sauté these for 5 minutes or so. Add all remaining ingredients and bring to a boil. Pour over meat, cover and bake at 275° for 2 or 3 hours, or until meat is tender.

Taste for seasoning, and if desired, thicken the sauce some more.

To prepare ahead of time: This can be cooked the day before or in the morning.

To freeze: This can be cooked and frozen.

MERYL'S MADNESS—A PERFECT
BEEF STEW FOR NON-COOKS   [serves about 6]

3 pounds beef stew (cut in
    large cubes)
1 can condensed mushroom
    soup, undiluted
⅓ cup Sherry

1 package dried onion soup,
    no liquid added
salt if needed
freshly ground black
    pepper

To add later:

quartered and sautéed fresh
    mushrooms
fresh peas

fresh cooked carrots or any
    kind of vegetable you
    prefer

Mix together the beef, mushroom soup, onion soup and Sherry. Place in a casserole, cover and bake at 350° for 1 hour. Reduce heat to 325° and bake about another 2 hours or until meat is tender. Remove from oven, cool, then refrigerate overnight. The next day, heat in oven, season with salt (if needed) and freshly ground black pepper and add the vegetables.

To prepare ahead of time: Both the flavor and the texture of the beef is better if this is cooked the day before as instructed in the above recipe.

To freeze: Yes, this freezes beautifully. Defrost, heat, and add the vegetables.

BEEF WITH SAUERKRAUT AND SOUR CREAM

[serves 4 to 6]

2 or 3 pounds lean stewing beef cut in 1½ inch cubes	½ to 1 teaspoon paprika
	1 cup tomato purée
	1 cup water
¼ cup oil or clarified butter	1 or 2 tablespoons sugar
2 onions, sliced	1 cup sour cream
1 clove garlic, mashed	2 cups sauerkraut
salt and pepper to taste	freshly chopped parsley

Sauté meat in the oil or butter until browned. Remove and set aside. Add onions to skillet and cook 5 or 6 minutes. Return meat to skillet and add garlic, salt, pepper, paprika, sugar, tomato purée, water, and stir. Cover tightly and simmer slowly until meat is nearly tender. Add sour cream and sauerkraut and continue cooking very gently until meat is very tender. Taste for seasoning. (Cooking will probably take 2 or 3 hours.) Serve hot with rice or noodles or mashed potatoes. Garnish with plenty of chopped parsley.

To prepare ahead of time: This can be made the day before or in the morning.

To freeze: This can be frozen.

LEG OF LAMB WITH A VEGETABLE BOUQUET

[serves 6 to 8]

1 leg of lamb
salt, pepper and paprika
1 dozen or more small
  boiling onions
2 pounds fresh peas
4 or 5 large boiling potatoes,
  cut into olive shapes
1 cauliflower divided
  into flowerets

6 large carrots, cut into 1-inch
  pieces, then ends
  rounded off
12 or more mushroom caps
1 ½ cups undiluted bouillon
2 tablespoons cornstarch
  diluted in ¼ cup cold
  water

Season leg of lamb with salt, pepper and paprika. Roast in a 350° oven for 2 or 3 hours depending upon weight and your taste. Baste occasionally.

Meanwhile prepare the vegetables. Shell peas and set aside. Cook cauliflower until just barely tender, drain and set aside. Do the same with the potatoes and carrots. Sauté the mushrooms briefly and season with salt and pepper. Cook onions, drain and set aside.

Place lamb on a very large heat-proof platter. Remove grease from roasting pan and deglaze the pan with the bouillon, then thicken the juices with the diluted cornstarch. Taste for seasoning.

Reheat the vegetables, each kind in a separate pan, sautéed in a little butter, seasoned lightly with salt and pepper. Cook the peas for about 3 minutes and drain. Arrange vegetables around the lamb in separate little bunches. Pour a little of the sauce over the lamb, serve the rest separately.

To prepare ahead of time: The leg of lamb can be roasted in the morning and the sauce prepared. (Leave at room temperature.) The lamb can then be reheated a half hour or so before serving. All of the vegetables can be cooked the day before or in the morning. Do the cooking in butter shortly before garnishing the lamb. (The peas cook such a short time that one should leave them raw until just before cooking them.)

Note: Hollandaise sauce can be served on the cauliflower bouquet if desired.

LEG OF LAMB WITH ONIONS AND ARTICHOKES

[serves 6 to 8]

1 leg of lamb
6 large fresh artichokes
3 large onions, quartered
salt, pepper and paprika

2 cups water (or beef stock)
1 tablespoon cornstarch
   dissolved in ¼ cup
   cold water

Place lamb, seasoned with salt, pepper and paprika, in a roasting pan. Place quartered onions around it. Roast for 1 hour at 400°. Meanwhile remove outer leaves of artichokes, trim away all tough parts with a scissors, cut in half and remove chokes, and then soak in water to which lemon has been added.

After lamb as cooked an hour, arrange artichokes cut side down around the lamb. Add water or beef stock and cover the roasting pan. Reduce heat to 300° and cook for another hour. Remove cover once again and roast another 30 minutes to an hour depending upon the weight of the lamb and just how done you like it.

Place leg of lamb on platter, arrange artichokes around it. Thicken sauce lightly with a little dissolved cornstarch, and pour a little of it over the lamb. Serve the rest of the sauce separately with the onions right in the sauce.

To prepare ahead of time: This can all be cooked in the morning, then reheated before serving time.

LEG OF LAMB WITH A SPICY SAUCE   [serves 6 to 8]

1 leg of lamb
salt and pepper
¼ cup chili sauce
1 ½ tablespooons Worcestershire sauce
2 tablespoons vinegar

1 large onion finely chopped
1 green pepper finely chopped
1 clove of garlic, mashed
¼ teaspoon thyme
1 cup beef stock

Mix together the chili sauce, Worcestershire, vinegar, onion, green pepper, garlic, thyme, and beef stock. Season the lamb and place in a roasting pan. Pour the combined mixture over the lamb and roast at 325° for 2½ to 3 hours, depending upon the size of the lamb. Baste frequently.

Remove lamb from roasting pan. Remove fat from the sauce. Serve the sauce with slices of the lamb. (If desired the sauce can be put in the blender and blended until smooth.)

To prepare ahead of time: This can be prepared in the morning. Leave the lamb at room temperature, then reheat in the oven before serving.

LEG OF LAMB, BUTTERFLY STYLE [serves 6]

    1 large leg of lamb, boned
        and flattened out—
        called butterflied

Marinade:

    1 sliced onion   ¼ teaspoon oregano
    1 clove garlic, mashed   ¼ teaspoon thyme
    ½ teaspoon black pepper   juice of 1 lemon
    1½ teaspoons salt   ½ cup red wine vinegar
    ½ teaspoon sweet basil   ¾ cup oil

Combine ingredients for the marinade. Marinate the lamb in this mixture all day, turning once or twice. Do this at room temperature. Broil on the barbecue or under an oven broiler, turning and basting with the remaining marinade. This takes from 40 to 50 minutes.

Note: This is delicious cold the next day.

A LYRICAL LAMB STEW [serves about 6]

2 to 3 pounds lamb stew meat
(weight after trimming)
salt and pepper
¼ cup butter or oil
1 large onion, finely chopped
2 large carrots, finely
chopped
3 stalks celery, finely chopped
¼ cup flour

1 cup dry white wine
3 cloves
½ teaspoon dried thyme
3 garlic cloves
1 bay leaf
½ teaspoon peppercorns
3 sprigs parsley
2 cups beef stock
salt and pepper to taste

For the vegetables:

½ pound fresh mushrooms,
quartered and sautéed
in butter
6 turnips, quartered and ends
trimmed, boiled just
until barely tender
2 pounds fresh peas, shelled
(or 1 package of frozen)

4 carrots, cut in large pieces,
ends trimmed, boiled
just until barely tender
1 or 2 dozen small boiling
onions, cooked until
barely tender

Season the lamb with salt and pepper, then brown quickly in the butter or oil. Remove to a large casserole and keep covered. Add the onion, carrots and celery to the skillet and sauté until the vegetables begin to brown, then sprinkle on the flour. Add the wine and beef stock and stir constantly until mixture begins to boil. Reduce heat and simmer for a minute. Place the cloves, thyme, garlic, bay leaf, peppercorns, and parsley into a piece of cloth or cheesecloth and tie into a bouquet garni, then add to the mixture. Pour over the meat in the casserole, cover and bake at 300° for 1½ to 2 hours, or until the meat is tender. Taste for seasoning and thicken more if desired.

Add the previously prepared vegetables to the stew and place in oven until everything is very hot. Serve with boiled or sautéed potato balls on the side.

To prepare ahead of time: This can be done the day before or in the morning. Reheat gently in the oven.

To freeze: This can be frozen. I recommend freezing it without the vegetables. After defrosting and reheating, add the above vegetables, or any others that you prefer.

LAMB CURRY SANS WORRY [serves about 6]

⅓ cup butter
2 onions, chopped
3 or 4 cups diced cooked
   lamb
3 tablespoons flour
2 ½ to 3 cups thickened lamb
   gravy (or can substitute
   some canned bouillon
   lightly thickened)

1 green apple, peeled and
   chopped
¼ teaspoon thyme
salt and pepper to taste
4 teaspoons good quality
   curry powder (or any
   amount you prefer)
1 package frozen peas
   (to be added later)

Sauté the onions in the butter until golden and tender. Add diced lamb and cook a little longer. Add apple and stir. Sprinkle flour over, stir, then add gravy or thickened stock and cook, stirring constantly, until mixture comes to a boil. Turn down heat, add salt, pepper, thyme, and curry powder. Simmer for about 30 minutes. Shortly before serving, pour boiling water over peas, drain, then add them to the curry. Serve with steamed white rice and assorted condiments such as: plumped raisins, toasted coconut, crisp bacon bits, chopped candied ginger, piñons or other toasted nuts, sliced bananas in a little lemon juice, chopped green onions, chopped green pepper, chopped hard cooked eggs, and of course, chutney.

To prepare ahead of time: This can be done the day before or in the morning, but add the peas shortly before serving.

To freeze: This can of course be frozen. Freeze without the peas.

Note: To simplify, leave out the peas.

SWEETBREADS AND MUSHROOM MARVEL [serves 4]

2 pairs of sweetbreads
¼ pound fresh mushrooms,
   sliced
1 thin slice of cooked ham,
   very finely chopped
1 onion, finely chopped

salt and pepper
6 tablespoons butter
flour
¼ cup tomato sauce
¼ cup Sherry

Soak sweetbreads in ice water for about an hour. Simmer in acidulated water for 15 minutes. Drain and put into ice water. When cool, dry and trim. Cut into thick slices. Season with salt and pepper and lightly dust with flour. Set aside.

Sauté the chopped onions and minced ham in 2 tablespoons of the butter, stirring until onions are tender and lightly browned—from 5 to 10 minutes. Add sliced mushrooms and sauté, stirring, for about 2 minutes. Add tomato sauce, cover and simmer for 10 minutes. Add Sherry and reduce some over high heat. Taste for seasoning. Keep warm.

Sauté the floured sweetbread slices in the remaining 4 tablespoons of butter, for 5 to 10 minutes or until beautifully browned. Combine with the sauce and reheat if necessary. Serve hot.

To prepare ahead of time: The sweetbreads can be cooked, trimmed and soaked in ice water in the morning. The sauce can be prepared in the morning. Sauté the sweetbreads shortly before serving.

BONED AND ROLLED LOIN OF VEAL MARSALA FOR TWELVE

2 loins of veal, boned and rolled, about 5 or 6 pounds each before boning
6 shallots, finely chopped
salt and pepper
½ cup melted butter

½ cup Marsala
½ to 1 cup stock (use veal bones to make stock)
1 or 2 tablespoons cornstarch dissolved in
½ cup cold water

Season veal, place in roasting pan, add shallots, and pour melted butter over. Roast at 300° for 2 to 3 hours, basting every 15 minutes, and turning the two roasts over once or twice during this time. Veal should have browned nicely and should be well done. Remove from the oven and place veal loins on a platter. Make a sauce by adding the Marsala and the stock to the roasting pan and scraping all of the good brown bits into the liquid. Thicken to taste with the dissolved cornstarch. Taste for seasoning.

Remove strings from veal. Place on an ovenproof dish and pour some of the sauce over. If veal has cooled off, cover lightly with foil and reheat in a 300° oven, remove from oven, cover with some more of the sauce and carve at the table. Serve additional sauce separately.

To prepare ahead of time: This can be cooked in the morning, left at room temperature, then reheated before serving as directed above.

LOIN OF VEAL IN A GARDEN [serves 6 to 8]

1 boned and then tied loin of veal (about 5½ pounds)
salt and pepper
1 onion, chopped
¼ cup melted butter
⅓ cup dry Vermouth
1 tablespoon cornstarch dissolved in ¼ cup cold water
2 pounds fresh peas
12 large mushrooms
5 potatoes (cut into olive shapes)
1 cauliflower (divided into flowerets)
2 or 3 cups fresh carrots (shaped into 1 or 1½ inch pieces)
Hollandaise sauce (optional for the cauliflower)—for a recipe see p. 34

Season the veal with salt and pepper, then roast in a 325° oven with the butter and chopped onion. Baste often. Roast about 20 to 25 minutes to the pound. Remove veal from roasting pan. Remove excess fat from pan, then deglaze it by adding the Vermouth and a little water or stock. Thicken to taste with the cornstarch dissolved in cold water. Strain the sauce.

Shell and cook peas for a few minutes, then drain. Cook potatoes just until tender, then roll in some melted butter. Same for the carrots and cauliflower. Sauté the mushrooms very briefly in some butter. Season all of the vegetables and keep them warm.

Arrange all of the warm vegetables around the roast veal. Spoon Hollandaise over the cauliflower. Carve at the table and serve the sauce for the veal separately spooning some on each slice of veal.

To prepare ahead of time: The vegetables can be cooked either the day before or in the morning. Reheat each kind separately in a little butter before arranging around the roast veal. The veal and sauce can be cooked in the morning. Reheat the veal lightly covered with foil before serving. Reheat the sauce. (Do not refrigerate the roast veal, just leave it at room temperature.)

VEAL TENDERLOINS BRAISED WITH
CARROTS AND ONIONS [serves about 8]

4 veal tenderloins (weighing
    about 1 pound each)
24 small boiling onions
10 small carrots
salt and pepper
flour

¼ cup clarified butter
    or oil
¾ cup water or stock
⅓ cup tomato purée or
    tomato sauce

Peel boiling onions. Peel carrots but leave them whole. Roll the veal tenderloins in flour. Sauté the veal in the oil or butter and keep turning them to brown on all sides. Add the onions and sauté a few more minutes. Add salt and pepper, water or stock, and tomato purée. Add the carrots and bring to a boil. Cover and place in a 275° oven and cook until veal is tender—about 1½ to 2 hours. Serve sliced with hot buttered noodles.

To prepare ahead of time: This can be prepared the day before or in the morning. Slice the veal and replace it in the sauce. Refrigerate, then reheat in a slow oven the following day.

To freeze: This can be frozen. After veal is tender, slice it and put it the sauce, then freeze. Defrost, then reheat gently in the oven.

VEAL WITH LEMON [serves 4]

2 pounds veal scallops,
    trimmed and flattened
salt and pepper
flour
¼ cup butter

½ cup Marsala or moderately
    dry Sherry
½ or 1 whole lemon, sliced
    (skin left on but seeds
    removed)

Season veal then roll lightly in flour, shaking off excess. Sauté quickly in the butter and remove pieces to another plate while continuing to brown the remaining scallops. Return to skillet when finished with the browning and add the Marsala or Sherry. Bring quickly to a boil, reduce heat and simmer with the sliced lemon (as much as your taste dictates) over low heat for about 10 minutes.

VEAL WITH APRICOTS AND PRUNES   [serves about 6]

3 pounds lean veal stew meat,
   cut in 1½ inch cubes
salt and pepper
¼ cup oil or clarified butter
2 onions, chopped
3 tablespoons flour

3 cups veal or beef stock
1 cup dried prunes
¾ cup dried apricots
1 cup (or more) fresh or
   frozen peas (optional)

Season the veal, then sauté in oil or butter until browned on all sides. Place it in a casserole. In same skillet sauté the onions until lightly browned, then sprinkle with the flour and stir in the beef stock (or veal stock if you have it). Cook over low heat and stir constantly until mixture comes to a boil. Pour over the veal, cover tightly and simmer over low heat—or bake at 300°—for about 1½ hours. Add apricots and prunes, then continue cooking until meat is tender —an additional 1 to 1½ hours. Taste for seasoning and add the peas if desired. Serve with noodles or steamed rice.

To prepare ahead of time: This can be cooked the day before or in the morning, to be reheated before serving.

To freeze: No problem, just freeze, then reheat after defrosting.

A QUICKLY DONE VEAL VERMOUTH   [serves 4]

2 pounds veal scallops,
   trimmed and flattened
salt and pepper
flour
½ cup butter

½ cup finely chopped
   green onions
⅓ cup finely chopped
   parsley
about ¾ cup dry Vermouth

Season veal with salt and pepper, then dip in flour, shaking off all of the excess flour. Brown quickly in the butter, removing pieces as they are done. Add the green onions and parsley to skillet, return veal to skillet and add the Vermouth. Bring to a boil and simmer for about 5 minutes, covered part of the time. Serve at once with sautéed potato balls or steamed rice.

VEAL SCALLOPS WITH MUSHROOMS AND CHEESE

[serves 6 to 8]

2 ½ to 3 pounds trimmed and flattened veal scallops
salt and pepper
flour
½ cup butter
½ pound fresh mushrooms, sliced
thinly sliced ham (Prosciutto or Danish)
thinly sliced Mozzarella cheese

1 cup brown sauce (I use beef bouillon and a thickening of about 2 tablespoons butter mixed with 2 tablespoons flour, a tablespoon or so of Sherry and sometimes a ½ teaspoon tomato paste)
½ cup grated Parmesan cheese
½ teaspoon dried basil

Season veal with salt and pepper, then roll in flour (shake off excess). Sauté veal in butter until bròwned on both sides, then transfer to a large shallow casserole (or better yet, two casseroles, so as to have them in a single layer). In same skillet, sauté the sliced mushrooms, season to taste, then add the 1 cup of brown sauce. Cover and simmer for a few minutes, then set aside.

Top each piece of veal with a thin slice of ham, then a thin slice of cheese. Spoon on the mushrooms and sauce, distributing them so that each piece of veal gets some of the mushrooms and the sauce. Combine the grated cheese with the dried basil. Sprinkle it over all.

Cover with foil and bake at 350° for 20 minutes, then uncover and bake an additional 10 minutes. (This timing is for veal at room temperature—if cold, it must be heated longer.)

To prepare ahead of time: This can be prepared the day before or in the morning and kept in the refrigerator. Take out of the refrigerator several hours before baking, then proceed as in the above recipe.

To freeze: This can be frozen. Defrost overnight in the refrigerator if possible. After defrosting proceed with the baking as in the above recipe.

VEAL CHOPS SUCCESS

[serves 3 or 6 depending upon size of veal chops]

6 thick veal chops
4 tablespoons butter
¼ pound fresh mushrooms, sliced
1 tablespoon flour
¾ cup stock or water
salt and pepper
¼ teaspoon thyme
½ cup sour cream
2 or 3 tablespoons Cognac

Sauté chops in the butter until lightly browned on both sides. Remove from pan. In this same skillet sauté the sliced mushrooms for a few minutes, adding a little more butter if necessary. Sprinkle with the flour, stir and reduce heat. Add remaining ingredients, stirring constantly until sauce comes to a boil. Simmer very slowly for 1 or 2 minutes. Return chops to pan, cover and simmer slowly for about 40 minutes, turning once. Serve with wild or brown rice.

To prepare ahead of time: These can be prepared in the morning, then reheated before serving. Thes can also be done the day before, bring to room temperature, then reheat covered.

To freeze: These can be frozen. Defrost, bring to room temperature, then reheat covered in a slow oven.

VEAL SCALOPPINE MARSALA FOR MANY

[serves 12 to 16]

6 pounds trimmed veal slices
1 cup flour
4 teaspoons salt
½ teaspoon pepper
¼ teaspoon paprika
2 pounds fresh mushrooms, sliced
butter
2 tablespoons flour
2 cups beef bouillon
1¼ cups Marsala

Cut veal into serving pieces. Combine flour, salt, pepper, and paprika and stir well. Place this in a paper bag. Add veal slices a few at a time and coat with the seasoned flour. Sauté veal slices quickly in butter, browning lightly on both sides. As they are browned remove them to a large roasting pan with a cover. Sauté the mushrooms in the same skillet with some additional butter (I usually do this in 2 batches).

When mushrooms are cooked, sprinkle with the 2 tablespoons of flour and stir. Add bouillon and Marsala and stir over low heat until mixture comes to a boil. Pour over the veal. Cover and place in a 325° oven for 30 to 40 minutes, or until tender.

To prepare ahead of time: This can be cooked the day before or in the morning.

To freeze: This freezes.

VEAL CORDON BLEU SIMPLIFIED [serves 4]

8 large thin slices of perfect veal, about 4" by 6"
salt and pepper
thin slices of ham (I use the packaged Danish sliced kind)

thin slices of Swiss cheese (or use Monterey Jack)
flour
1 egg beaten lightly with a little water
dry bread crumbs
oil or shortening

For the sauce:

½ cup butter, melted
juice of half a lemon
1 tablespoon finely chopped parsley

1 tablespoon finely chopped green onions (optional)

Pound the veal slices until very thin. Season lightly with salt and pepper. Place a thin slice of ham and then one of cheese on 4 of the veal slices. Make sure that neither the ham nor the cheese sticks out over the veal. Top these with the remaining slices of veal. Pound edges together as much as possible, using the palm of the hand. Chill if possible for an hour or longer. These are now what I would call veal sandwiches.

Flour the veal sandwiches completely, dip in the beaten egg, then dip in the dry bread crumbs, covering them completely. Place these on a tray lined with more bread crumbs and place uncovered in the refrigerator.

Shortly before serving, sauté these veal sandwiches in oil or shortening for about 5 minutes on a side. Remove from the skillet and place on a heatproof serving dish. Place in a 325° oven for 15 to 20 minutes. Serve with the sauce, previously prepared, poured over.

Sauce: Combine the butter, lemon juice and parsley (onion if desired) and heat gently.

To prepare ahead of time: The "veal sandwiches" can be prepared up to the point of sautéing them. Keep them refrigerated uncovered as in above recipe until ready to cook.

A SUPER SUPPER OF SMOKED PORK CHOPS, SAUERKRAUT AND SAUSAGES [serves 4]

1 onion, chopped
1 large carrot, chopped
3 tablespoons butter
1 tablespoon chopped
    parsley
salt and pepper to taste
2 cups sauerkraut (drain it, rinse with cold water, drain, rinse, and drain again)

½ cup dry white wine
1 can beef bouillon, undiluted
4 very thick smoked pork chops
4 Polish sausages, or knockwurst, or any other kind of your choosing

Sauté onion and carrot in the butter until tender, about 5 to 10 minutes. Add seasonings, wine, bouillon and sauerkraut. Place in a large casserole, cover and bake at 350° for at least 2 hours, but three are even better. Remove cover, add pork chops and sausages and return to oven for an additional 40 to 45 minutes. (During this last baking period spoon some of the sauerkraut and juice over the chops and sausages.)

Serve with hot boiled potatoes and icy cold beer.

To prepare ahead of time: This can be prepared the day before or in the morning.

PARTY PORK CHOPS [serves 6]

6 large loin pork chops, cut
    about 1¼ inches thick
salt and pepper
flour
6 tablespoons raw rice
6 slices of tomato

6 thin slices onion
6 generous tablespoons of
    shredded raw carrots
6 slices green pepper
1½ cups tomato juice

Season chops with salt and pepper. Flour lightly, then sauté in a little oil until browned on both sides. Drain off excess fat and remove skillet from heat while doing the following: On each chop place 1 tablespoon of raw rice, next a slice of tomato, then 1 tablespoon shredded carrot, then the onion slice and green pepper. Now, spoon some of the tomato juice over each chop and pour the remaining juice in the bottom of the skillet (or do all of this in a large heatproof serving casserole). Cover tightly and bake 1 to 1½ hours at 350° or until chops are tender and rice is cooked.

To prepare ahead of time: This can all be done in the morning, then reheat before serving.

PANDORA'S PORK CHOPS WITH WHITE WINE
[serves 8]

8 very thick loin pork chops,
    as lean as possible
salt and pepper
1 tablespoon butter

1 can mushroom soup,
    undiluted
1 cup dry white wine

Sauté the pork chops in the butter until browned on both sides, season with salt and pepper and remove any excess fat from the pan. Add soup and wine, stir and bring to a boil. Cover and simmer (or put in a 325° oven) until tender. Remove chops from pan, reduce the sauce rapidly to desired consistency, then pour over the chops and serve.

To prepare ahead of time: These can be prepared in the morning, or the day before, then reheated in a 325° oven (covered).

To freeze: These can be frozen. Freeze in the sauce. After defrosting reheat in a 325° oven (covered).

MARY CULLIN'S BARBECUED SPARERIBS

1 ½ cups pineapple juice
¼ cup brown sugar
½ cup chili sauce
1 cup tomato ketchup
1 teaspoon celery seeds

1 onion, finely chopped
dash of nutmeg
salt and pepper
6 to 8 pounds lean pork
    spareribs

Season the ribs with salt and pepper. Place in a large roasting pan and bake at 450° for 30 minutes, turning once or twice, and removing the fat as it cooks down.

Combine the other ingredients and pour this sauce over the ribs. Reduce heat to 300° and bake, basting and turning occasionally for about another hour—or until tender.

To prepare ahead of time: This can be done the day before or in the morning.

To freeze: Yes, these freeze beautifully.

HAM WITH CHERRY SAUCE   [serves 6]

6 rather thick slices of baked
    ham or ham which you
    plan to sauté
½ cup sugar
pinch of salt

1 tablespoon cornstarch
1 1-pound can tart cherries
    with all of the juice
    (these are the kind used
    for making pie)

Make the sauce first: Mix the sugar, salt and cornstarch together and then mix with the cherries and juice. Cook over low heat, stirring constantly until it comes to a full boil. Reduce heat and simmer for about 1 minute.

Heat the slices of baked ham quickly under a broiler, or sauté slices of ham in a little butter. Serve each slice with some of the hot cherry sauce.

To prepare ahead of time: Your ham can be baked a day or more ahead of time. Your sauce can be prepared the day before or in the morning, then reheated before serving.

HERCULES' HAM ROLLS IN SOUR CREAM [serves 6]

12 large thin slices of boiled
    or baked ham
3 tablespoons of butter
1 large onion, finely chopped
1 garlic clove, mashed
1 tablespoon chopped parsley
½ cup fine, dry bread crumbs
1 cup cooked ham, ground

½ cup grated Parmesan
    cheese
2 teaspoons Worcestershire
    sauce
3 egg yolks
¾ cup light cream
¼ cup Sherry
salt and pepper as needed

For the sauce:

3 tablespoons butter
2 tablespoons flour
1 egg, beaten
3 tablespoons grated
    Parmesan cheese

1 ½ cups sour cream
½ teaspoon salt
¼ teaspoon pepper
chopped chives or finely
    chopped green onions

Sauté the onions and garlic in the 3 tablespoons of butter until lightly browned. Combine with the parsley, bread crumbs, ground ham, cheese, egg yolks, cream and Worcestershire, mixing thoroughly. Cook slowly over low heat for just a minute or two. Stir in the Sherry. Taste for seasoning. Place a generous spoonful of this mixture on a slice of ham and roll up. Continue this until all have been rolled and placed in a shallow casserole.

Make the sauce by melting the butter with the flour, adding the remaining ingredients and stirring over low heat until mixture boils. Then spoon this sauce over the ham rolls. Bake uncovered in a 350° oven until hot and bubbly—20 to 30 minutes if they are at room temperature. Garnish with the chopped chives or chopped green onions.

To prepare ahead of time: These can be prepared the day before or in the morning, then baked before serving.

To freeze: These can be frozen. Freeze after pouring the sauce over the rolls. Defrost, then proceed with the baking.

Special Entrées

Special Entrées

A NOBLE SPAGHETTI CARUSO [serves 4 to 6]

1 large onion, finely chopped
1 green pepper, finely chopped
2 tablespoons olive oil
2 cups tomato purée
1 cup tomato sauce
¼ teaspoon sweet basil
¼ teaspoon oregano
⅛ teaspoon thyme

salt and pepper to taste
2 tablespoons olive oil
¾ pound fresh mushrooms, cut in halves or quarters
1 pound fresh chicken livers, cut in halves or quarters
flour
butter
½ pound spaghettini

Make the sauce: Sauté the onion and green pepper in the 2 tablespoons oil for about 5 to 7 minutes. Add the tomato purée, tomato sauce, sweet basil, oregano, thyme, and salt and pepper. Simmer over very low heat for about 1 hour or a little longer.

Sauté the mushrooms quickly in 2 tablespoons oil, season, then set aside.

Flour the chicken livers, then sauté in butter until tender and just done—don't overcook them. Season with salt and pepper.

Add the sautéed mushrooms and livers to the tomato sauce and keep warm over low heat, but do not boil.

Cook spaghettini in plenty of boiling, salted water until the "al dente" stage, that is, until tender but just a little chewy. Drain, then stir in a little butter.

Serve each person with some of the spaghettini and a generous topping of the Caruso sauce. If you like, grated Parmesan cheese can be passed.

To prepare ahead of time: The sauce can be made the day before or in the morning. Reheat slowly and not too long so as not to toughen the livers and mushrooms.

To freeze: The sauce with the livers and mushrooms can be frozen. Reheat slowly and not too long so that the chicken livers do not cook too much.

AN ITALIAN TOMATO FOUNDATION FOR FINITE FRIVOLOUS FOLLIES

[makes enough sauce to serve about 6 to 8]

3 or 4 cloves garlic, mashed
4 large onions, chopped
½ cup olive oil
2 cups canned stewed tomatoes
4 cups canned tomato purée
1 can tomato paste (6 ounces)
½ cup dry red wine

1 ½ cups beef stock (canned bouillon)
1 ½ teaspoons salt (about)
pepper
1 tablespoon sugar
1 teaspoon dried basil
½ teaspoon dried oregano
½ teaspoon dried thyme

Sauté garlic and onions in the oil for 5 to 10 minutes, stirring occasionally. Add remaining ingredients and simmer for 1 ½ to 2 hours. Taste for seasoning.

Serve this with any of the following: (*Plus some kind of cooked pasta*)

meatballs
sautéed chicken livers
diced baked ham, briefly sautéed
sautéed jumbo shrimp

a combination of cooked lobster and crab meat
sautéed pork chops
canned tuna broken up into large pieces

To prepare ahead of time: The sauce can be made days ahead of time (or in the morning), just reheat before using and add the choice of meat or fish.

To freeze: The sauce freezes very nicely. It can, of course, be made in very large quantities, then frozen in smaller portions.

LYRA'S LASAGNA

1 pound wide lasagna noodles, cooked and drained, then rinsed with cold water and drained again
1 small Mozzarella cheese, thinly sliced

¼ pound grated Parmesan cheese
1 pound Ricotta Cheese
Tomato-Meat sauce (recipe follows)

Tomato-Meat Sauce:

3 tablespoons oil
2 cloves garlic, mashed
2 onions, chopped
2½ pounds ground round
½ pound fresh mushrooms, sliced
3 cups canned tomatoes

3 cans tomato paste (6-ounce size)
4 cups beef stock (can use canned beef bouillon)
½ teaspoon dried sweet basil
½ teaspoon dried oregano
salt and pepper to taste

Sauté the onions and the garlic in the oil for about 3 or 4 minutes. Add the ground round and sauté until lightly browned. Place all in a large saucepan. Sauté the mushrooms for a few minutes, then add to the beef. Add all of the remaining ingredients and simmer slowly uncovered for about 1½ to 2 hours. Stir occasionally.

To assemble: Place a layer of the drained noodles in a casserole, then some of the sliced Mozzarella, then sauce, then some Ricotta, then the Parmesan cheese. Continue in this fashion until ingredients are used up, ending with the Parmesan on top. THERE SHOULD BE SAUCE LEFTOVER WHICH YOU WILL SERVE ON THE SIDE. Bake the lasagna in a 350° oven for 30 to 45 minutes, or until hot and bubbling.

To prepare ahead of time: This can be made the day before or in the morning. Do the baking before serving.

To freeze: This can be frozen. Freeze the lasagna and the extra sauce separately. Defrost, then proceed with the baking as directed in the above recipe.

A SIMPLE SEAFOOD WITH SPAGHETTI [serves 4]

3 garlic cloves, mashed
1 onion, chopped
¼ cup oil
3 large ripe tomatoes, peeled
 and chopped (or sub-
 stitute canned)
1 can tomato sauce (8 ounces)
1 teaspoon salt (about)

⅛ to ¼ teaspoon black pepper
¼ teaspoon oregano
¼ teaspoon sugar
12 to 18 raw shrimp, peeled
 and deveined
1 can minced clams (7 ounce)
½ to 1 pound spaghetti

Sauté garlic and onion in the oil for about 5 minutes. Add the tomatoes, tomato sauce, salt, pepper, oregano, and sugar. Cover and simmer slowly for 1 hour. Remove cover, add shrimp and simmer 5 to 10 minutes. Add clams and simmer an additional 5 minutes. Keep sauce hot but do not continue to cook or the seafood will toughen.

Cook the spaghetti in plenty of salted boiling water to which you have added a tablespoon of oil. Cook to the "al dente" stage—tender but chewy. Drain and then if desired, add a little butter.

Serve on very hot plates with a generous portion of the sauce on each serving of the spaghetti.

To prepare ahead of time: The sauce can be prepared days ahead of time (or in the morning). Remember to reheat very gently so as not to overcook the seafood.

To freeze: The sauce can be frozen. Remember to reheat very gently so as not to overcook the seafood.

TORTELLINI IN GENTLE WHITE WINE SAUCE
[serves 4 to 6]

½ pound tortellini (or any
 desired pasta shape)
4 tablespoons butter
3 tablespoons flour

½ cup dry white wine
2 cups cream
salt and pepper
grated Parmesan cheese

Make the sauce: Melt butter, stir in flour, then cook over low heat without browning the flour, for about 5 minutes. Remove from heat and when it has stopped bubbling, add wine. Return to heat and cook, stirring constantly, until mixture comes to a boil. Add cream and salt and pepper. Simmer, stirring occasionally, for about 10 minutes. Taste for seasoning.

Cook the tortellini to the "al dente" stage—tender but still a little chewy—and drain. Serve very hot with the white wine sauce, topped with a generous amount of the grated Parmesan cheese.

To prepare ahead of time: The sauce can be prepared the day before or in the morning, reheat to use. Do not combine the pasta with the sauce until shortly before serving.

To freeze: The sauce can be frozen, however, it is such a simple preparation that it doesn't seem practical. The tortellini in the sauce can be frozen, but I would recommend this as a means of saving what is leftover for family use.

MANY MANICOTTI WITH TWO SAUCES
[enough for 16 manicotti shells]

16 manicotti shells, cooked, until just barely tender, cooled in cold water, then drained (use the packaged variety)

For the stuffing:

1 onion, finely chopped	salt and pepper to taste
2 tablespoons butter	3 tablespoons Cognac
4 cups ground cooked veal (leftover roast veal is very good)	1 cup Mornay sauce (see recipe below)

For the Mornay sauce:

½ cup butter	salt and pepper
½ cup flour	1 ½ to 2 cups grated Parmesan cheese
4 cups milk	
½ teaspoon nutmeg	

For the Tomato sauce:

1 onion, finely chopped	2 cups chicken stock (can use water plus chicken concentrate)
¼ cup oil	
2 cups canned tomatoes	
2 cups tomato purée	½ teaspoon oregano
1 cup tomato sauce (canned)	½ teaspoon sweet basil
	salt and pepper

Make the Mornay sauce: Melt butter, stir in flour and then gradually add the milk and bring to a boil, stirring all the while. Reduce heat and simmer slowly for about 10 minutes. Add seasonings and taste. Add more milk if sauce seems too thick. Stir in the grated cheese over low heat until completely melted.

Make the tomato sauce: Sauté the onion in the oil, add remaining ingredients and simmer for about 20 to 30 minutes. Taste for seasoning.

Make the stuffing: Sauté the onion in the butter, add the ground veal and cook over low heat for several minutes, season and add the Cognac. Stir in the 1 cup Mornay sauce. Taste for seasoning and set aside.

To assemble: Place the tomato sauce in the bottom of one or more shallow casseroles. Stuff the manicotti shells with the veal mixture (do this with a small teaspoon or with a pastry bag and tube). Place the stuffed shells on top of the tomato sauce. Spoon the Mornay sauce over each stuffed manicotti. Heat in a 350° oven until very hot. You can add more Parmesan cheese on top and brown under broiler at the end if desired.

To prepare ahead of time: This can be prepared a day or two ahead of time (or in the morning) and kept refrigerated until an hour or two before serving. Do the final baking before serving.

To freeze: This can be frozen. Freeze before baking. After defrosting, proceed with the baking as in the above recipe.

MARIA MEDELLIN'S CHILAQUILES LA SONORA

[serves about 12]

1 ½ dozen tortillas, cut in sixths
oil or shortening for frying

For the sauce:

4 tablespoons oil
4 tablespoons flour
2 10½-ounce cans of
    enchilada sauce

3 ½ cups chicken stock
    (about 2 cans)
good pinch of dried oregano
½ to 1 teaspoon of ground
    cumin seeds

For the filling:

2 pounds ground round
¾ cup warm water
1 clove garlic, mashed
onion salt

1 pound Cheddar or Jack
   cheese, grated
½ onion, finely chopped
2 or 3 green chilis, finely
   chopped (optional)

For the topping:

1 or 2 cups sour cream
plenty of pitted ripe olives

Fry the tortilla pieces in oil or shortening until brown, then drain on paper towels and set aside.

Prepare the sauce: Heat oil, stir in flour, then add enchilada sauce and chicken broth, and stir until sauce comes to a boil. Add oregano and cumin. Simmer gently for 20 to 30 minutes.

Simmer the ground round in the warm water with the garlic until water has completely evaporated and meat browns lightly. Season to taste with onion salt. Remove from heat and set aside.

In a very large casserole (or two) place a layer of the tortillas. Next place a layer of grated cheese along with a little onion and some chopped chilis. Repeat this layering ending up with the cheese. (Preparation ahead can be done to this point.)

Before serving pour prepared sauce over the top of the casserole. Place in a 350° oven until quite warm (about 30 to 60 minutes) depending upon temperature of the ingredients). Remove from oven, top with dabs of sour cream and pitted olives. Return to oven until piping hot, then serve.

To prepare ahead of time: This can be partly prepared ahead of time (day before or in the morning) and refrigerated—without the sauce poured over the top. Pour sauce on top before baking, then proceed as in above recipe.

To freeze: This freezes, but the texture is not quite the same. Of course, you can take advantage of the fact that frozen tortillas and frozen ground round can be used to prepare this dish.

Note: This is a delightfully easy, but superb dish, to make for a large gathering, and it can be doubled or tripled if needed; similarly, it can be cut in half if it is wanted to serve just family or a few friends.

TWENTY ENCHILADAS

20 corn tortillas
oil or shortening for frying
the tortillas

For the enchilada sauce:

¼ cup oil
1 clove garlic, mashed
1 large onion, finely chopped
8 tablespoons flour (½ cup)
4 cups tomato sauce (canned)
2 teaspoons salt (about)

4 cups grated Cheddar
cheese (or more)
2 cups sliced ripe olives,
well drained

4 cups beef stock
2 tablespoons chili powder
(or to taste)
1 teaspoon dried oregano
1 10-ounce can Mexican
enchilada sauce

For the filling:

1 large onion, finely chopped
and a little oil
½ pound Chorizo (Mexican
sausage)
1 pound lean ground chuck

salt to taste
2 tablespoons of the enchilada
sauce which you have
prepared

Make the sauce: Sauté the garlic and onion in the oil, sprinkle with the flour, stir and then add the tomato sauce, beef stock, and remaining ingredients. Cook, stirring constantly, until sauce comes to a boil. Reduce heat and simmer slowly for 45 minutes to an hour. Taste for seasoning.

Make the filling: Sauté chopped onion in a little oil. Remove skin from the chorizos and add the sausage to skillet. Mash with a fork and cook until well done. Remove any excess fat. Add beef and cook until browned, then add the enchilada sauce and salt to taste. Set aside.

To assemble: Fry each tortilla in hot shortening or oil for about 30 seconds, just enough to soften, drain on paper towels. Place a spoonful of prepared filling on each tortilla. Add some of the grated cheese and a small spoonful of the ripe olives. Roll up and place in a large shallow casserole (or casseroles). Spoon enchilada sauce over the rolled tortillas. Sprinkle with the extra cheese and sliced olives. Bake at 350° until hot and bubbling—about 30 minutes.

To prepare ahead of time: The sauce and the filling can be prepared a day or two ahead of time and kept refrigerated. The tortillas can be fried and filled the morning of the party and left at room temperature with the sauces poured over.

To freeze: These can be frozen, however, the somewhat chewy texture of the tortillas is usually changed—the tortillas become much softer.

FRESH CORN AND GREEN CHILI CASSEROLE (MARY HILL'S) [serves 8]

4 very large ears of corn (or 6 small ones)— enough to make 2 cups
½ cup melted butter
2 eggs, beaten
½ cup yellow cornmeal
1 ½ teaspoons salt (or a little less)

1 cup sour cream
1 generous cup diced Monterey Jack cheese (about 7 or 8 ounces)
1 can green peeled chilis (4-ounce)

Scrape the kernels from the ears of corn (grate on a grater or use a regular corn scraper). Place the 2 cups of grated corn in a large bowl and add the melted butter, eggs, cornmeal, salt, sour cream and diced cheese. Rinse all of the seeds out of the chilis. Chop the chilis and add them to the mixture. Pour into a greased casserole and bake at 350° for 40 to 60 minutes, or until firm to the touch and golden brown.

To prepare ahead of time: This can be baked the day before, then reheated before serving. It is equally delicious cold for lunch with a green salad.

To freeze: This can be frozen. Freeze after baking. Defrost, then reheat in oven before serving.

RICE, GREEN CHILI, JACK CHEESE
AND SOUR CREAM HEAVEN [serves 6]

1 can green peeled chilis
(4-ounce)
2 cups sour cream
1 teaspoon salt

½ pound Monterey Jack
cheese
3 cups cooked dry rice

Remove seeds from chilis and chop the chilis. Combine the chopped green chilis with the sour cream and salt and set aside. Cut the cheese into thin strips.

Place 1 cup of the rice in the bottom of a 1½ quart casserole and spoon on ⅓ of the sour cream mixture, then top with ⅓ of the cheese strips. Repeat this procedure twice more. Bake covered at 350° for about 20 minutes. Then bake uncovered about 10 minutes. Bake only long enough for everything to be very hot, but do not over-bake or the casserole of rice will change its texture and dry out.

To prepare ahead of time: This can be assembled the day before or in the morning, then bake before serving.

To freeze: Freeze this unbaked. Defrost, then proceed with the baking as in the above recipe.

COTTAGE CHEESE CASSEROLE HOT OR COLD
[serves 4]

2 cups cottage cheese
4 large eggs
about ½ teaspoon salt

¼ teaspoon pepper
dash of paprika

Beat eggs, stir in other ingredients and pour into a lightly greased casserole. Bake until firm to the touch—about 40 to 60 minutes—at 325°. Serve hot or cold with a lightly dressed green salad.

To prepare ahead of time: This can be baked the day before and served cold the next day. It can be reheated also, but it is better if one is going to eat it hot, baked just before serving.

KATHARINA MARMOR'S EGG BARLEY
CASSEROLE VARIATIONS

1 cup Manischewitz's egg barley	1 tablespoon chicken fat or sweet butter
2 cups chicken soup or equivalent	1 medium onion, chopped
	¼ teaspoon salt

I. Egg Barley Casserole

Sauté onion and barley in fat until golden yellow. Add soup and salt. Bring to a boil. Stir once, then cover tightly and simmer over low heat for about 25 to 30 minutes. The egg barley should be moist and shiny.

II. Egg Barley Casserole Variation

Use the same ingredients as listed above. Put the barley in a casserole, allowing space for 3 times expansion. Heat soup to boiling. Add fat or butter and, if desired, substitute 1 tablespoon onion flakes for the chopped onion. Pour over the barley. Place in a 450° oven and allow to come to a boil once more. Stir, then cover, and reduce oven to 300°. Bake, covered for 25 to 30 minutes.

III. Egg Barley Casserole with mushrooms

Sauté one-half pound of fresh mushrooms (sliced) in sweet butter and mix into either of the above casseroles just before serving.

IV. Egg Barley Casserole with almonds

Sauté ½ cup blanched, slivered almonds in butter and mix into either of the above casseroles just before serving.

MONTE CRISTO SANDWICHES   [serves 4]

bread and butter (3 slices for each sandwich)	thin slices of Monterey Jack cheese
sliced white meat of cooked chicken or turkey	3 eggs
thin slices of boiled ham	⅓ cup milk
	salt and pepper

Remove crusts from the bread. Butter the first slice, then cover with sliced chicken or turkey. Season lightly. Butter middle slice on each side and place over the chicken slices. Place ham and cheese on top of the bread. Butter third slice and place buttered side down over ham-cheese. Cut sandwiches in two and fasten with toothpicks. Beat eggs slightly with the milk. Dip sandwiches in egg mixture, placing them on a plate after they have been dipped. Sauté in butter on both sides until browned. Remove toothpicks and serve with strawberry jam on the side. These can be kept warm a short time in a 350° oven.

To prepare ahead of time: The sandwiches can be assembled the day before or in the morning. They must be kept tightly wrapped in the refrigerator. Dip in egg and sauté shortly before serving.

A VERSATILE CHEESE ENTRÉE FOR LUNCH, SUPPER, OR APPETIZER

[serves 8 as an entrée, 16 or more as an appetizer]

10 slices of good quality white bread
softened butter
¾ pound Cheddar cheese grated
¾ pound Monterey Jack cheese, grated
8 eggs, slightly beaten
3 to 4 cups light cream

1 teaspoon brown sugar
¼ teaspoon paprika
1 ½ teaspoons salt
½ teaspoon onion powder
¼ teaspoon pepper
⅛ teaspoon cayenne
1 teaspoon Worcestershire sauce
1 teaspoon dry mustard

Butter the bread, then cut in cubes. Grease a large, shallow baking dish and line it with half of the bread cubes. Sprinkle with half of the cheese, then repeat: bread, then cheese. Combine remaining ingredients and pour over the bread-cheese. Refrigerate 8 to 24 hours before baking. Bake in a 325° oven for about an hour or so. Serve hot as an entrée (or cold for lunch) or cut in small squares and serve as an appetizer.

To prepare ahead of time: This is best if assembled the day before, then baked the following day. It is also helpful to note that if baked, it will reheat very well.

To freeze: Bake before freezing. Defrost, then reheat and serve.

Note: It is easier to cut this in small squares for appetizers if it is baked, chilled and then cut. To serve as a hot appetizer, place the small squares on cookie sheets, heat in a 350° oven, then serve with toothpicks.

A DOMESTIC VERSION OF A
FRENCH CHEESE SOUFFLÉ [serves 4]

¼ cup butter
¼ cup flour
1 cup milk
⅓ pound Cheddar cheese,
grated (or imported
Swiss)

¼ cup grated Parmesan
cheese
¾ teaspoon salt
⅛ teaspoon nutmeg
6 egg yolks
8 egg whites

Melt butter, stir in flour. Add the milk gradually and cook over low heat, stirring constantly, until mixture comes to a boil. Remove from heat and stir in cheese until melted. Add salt and nutmeg. Beat egg yolks slightly and add to the mixture. Beat the egg whites until stiff but not dry. Fold gently into the egg-cheese mixture. Pour into a generously greased 1½ quart casserole or soufflé dish which has a waxed paper collar attached (also greased), and bake in a 375° oven for 35 to 40 minutes. Serve at once.

To prepare ahead of time: The soufflé mixture can be prepared in the morning up to the point of beating the egg whites. Place it in a large bowl, cover with plastic wrap and leave at room temperature. About 45 minutes before serving the soufflé beat egg whites and proceed as in the above recipe.

MUSHROOM-ONION QUICHE LORRAINE
[serves 6 to 8]

enough pie pastry to make a
shell 9 to 10 inches in
diameter
1 small onion, very finely
chopped
¼ cup butter
½ pound fresh mushrooms,
sliced

¼ pound bacon, sautéed and
drained
½ pound Cheddar cheese,
grated
½ teaspoon salt, or to taste
¼ teaspoon nutmeg
⅛ teaspoon pepper
2 large eggs or 3 medium
¾ cup milk

Line a fairly deep pie dish of at least 9 inches in diameter with pastry and chill in refrigerator for at least 30 minutes.

Sauté the chopped onion in the butter for about 3 or 4 minutes. Add sliced mushrooms and continue cooking for an additional 4 or 5 minutes. Remove from heat and cool slightly

Remove pie shell from refrigerator and sprinkle bottom with the bacon crumbled. Next, cover with the onion-mushroom mixture, then cover with the grated cheese.

Beat together slightly the eggs, milk, salt, nutmeg, and pepper. Pour this mixture over the filled pie shell. Bake at 450° for 12 minutes. Reduce oven to 300° and bake 35 to 40 minutes or until custard is set.

To prepare ahead of time: This can be baked the day before or in the morning. Reheat to serve.

To freeze: Bake, then freeze. Defrost, then reheat to serve.

Note: This is delicious served hot with a green salad either for supper or for lunch. However, I find it equally good cold the next day.

EGGS GLORIFIED IN THE CHIMAY WAY   [serves 4]

6 hard-cooked eggs
¼ pound mushrooms, finely
    chopped
½ small onion, finely chopped
2 ½ tablespoons butter
juice of half a lemon

3 tablespoons finely
    chopped parsley
salt and pepper
¼ cup grated Parmesan cheese
    (for topping)

For the Mornay sauce:

3 tablespoons butter
3 tablespoons flour
2 cups milk (or a little
    more if needed)

salt and pepper (about ¾
    teaspoon salt)
⅛ teaspoon nutmeg
¼ pound Swiss cheese, grated
3 egg yolks

Make the sauce first: Melt butter, stir in flour, then add milk and stir constantly until mixture comes to a boil. Reduce heat and simmer. Add salt, pepper and nutmeg. Stir in the Swiss cheese. Cool slightly, then beat in the egg yolks and set aside. (Taste for seasoning.)

Slice eggs in half lengthwise. Remove yolks and put them through a sieve into a bowl. Sauté the chopped onion in the 2 ½ tablespoons of butter for a few minutes. Add mushrooms, salt and pepper and lemon juice and sauté for a few minutes more. Combine with the mashed egg yolk. Stir in the parsley. Add 1 to 3 tablespoons of the prepared Mornay sauce, enough to moisten well, but not too much. The mixture must hold its shape. Fill the egg whites with this mixture and place the stuffed eggs in a large shallow casserole or in individual ones.

Cover each egg with some of the Mornay sauce. Let them stand a few minutes, then coat each egg again with the sauce, then add remaining sauce to the sides and around the eggs. Use all of the sauce. Sprinkle tops with the grated Parmesan. Bake at 375° for 10 to 20 minutes—or until very hot, then brown under the broiler.

To prepare ahead of time: This can be prepared in the morning and baked in the evening. Leave eggs at room temperature, well covered with plastic wrap. They lose something if they have been refrigerated. Of course, the eggs can be hard-cooked the day before.

Note: This amount makes enough to serve 12 persons as a first course, giving each guest one stuffed half an egg. Three such halves make an ample lunch with a green salad and rye toast.

VARIATION ON NASI-GORENG: FRIED RICE WITH SHRIMP, CHICKEN AND HAM   [serves 6 to 8]

4 cups cooked rice
¼ cup oil
2 cloves garlic, mashed
2 large onions, chopped
1 ¼ teaspoons salt (about)
¼ teaspoon pepper
1 ¼ teaspoons ground coriander
½ teaspoon ground cumin

½ teaspoon chili powder
⅛ teaspoon mace
2 cups cooked shrimp
2 cups cooked diced chicken (largish pieces)
1 cup cubed cooked ham
2 generous tablespoons chunk style peanut butter

Sauté onions and garlic in oil until tender and lightly browned. Add rice and stir over heat until just barely browned. Add remaining ingredients and stir-fry for about 3 to 5 minutes BUT DO NOT

ADD PEANUT BUTTER UNTIL LATER. Just before serving stir in peanut butter; cover lightly with foil and heat in a 375° oven until very hot, but do not overcook.

To prepare ahead of time: This can be done the day before or in the morning. Do not bake until shortly before serving.

To freeze: Yes, this can be frozen. Defrost, then heat as in the above recipe.

Note: I like to serve this with a sliced banana salad, or with cold spiced fruit.

A JOYOUSLY JUMBLED JAMBALAYA [serves about 6]

1 onion, finely chopped
1 green pepper, finely
   chopped
½ cup butter
3 cups diced baked ham
   (about 1 pound)
1½ cups cooked shrimp
   (cut in largish pieces)

salt, only if needed
pepper
1 cup tomato purée
1 cup tomato sauce
½ cup dry Sherry
2 cups cooked rice

Sauté onion and green pepper in butter until tender and lightly browned. Add diced ham and cook another minute or two, then stir in the tomato purée, tomato sauce, Sherry, salt and pepper. Simmer covered for about 10 or 15 minutes. Taste for seasoning, then add the shrimp and the rice and heat, but do not boil. Or you can put it in the oven at 350° to heat. Do not overcook or the shrimp will toughen and the rice will dry out.

Too prepare ahead of time: This can be assembled the day before or in the morning. Bake before serving.

To freeze: This can be frozen. Freeze before the final heating or baking. Defrost, then heat in a 350° oven until hot, but do not overcook.

A CASSEROLE FOR THOSE WHO LIKE POTATOES, CABBAGE AND SAUSAGES [serves 4 to 6]

4 large potatoes, peeled,
  boiled and drained
1 medium-size cabbage

1 pound link pork sausages
  (or more if desired)
salt and pepper

Slice cabbage for cooking. Cook cabbage about 5 minutes in salted water and drain. Brown sausages in a skillet and set aside. Cut boiled potatoes into cubes or slices.

Place a layer of potatoes in a casserole. Then place a layer of cabbage and season well with salt and pepper. Top with a layer of the sausages, and then repeat the layering. Pour a little of the fat left from sautéing the sausages over all. Bake in a 350° over for about 40 minutes.

To prepare ahead of time: This can be prepared the day before or in the morning. Reserve the baking until the following day, if prepared the day before. If prepared in the morning, leave at room temperature, then bake in the evening before serving.

NOODLES WITH ALMONDS [serves 10 to 12]

12 ounces packaged dry
  noodles
½ cup butter
½ cup grated Parmesan
  cheese

1 cup sour cream
1 cup diced almonds
salt and pepper to taste

Cook noodles in boiling salted water until tender but not mushy. Drain and rinse with boiling water. Combine with the remaining ingredients and place in a casserole. Heat in a 350° oven for about 20 to 30 minutes.

To prepare ahead of time: This can be assembled the day before or in the morning. Do the final oven heating before serving—the casserole lightly covered with foil.

To freeze: This freezes. Freeze before the oven heating. Defrost, cover lightly with foil, then heat in a 350° oven until hot.

VERMICELLI CASSEROLE   [serves 6 to 8]

½ pound fresh mushrooms,   ¾ cup stewed tomatoes
   sliced   1 ½ cups hot chicken stock
1 small onion, chopped   salt and pepper to taste
¼ cup butter or olive oil   ½ cup grated Cheddar
½ pound vermicelli   cheese

Sauté the mushrooms and onion in the oil for 5 or 6 minutes. Add the
vermicelli and continue to sauté, stirring for another 5 minutes. Add
the tomatoes, chicken stock, salt and pepper to taste. Bring to a boil.
Transfer to a casserole. Cover tightly and bake in a 300° oven for
about 40 minutes. Remove cover. Sprinkle cheese on top. Bake uncovered an additional 15 minutes. Serve very hot.

To prepare ahead of time: This can be done the day before or in the
morning, but do not add the cheese. Shortly before serving, reheat,
sprinkle with cheese and continue as in the above recipe.

To freeze: This freezes. It is best to freeze it without doing the last
15 minutes of baking. Defrost, reheat, then add cheese and proceed as
in above recipe.

Vegetables

Vegetables

JO ANNE COTSEN'S FOUR VEGETABLE COMBINATION: EGGPLANT, TOMATO, SPINACH AND MUSHROOM [serves 8]

1 eggplant	nutmeg
butter and olive oil	4 large tomatoes
salt and pepper	8 large mushroom caps
2 packages chopped frozen	
spinach	

For the cheese sauce:

2 tablespoons butter	1 cup milk
2 tablespoons flour	1 cup grated Cheddar
salt, pepper and nutmeg	cheese

Make the cheese sauce: Melt butter, add flour and then gradually add the milk, stirring constantly until mixture comes to a boil. Add seasonings and simmer for a few minutes. Stir in the grated cheese, then set aside.

Wash eggplant, but do not peel. Cut into eight ½ to ¾ inch slices. Sauté in butter and olive oil (about half and half) until tender and browned but not mushy. Drain on paper towels.

Cook spinach about 1 minute. Drain thoroughly, then season with salt, pepper, and a little nutmeg.

Peel tomatoes by first dipping them in boiling water. Cut each one in half.

Sauté mushroom caps briefly in butter.

To assemble: Arrange eggplant slices in a large shallow casserole, or on an ovenproof platter. Top each slice with half a tomato. Next place a spoonful of the spinach on each tomato half. Top with a mushroom cap (or reserve mushroom cap and add later). Spoon cheese sauce over each and heat thoroughly in a 350° oven, then place under a broiler to brown.

To prepare ahead of time: The vegetables can be prepared and assembled in the morning. (Cover and leave at room temperature.) Put cheese sauce on later, then proceed as in the above recipe. The cheese sauce can be prepared the day before.

To freeze: The cheese sauce can be frozen. Reheat and stir over very low heat.

Note: Jo Anne says, "This is especially good because it takes up little room on a crowded plate; men like it; and it's good with roasts!"

EGGPLANT PARMIGIANA [serves 4 to 8 depending upon whether or not it is a main course or a vegetable on the side]

1 medium eggplant, peeled and sliced in circles ¼ inch thick
flour
olive oil
2 cups tomato sauce or tomato purée
salt and pepper
½ pound Mozzarella cheese, thinly sliced
½ cup grated Parmesan cheese
oregano

Dust eggplant slices lightly with flour, then sauté them in the oil until browned on both sides. Drain on paper towels.

In a large shallow casserole pour a thin layer of the tomato sauce (or purée), then add a layer of the eggplant slices, then season with salt, pepper, and a light sprinkling of oregano, then a thin layer of Mozzarella, then a sprinkling of the Parmesan. Repeat until ingredients are used up. Bake at 350° for 30 to 35 minutes, and if not sufficiently browned, place under the broiler for a few minutes.

To prepare ahead of time: This can be assembled the day before or in the morning, reserve the final baking until before serving.

To freeze: This freezes. Freeze before the final baking. Defrost, then proceed with the baking as in the above recipe.

FRESH GREEN BEANS WITH TOMATO AND ONION
[serves 8]

2 pounds fresh green beans
(cut any way you prefer)
1 large'can of tomatoes
(about 3 cups)

1 clove garlic, mashed
¼ cup melted butter
1 onion, finely chopped
salt and pepper to taste

Combine all of the ingredients and cook very slowly in a 325° oven, or simmer on top of the stove, covered for 45 minutes or longer—until beans are tender but not mushy. Taste for seasoning, then serve.

To prepare ahead of time: This can be done the day before or in the morning. Reheat to serve.

To freeze: This can be frozen. Reheat to serve.

Note: Green beans cooked this way will not retain their bright green color, however, the taste is excellent.

BROCCOLI WITH OLIVES
[serves 4]

2 pounds fresh broccoli
½ cup sliced pimento stuffed
green olives

2 tablespoons melted butter
1 tablespoon lemon juice
salt and pepper

Cook broccoli (after trimming it) in plenty of boiling water—uncovered. Cook until tender but not mushy. Drain it and place in a heatproof serving dish or casserole. Scatter olives over the broccoli and sprinkle with the lemon juice and melted butter. Season to taste with salt and pepper.

To prepare ahead of time: This can be prepared the day before or in the morning. Bring to room temperature. Cover lightly with foil and reheat in a 350° oven.

To freeze: Use the freezing process for any leftovers, but do not freeze as a beforehand procedure.

CARROTS AND MUSHROOMS [serves 6 to 8]

4 cups sliced raw carrots
¼ pound fresh mushrooms
  briefly sautéed in butter
  or 1 can sliced mush-
  rooms

salt and pepper to taste
¼ cup or more of melted
  butter

Cook carrots until just barely tender. Drain, then mix with the mush-rooms, butter, and salt and pepper. Place in a serving casserole and reheat in a 350° oven until very hot.

To prepare ahead of time: This can be done the day before or in the morning. Reheat before serving.

To freeze: These freeze but I think they lack quite the perfect texture that they have before freezing.

CARROTS WITH CELERY [serves about 8]

4 cups thinly sliced carrots
4 cups thinly sliced celery
3 green onions, finely chopped

½ cup butter
salt and pepper to taste

Sauté the carrots and celery in the butter over very low heat, keep-ing them covered part of the time to develop steam. As soon as they have begun to exude some juice, cover tightly and cook over low low heat until tender (or bake in a 350° oven until tender). Add the green onion, salt, and pepper and serve.

To prepare ahead of time: This can be prepared the day before or in the morning. Reheat to serve.

To freeze: This can be frozen if you serve the carrots on the very well cooked side. They cannot after freezing keep their crisp under-cooked texture, however, this is a matter of individual taste.

LOVELY LURING LENTILS [serves 4 to 6]

1 cup lentils
3 cups water
1 clove garlic, mashed
3 small or 2 medium onions,
    finely chopped

¼ cup butter
salt (about 2 teaspoons)
pepper (about ½ teaspoon)

Cook lentils, water and garlic slowly (covered), for about an hour, or until lentils are soft. Meanwhile sauté the finely chopped onion in the butter until very tender and lightly browned. When lentils are tender, purée or mash about ⅓ of them. Then mix this purée with the remaining lentils, onions, salt and pepper, and simmer uncovered until thickened. Taste for seasoning. Serve hot as a vegetable-starch.

To prepare ahead of time: This can be done the day before or in the morning.

To freeze: This freezes.

Note: These are especially good with something like smoked tongue or baked ham.

PEAS IN ARTICHOKE BOTTOMS [serves 6]

12 small canned artichoke
    bottoms
1 package frozen peas

3 tablespoons butter
salt and pepper

Cook frozen peas and drain. Put half of them through a food mill or purée in a blender. Combine the mashed peas with the remaining half which are not mashed. Add butter and seasoning to taste.

Rinse artichoke bottoms in cold water and dry on paper towels. Sprinkle them lightly with salt and pepper.

Place artichoke bottoms on an ovenproof dish and fill them with the pea mixture. Cover lightly with foil and heat in a 350° oven. Serve 2 per guest when they are hot.

To prepare ahead of time: These can be assembled the day before or in the morning. Heat in the oven before serving.

MARGARET HALL'S ESCALLOPED GREEN PEPPERS

[serves 6]

4 large green peppers, seeded,
    then put through the
    meat grinder
30 or 40 saltines, crumbled

salt and pepper, to taste
⅓ cup butter
about 2 cups light cream

Cover the ground peppers with boiling water and cook 3 minutes, then drain. Place a layer of these peppers in a greased shallow casserole, then a layer of crumbled crackers, then dot with butter. Repeat this procedure ending with the crackers. (Lightly salt and pepper the green peppers as you layer them in the casserole.) Pour cream over all, enough to moisten, but not soupy. Bake at 325° for 30 to 40 minutes.

To prepare ahead of time: This can be done the day before or in the morning. Reheat to serve.

Note: A little cheese can be grated on the top before baking if desired.

RED AND GREEN PEPPERS WITH MUSHROOMS

[serves about 6]

1 green pepper, cut in largish
    pieces
1 red pepper, cut in largish
    pieces

¾ pound fresh mushrooms,
    sliced about ¼ inch
    thick
3 green onions, chopped
¼ cup butter
salt and pepper

Sauté mushrooms in the butter, season with salt and pepper. Do not overcook. Add the vegetables and stir over high heat for a minute or two. Remove from heat and serve at once—or set aside and when ready to serve, heat quickly and briefly, then serve.

To prepare ahead of time: The vegetables can all be sliced in the morning, ready to cook. The final preparation only takes minutes so it is really not worth the attempt to cook them far ahead of time. As mentioned above they can be cooked a short time before you plan to serve, then reheated briefly and served.

142

GRATED POTATO PANCAKES [serves 6 to 8]

4 large potatoes, grated
   (about 2 cups of grated
   potatoes)
1 teaspoon salt
¼ teaspoon pepper

2 eggs
1 tablespoon flour
2 or 3 tablespoons grated
   onion

Combine all of the ingredients. Drop spoonfuls of the potato mixture into a skillet in which ¼ inch vegetable shortening or oil has been heated and brown the pancakes over moderate heat. Make certain that they are well browned on both sides and thoroughly cooked. Drain on paper towels and serve.

To prepare ahead of time: These do lend themselves to beforehand preparation very nicely. If you cook them in the morning, place the pancakes on large cookie sheet pans and place them in a 375° oven (uncovered) until very hot, then serve.

To freeze: These freeze very beautifully too. Cook the pancakes, then freeze them in foil pans between layers of plastic wrap. Defrost, then reheat as directed above—in a 375° oven.

BRIOCHE POTATOES [serves 6 to 8]

3½ pounds of potatoes
½ cup butter
salt and pepper to taste
4 egg yolks

1 egg diluted with 1 tablespoon milk, then beaten
   slightly

Boil potatoes until tender, then put through a ricer or a food mill. Add the butter, salt, and pepper and beat with an electric beater. Add egg yolks one at a time and beat until thoroughly combined.

Form potato mixture into brioche shapes using a floured board. Place them on a greased baking pan or in a heatproof serving dish. Brush with the diluted beaten egg mixture and bake at 300° until hot and browned on top. Serve at once.

To prepare ahead of time: These can be readied in the morning, covered with plastic wrap, then baked before serving. I do not recommend doing them the day before, but you can freeze them.

To freeze: Freeze these after forming the potato mixture into brioche shapes. Defrost them for not more than 45 minutes to an hour, then proceed with the baking as directed above. They will, of course, take longer to bake under these circumstances.

WHIPPED POTATOES WITH GREEN
PEPPER, ONION, AND CHEESE [serves 10 to 12]

4 pounds potatoes
6 ounces cream cheese
¼ cup butter
¼ pound Cheddar cheese, grated
½ cup grated Parmesan cheese
2 egg yolks

1 egg
salt and pepper
1 green pepper, finely chopped
4 green onions, finely chopped
⅓ to ½ cup finely chopped pimento
milk if necessary to moisten

Peel, then boil the potatoes and put them through a ricer. Whip them with an electric beater, gradually adding the butter, cream cheese, Cheddar, Parmesan, egg yolks and whole egg. Season to taste and then beat again, adding milk to moisten if necessary. Add the green pepper, green onions, and pimento and combine thoroughly. Place in a casserole and heat in a 350° oven until hot, puffy and lightly browned.

To prepare ahead of time: This can be prepared the day before or in the morning. Do the final baking before serving.

To freeze: This can be frozen. Defrost partially, then proceed with the baking as directed in the above recipe.

POTATOES AU GRATIN [serves 6 to 8]

5 cups cubed, boiled potatoes
salt and pepper
2 tablespoons butter
2 tablespoons flour

½ teaspoon salt
1½ cups milk
1 cup grated Cheddar cheese (generous)

Make a cream sauce: Melt the butter, then stir in the flour and add the milk, stirring constantly, until the mixture comes to a boil. Simmer for a few minutes, adding the salt. Place the cubed potatoes in a large bowl and season lightly with salt and pepper. Add the cream sauce and stir gently until potatoes are well coated. Place the potatoes either in one large shallow casserole, or in individual ones. Cover with the grated cheese. Bake in a 400° oven until hot and browned. If necessary, place under the broiler for a minute or two to brown.

To prepare ahead of time: These can be assembled the day before or in the morning, then baked before serving.

To freeze: These can be frozen. Freeze after the potatoes have been combined with the cream sauce and topped with the cheese. Defrost, then proceed with the baking as directed above.

POTATOES BOULANGÈRE [serves about 6]

5 medium-size potatoes, thinly sliced
1 small onion, thinly sliced
1 tablespoon finely chopped parsley

3 tablespoons butter
1 ½ to 2 cups undiluted beef bouillon (canned is fine)

Place a layer of the sliced potatoes in a greased casserole; next place a layer of the sliced onion, then sprinkle with some of the parsley. Repeat this procedure until all of the ingredients have been used up. Dot the top with butter. Pour the bouillon over all and bake in a 375° oven for 1 ½ to 2 ½ hours, or until potatoes are done and the top is well browned.

To prepare ahead of time: These can be baked the day before or in the morning. Reheat before serving.

To freeze: These freeze. Bake the casserole, cool, then freeze. Defrost, then reheat to serve.

Note: Salt and pepper is usually not needed because of the use of undiluted bouillon, however, this is a matter of taste.

LILLIE MAE HENDRICK'S
SOUTHERN SWEET POTATO BALLS

5 large yams, boiled in their
    skins, peeled, then
    mashed
1 egg (or 1 or 2 egg yolks)
2 tablespoons brown sugar
1 tablespoon white sugar

a little nutmeg
a little cinnamon
1 cup crushed cornflakes
1 tablespoon flour
marshmallows, cut in half
additional crushed cornflakes

Combine the mashed yams with the egg, sugars, spices, flour, and the 1 cup of crushed cornflakes. Chill thoroughly, if possible, overnight.

Form mixture into balls, pressing a half a marshmallow into the center of each. Roll each ball in crushed cornflakes and chill again for at least 30 minutes.

Take balls out of regrigerator about 5 minutes before ready to cook. Fry in deep fat for 1 or 2 minutes, drain and keep warm in a moderate oven until ready to serve them.

To prepare ahead of time: These are best prepared a day ahead of the party, and as mentioned above, rolled into balls and chilled again.

To freeze: Yes, these do freeze. Defrost for several hours, then proceed with the cooking.

SIMPLY DONE CANDIED SWEET POTATOES [serves 4]

4 sweet potatoes (or yams)
    boiled with skins until
    barely tender
¾ cup brown sugar (packed)

¼ teaspoon salt
2 tablespoons butter
2 tablespoons water

Peel and then cut potatoes in half lengthwise. Place them in a heatproof casserole. Bring sugar, salt, butter, and water to a slow boil. Pour this sauce over the potatoes and then bake them in a 350° oven for 30 to 40 minutes. Baste occasionally, and if desired, turn the potatoes once or twice.

To prepare ahead of time: These can be assembled the day before or in the morning, then baked before serving.

To freeze: These do freeze. Bake, but not too long, and then freeze. Defrost, then finish the baking and basting process.

YAM CASSEROLES WITH CANDIED MARRONS

[serves 6]

4 very large yams
3 tablespoons butter
pinch of salt
¼ teaspoon ginger
¼ teaspoon nutmeg
½ teaspoon cinnamon
⅓ cup sugar

2 eggs, beaten
candied marrons (either
    those in syrup or those
    which are glacéed, need
    about 1 for each serving)
brown sugar

Cook yams until tender, peel, then put through a ricer. Whip the potatoes with the butter, ginger, nutmeg, sugar, salt, eggs, and cinnamon. Spoon potatoes into individual casseroles. Top them with either one whole marron or with the marron pieces. Sprinkle with brown sugar and bake in a 400° oven for about 30 minutes.

To prepare ahead of time: These can be assembled the day before or in the morning and refrigerated. Bring to room temperature, then bake as in the above recipe.

To freeze: This can be frozen. Defrost, then proceed with the baking as in the above recipe.

RATATOUILLE

[serves about 8]

1 medium-size eggplant
2 large onions, coarsely
    chopped
1 clove of garlic, mashed
⅓ cup olive oil
2 or 3 green peppers, seeded
    and cut in large pieces

2 or 3 red peppers, seeded
    and cut in large pieces
salt and pepper
¼ teaspoon ground coriander
1 6-ounce can tomato paste
1 ½ cups canned tomatoes

Dice the eggplant in ½ inch cubes, leaving the skin on. Sauté the onions and garlic in the olive oil over medium heat for about 5 to 10 minutes, until soft and lightly browned. Add cubed eggplant and cook, stirring frequently, until eggplant is very well browned. Add the sliced peppers and cook over medium heat, stirring, for about 5 to 7 minutes. Add salt and pepper, coriander, tomato paste, and canned tomatoes, and stir. Reduce heat and cover. Simmer for about 30 minutes. Serve either hot or cold.

To prepare ahead of time: This can be prepared a day or two ahead of time. Serve cold, or reheat in a casserole in the oven to serve hot.

To freeze: This can be frozen. Defrost, then reheat to serve hot. If serving cold, stir it gently and thoroughly.

SIX INDIVIDUAL SPINACH SOUFFLÉS

2 packages frozen, chopped spinach	salt, garlic powder, and pepper to taste
4 tablespoons butter	1 cup milk or cream
4 tablespoons flour	4 egg yolks
	6 egg whites

Put spinach through the meat grinder (even though it is already chopped) and drain it thoroughly.

Melt the butter, stir in the flour, and then add the milk and seasonings. Bring to a boil, stirring constantly. Remove from the heat and beat in the egg yolks, using a wire whisk if possible. Stir in the spinach.

Beat egg whites until stiff but not dry. Fold them into the spinach mixture and pour into six well greased individual soufflé dishes or casseroles. Bake at 375° for 30 to 40 minutes, then serve at once.

To prepare ahead of time: The soufflé mixture can be prepared in the morning up to the point of beating the egg whites. Put the spinach mixture in a large mixing bowl and cover tightly with plastic wrap. About 45 minutes before serving, beat the egg whites and proceed as in the above recipe.

A PART GREEK, PART FRENCH, SPINACH PIE

[serves 8 to 10]

enough French puff pastry to make a top and bottom crust for a 10-inch pie (make your own from a standard recipe, or buy it from your pastry shop by the pound)

2 packages frozen chopped spinach

½ cup olive oil

2 large onions, finely chopped

4 cloves garlic, mashed

⅓ cup raw rice

1¼ teaspoons mixed fine herbs

3 teaspoons salt

½ teaspoon pepper

⅓ cup chopped fresh mint

½ cup chopped fresh parsley

3 eggs

⅓ pound Cheddar cheese, grated

Put spinach through the meat grinder (even though it is already "chopped"). Sauté the onions in the oil gently for about 5 minutes. Add the garlic, herbs, parsley, mint, rice, and cook an additional 3 minutes. Add ground spinach and cook for 5 or 6 minutes. Add salt and pepper. Set aside to cool.

Roll out half of the puff pastry and line a 10-inch round shallow casserole or pie dish. Beat the eggs lightly and stir in the cheese. Combine the egg-cheese mixture with the spinach mixture and pour into the lined pan. (Sprinkle with extra cheese, if you like.) Roll out other half of the puff pastry and cover the top. Seal by wetting edges. Make a cut-out design in the pastry top.

Bake at 425° for 15 minutes. Reduce to 350° and bake an additional 45 minutes or an hour, or until pastry is golden brown.

To prepare ahead of time: This can be baked in the morning and reheated in the evening. This can be baked the day before and is very good served cold for lunch. (I do not think the flavor is as good, nor the texture of the puff pastry quite as good, if it is baked the day before to be served hot the following day.)

To freeze: Puff pastry can be frozen by itself but I do not like to recommend freezing the pie. Of course, it certainly is a procedure one can use to take care of leftovers.

SPINACH, MUSHROOMS AND ONION
CASSSEROLE FOR SIXTEEN

4 packages of frozen spinach
1 medium-size onion
1 pound fresh mushrooms
3 tablespoons butter

3 tablespoons flour
1 ½ cups milk
salt, garlic powder, and pepper
4 eggs

Put the spinach, onion, and the mushrooms through a meat grinder.

Melt the butter, stir in the flour, and add the milk, stirring constantly, until the mixture comes to a boil. Stir in the spinach mixture and season. Simmer over low heat for 2 or 3 minutes. Beat the eggs and add them to the spinach. Pour into a large well greased casserole and bake at 350° for about an hour, or until firm to the touch.

To prepare ahead of time: This can be baked the day before or in the morning. Reheat in the oven before serving.

To freeze: This can be frozen after baking. Defrost, then reheat in the oven before serving.

MARY CULLIN'S STUFFED SUMMER SQUASH

[serves 12]

12 large summer squash
1 can cream style corn
   (about 2 cups)
¼ cup butter

salt and pepper to taste
¼ pound Cheddar cheese,
   grated

Cook squash until just barely tender. Drain. Cut off a slice from the top of each squash and scoop out the juicy part. Chop up about four of these slices to be added later to the corn filling.

Cook the creamed corn with butter, salt, and pepper over medium heat in a small skillet. Stir frequently and add the chopped squash mentioned in the above paragraph. Cook and stir until very thick.

Season the insides of the squash with a little salt and pepper. Sprinkle the bottom of each one with a little of the grated cheese. Spoon in the corn mixture, and then top each with some of the remaining cheese. Bake at 350° only until hot and bubbly, browning under the broiler if needed. Don't overcook the squash.

To prepare ahead of time: These can be assembled the day before or in the morning, then baked before serving.

JO ANNE COTSEN'S YELLOW SQUASH AND FRESH CORN [serves about 8]

    1 pound small yellow crook   salt and pepper
        neck squash, sliced   fine herbs
        ⅓ inch thick   butter
    4 or 5 ears of corn

Cook squash briefly in salted water—only until barely tender, then drain.

Cook corn briefly, drain, then cut off the kernels.

Combine squash and corn kernels in a casserole. Dot with butter and season with salt, pepper, and fine herbs. Cover and bake in a 350° oven only until hot. Do not overcook.

To prepare ahead of time: This can be prepared in the morning or the day before. Before serving heat in an oven as directed above.

Note: Jo Anne says, "This is a pretty and different vegetable combination—for that change and variety we all seek."

TOMATOES STUFFED WITH RICE AND PECANS

[serves 12]

12 tomatoes, hollowed out for stuffing	1 cup pecans, chopped
	½ cup butter
salt and pepper	6 cups cooked rice

Sauté the pecans in the butter. Toss with the cooked rice and season with salt and pepper.

Season the insides of the tomatoes with salt and pepper. Stuff the tomatoes with the rice mixture. Place in a shallow baking dish, cover lightly with foil and bake at 375° for 20 to 25 minutes.

To prepare ahead of time: All but the baking can be done the day before or in the morning.

To freeze: The rice-pecan mixture can be frozen. Defrost completely, stuff the tomatoes, and then do the baking.

TOMATOES STUFFED WITH RICE, CHEESE, AND ARTICHOKES

[serves 6]

6 medium-size tomatoes	½ cup diced artichoke bottoms (cooked)
1 cup cooked rice	
4 tablespoons butter	1 tablespoon finely chopped parsley
½ cup diced Mozzarella cheese	salt and pepper to taste
3 tablespoons grated Parmesan cheese	

Cut a slice from the top of each tomato, remove pulp and seeds, then invert to drain.

Melt butter and mix with the rice, Mozzarella, 2 tablespoons of the grated Parmesan, artichoke bottoms, parsley, salt and pepper. Season the insides of the tomatoes lightly. Stuff tomatoes with the rice mixture and sprinkle the remaining grated Parmesan on the tops. Place in a 350° oven and bake for about 25 minutes.

To prepare ahead of time: All but the baking can be done the day before or in the morning.

To freeze: Only the rice mixture can be frozen. Defrost completely and then stuff the tomatoes.

152

GERTIE LEE SHORT'S ZUCCHINI SLIPPERS [serves 8]

8 zucchini (about 7 or 8
    inches long)
1 ½ cups shredded sharp
    Cheddar cheese
½ cup small curd cottage
    cheese

½ teaspoon salt
⅛ teaspoon pepper
2 tablespoons fresh chopped
    parsley
few drops Tabasco
2 eggs, beaten

Clean the zucchini but do not peel. Cook in boiling, salted water for 10 minutes, drain and cool slightly. Cut each zucchini in half lengthwise. Scoop out center pulp and discard. Turn halves upside down to drain.

Combine remaining ingredients. Fill each shell with some of the mixture and arrange them in a greased shallow casserole. Bake uncovered for about 15 to 20 minutes. Turn oven up to 450° and bake for about 5 more minutes or until the tops are browned (or put under the broiler briefly).

To prepare ahead of time: These can be assembled the day before or in the morning. Bake them before serving.

Note: This makes an interesting appetizer sliced and served with cocktail picks.

QUICKLY DONE BAKED TOMATOES
WITH MUSTARD

firm tomatoes, cut in half
prepared yellow mustard
dry bread crumbs

salt and pepper
butter

Place tomatoes in a greased shallow casserole, cut side up. Season, then cover with mustard and sprinkle with bread crumbs. Dot with butter and bake at 375° for about 15 minutes.

Note: These are particularly good with roast beef or broiled steaks.

Salads

Salads

CAESAR SALAD [serves 4 to 6]

1 very large head of romaine, washed, dried and chilled
2 anchovies, finely chopped
2 slices firm white bread, cubed
2 tablespoons butter

1 clove garlic, mashed
2 tablespoons oil
½ cup grated Parmesan cheese
1 egg coddled, then cooled, (cooked one minute)

For the dressing:

½ cup lemon juice
2 tablespoons red wine vinegar
½ teaspoon salt
¼ teaspoon pepper

½ teaspoon dry mustard
½ teaspoon Worcestershire sauce
1 clove garlic, mashed
oil to fill the cup

Make the salad dressing: Mix all ingredients together in a 1 cup measure and then whip together in a jar or with a whisk. Chill until ready to use.

Sauté bread cubes in the oil and butter, with the garlic added to the oil. Set aside.

Tear romaine into a salad bowl and sprinkle with the chopped anchovies. Cover with a damp towel and refrigerate.

Just before serving: Add egg to dressing, sprinkle cheese on the salad, and add dressing to the salad. Toss. Add croutons and toss again, then serve at once.

To prepare ahead of time: The salad dressing can be prepared a day or two ahead of time. The salad can be readied in the morning and kept refrigerated. Combine the two as in the above recipe just before serving.

AVOCADO, TOMATO, AND LETTUCE SALAD

[serves 10]

1 large head of lettuce
4 tomatoes, sliced
3 avocados, peeled and sliced
6 green onions, finely chopped

chopped black ripe olives
  (about ½ cup)
French dressing

Line an oblong platter with the lettuce. Place the sliced tomatoes in a row down the center of the platter. Place the sliced avocados down either side of the tomatoes. Sprinkle with the chopped green onions and chopped ripe olives. Chill, covered with plastic wrap for a short time, then pour French dressing over all and serve.

To prepare ahead of time: The platter can be arranged a few hours ahead of time if you dip the avocado slices in a little lemon juice. Cover tightly with plastic wrap and keep refrigerated until ready to serve.

A FAVORITE FAMILY COLE SLAW

[serves 6 to 8]

1 large whole solid cabbage,
  finely shredded
3 green onions, finely
  chopped

1 green pepper, finely
  chopped

For the dressing:

½ cup mayonnaise
½ cup sour cream (or all
  mayonnaise can be used)
3 or 4 tablespoons red
  wine vinegar

1 teaspoon salt
¼ teaspoon pepper
¼ cup sugar (or more
  if you like)

Combine ingredients for the dressing and set aside. Combine the cabbage, green onions, and green pepper in a large bowl. Pour dressing over the cabbage and toss until thoroughly mixed. Chill for several hours, then serve.

To prepare ahead of time: This can be prepared a day or two ahead of time. Keep refrigerated covered with plastic wrap. Stir very well just before serving.

158

ENDIVE SALAD WITH OLIVES, BEETS AND EGGS

Belgian endive, cut in
  quarters lengthwise
chopped pickled beets

chopped ripe olives
chopped hard-cooked eggs
French dressing

Use one endive per serving. Place the quartered pieces on one large serving platter (or on individual serving plates) and sprinkle each one with some of the pickled beets, olives, and eggs. Spoon French dressing over each.

To prepare ahead of time: The chopped beets, olives and hard-cooked eggs can be prepared ahead of time and kept refrigerated in small covered containers. The rest is just an assembly job.

GREEN SALAD WITH GREEN GRAPES

2 heads of Romaine lettuce
2 cucumbers

¼ cup chopped fresh dill
1 cup fresh seedless green grapes

For the dressing:

½ cup lemon juice
1 ½ cups salad oil
1 teaspoon salt

¼ teaspoon pepper
1 teaspoon sugar

Combine all of the ingredients for the dressing and mix thoroughly. Chill until ready to use.

Combine romaine, thinly sliced cucumbers and fresh dill in a large salad bowl. Cover with a damp towel (or with plastic wrap) and refrigerate. Just before serving sprinkle the top of the salad generously with the grapes, add the dressing, and toss. Serve, and be sure to give each person some of the grapes (occasionally they sink to the bottom of the salad bowl).

To prepare ahead of time: The salad can be arranged in a bowl, covered, and refrigerated until shortly before serving time. The salad dressing can be made a day or two ahead. Combine just before serving.

CUCUMBERS IN DILLED SOUR CREAM   [serves 8 to 10]

3 or 4 cucumbers, peeled and
   sliced
1 part vinegar and 1 part
   water, enough to cover
   cucumbers
a little salt
1 tablespoon sugar

2 cups sour cream
salt and pepper
2 tablespoons lemon juice
2 tablespoons tarragon vinegar
½ cup chopped fresh dill
2 green onions finely chopped

Marinate the sliced cucumbers in the vinegar, water, salt and sugar for at least 1 or 2 hours. Drain thoroughly.

Mix remaining ingredients together, then stir in the drained cucumbers and chill until ready to serve.

To prepare ahead of time: The cucumbers can be marinated the day before and the sour cream mixture can be combined the day before. The two can be combined in the morning of the day on which they are to be served. Keep them refrigerated until time to serve.

RADISH, OLIVE, CABBAGE, AND MUSHROOM SALAD
[serves 4 to 6]

1 cup sliced radishes
1 cup chopped celery
2 cups finely shredded
   cabbage
½ pound fresh mushrooms,
   sliced

¼ cup olive oil
salt and pepper
3 green onions, finely chopped
some chopped fresh dill
⅔ cup sliced black ripe olives
French dressing

Sauté the fresh mushrooms in the olive oil and season with salt and pepper. Do not overcook them.

Combine the sautéed mushrooms with the other ingredients and chill.

To prepare ahead of time: This can be prepared the day before or in the morning. Chill until ready to serve.

GREEN PEPPER, CUCUMBER AND RADISH SALAD

[serves about 6]

2 cucumbers, peeled and
    sliced
1 tomato diced
2 cups chopped green pepper
½ cup sliced radishes
½ cup sliced ripe olives
4 green onions, finely chopped

⅓ cup canned anchovies (the
    kind rolled with capers)
¼ cup olive oil
¼ cup red wine vinegar
garlic salt
pepper
1 tablespoon chopped parsley

Combine the cucumbers, tomato, green pepper, radishes, olives, onions and anchovies in a bowl and chill. Meanwhile mix the oil, vinegar and seasonings together. Pour over the vegetables and toss. Garnish with more chopped parsley.

To prepare ahead of time: This can be done in the morning.

Note: This is particularly attractive if served in very small individual bowls.

ROASTED GREEN AND RED PEPPERS [serves 16 to 25]

5 large green peppers
5 large red peppers (if red
    ones are out of season,
    use all green)

1 ⅓ cups olive oil (or other
    salad oil)
⅔ cup wine vinegar
salt and pepper to taste

Place the peppers on a broiler rack under the flame. Keep turning until the peppers are very well blistered on all sides. Remove from the broiler. Put the peppers in a large paper bag and close it tightly. Let them steam for 20 to 30 minutes. Then slip off the skins and remove all seeds. Cut the peppers into strips.

Combine the remaining ingredients and pour over the peppers. Chill at least several hours.

This is particularly pleasant for a buffet table instead of the more usual salad. It is equally nice as an appetizer.

To prepare ahead of time: This can be prepared a day or two ahead of time. Keep refrigerated until ready to use.

MINIATURE GARDENS, VINAIGRETTE

cherry tomatoes
canned string beans (or better
    yet, freshly cooked ones)
tiny canned carrots
large black ripe olives

stuffed green pimento olives
artichoke hearts
sprigs of parsley or tufts of
    watercress
French dressing

Marinate the string beans and the carrots in separate bowls in French dressing.

Before serving, arrange the tomatoes, string beans, two kinds of olives, artichoke hearts, and the parsley or watercress in individual flat, shallow dishes to look like miniature gardens. Keep colors separate, that is, carrots in one place, tomatoes in another, and so on. Spoon more French dressing on these vegetables just before bringing them in for the guests.

To prepare ahead of time: The carrots and green beans can be marinated the day before. The "gardens" can be arranged and kept refrigerated in the morning. Cover them tightly with plastic wrap. Shortly before serving, spoon on the dressing.

ZUCCHINI, TOMATO, AND ARTICHOKE PLATTER

small zucchini, cooked only
    until barely tender
sliced tomatoes

artichoke hearts
seasoned French dressing

Slice the zucchini lengthwise and arrange on a large round platter, alternating them with the sliced tomatoes. Arrange the artichoke hearts in the center of the platter. Spoon French dressing over all and chill. Shortly before serving spoon a little more dressing on the vegetables.

To prepare ahead of time: The zucchini can be cooked the day before and chilled. The platter can be arranged in the morning, covered with plastic wrap and kept refrigerated until serving time.

COLD ASPARAGUS WITH A
CHILLED SPECIAL SAUCE [serves 10]

6 pounds of fresh asparagus
1 cup Hollandaise sauce
   (page 34, or use any
   favorite recipe)
1 cup sour cream

salt and pepper
½ to 1 cup sliced pimento
½ cup finely chopped green
   onions
¼ cup finely chopped parsley

Combine the Hollandaise sauce (chilled) with the sour cream and season with salt and pepper. Chill until ready to serve.

Cook asparagus until just tender. Drain, rinse with cold water, drain thoroughly and chill.

Arrange asparagus on one large platter, or on individual plates. Spoon the sauce over the tips. Decorate with the pimento slices, green onions, and parsley. Serve very cold.

This is especially good as a first course.

To prepare ahead of time: The asparagus can be cooked the day before and kept refrigerated. The sauce can also be done the day before and chilled. The sauce should be put on the asparagus just before serving.

HOLMBY AVENUE SALAD [serves 4]

1 7-ounce can of tuna,
   well drained
1 cucumber, seeded and
   sliced
1 green pepper, sliced
1 sweet red pepper, sliced
   (or use some pimento)
1 cup sliced celery

1 hard-cooked egg, diced
¾ cup cooked green beans
3 green onions, finely chopped
½ cup sandwich spread
   (or mayonnaise)
1 tablespoon red wine vinegar
salt and pepper to taste

Combine, chill and serve. This is delicious served with ripe, chilled tomatoes.

To prepare ahead of time: The egg and the beans can be cooked the day before (or you can use canned green beans). The rest can be combined in the morning.

TOMATOES COLDLY STUFFED

medium-size tomatoes	finely chopped celery
canned baby string beans	mayonnaise
canned petit pois (peas)	anchovy paste

Dip tomatoes in boiling water, remove and peel. Cut a slice off the top of each, and carefully remove tomato pulp and seeds. Turn upside down to drain, then chill.

Drain string beans and peas. Mix together equal amounts of string beans, peas and celery. Add mayonnaise and anchovy paste to your taste. Add salt and pepper if needed. Chill.

Stuff tomatoes with the vegetable mixture. Place tomatoes on a lettuce-lined platter and serve very cold.

To prepare ahead of time: The vegetable mixture can be prepared the day before, then stuff the tomatoes the following morning, cover with plastic wrap and keep refrigerated until time to serve.

A BUFFET ARRAY OF CHILLED VEGETABLES

[serves 10 to 12]

1 cauliflower, divided into flowerettes, cooked and chilled	2 dozen cherry tomatoes, chilled
2 cans (No. 2) of white asparagus, chilled	3 or 4 cups cooked baby carrots, chilled

For the dressing:

1 cup sour cream	1 tablespoon prepared horseradish
½ cup mayonnaise	
1 teaspoon lemon juice (or more if desired)	¼ teaspoon paprika
¼ teaspoon dry mustard	salt and pepper to taste

Combine all of the ingredients for the dressing and chill. Arrange the chilled vegetables in separate mounds on a large platter. Place the sour cream dressing in a bowl in the center of the platter and serve.

To prepare ahead of time: This can be prepared the day before, however, do not arrange the platter until the following day.

STRING BEANS MARINATED WITH
CORN AND CARROTS (Mary Cullins') [serves 12 to 18]

3 pounds fresh green string beans
⅔ cup finely chopped raw carrots
½ cup finely chopped green onions
1 green pepper, finely chopped
⅔ cup finely sliced celery
1 cup whole kernel corn (canned)
1 small jar pimento strips
1 cup vinegar
¼ cup water
½ cup sugar
1 clove garlic, mashed
salt and pepper to taste
½ cup salad oil

Cut the beans lengthwise (that is, French style) and cook them only until barely tender. Drain and set aside while you prepare the marinade. Combine all of the vegetables and place in a bowl. Mix together the vinegar, water, sugar, garlic, salt, pepper, and salad oil and pour over the chopped vegetables. Add the green beans and marinate, stirring about once a day, for two to three days. Serve chilled.

This is perfect for a buffet dinner or supper.

To prepare ahead of time: This really needs to be done at least one day ahead.

WILD RICE AND SHRIMP SALAD
WITH CURRY DRESSING
[serves 12 to 18 as part of a late supper]

¾ pound wild rice, cooked and cooled
¾ pound fresh mushrooms, sliced
4 tablespoons olive oil
¾ pound raw peeled shrimp (or more)
5 hard-cooked eggs, diced
8 green onions, finely chopped
1 clove garlic, mashed
4 tablespoons lemon juice
1 cup sour cream
1 cup mayonnaise
⅛ teaspoon oregano
⅛ teaspoon thyme
salt and pepper to taste
1 or 2 teaspoons curry powder

Sauté the mushrooms in the oil for about 4 or 5 minutes. Add the raw shrimp and sauté them another 5 minutes or less, just until shrimp are cooked. Remove from heat. Place the cooled rice in a large bowl. Add the mushrooms, shrimp and the diced hard-cooked eggs. Mix gently, but thoroughly. Season with salt and pepper. Meanwhile prepare the curry dressing:

Mix together the lemon juice, sour cream, mayonnaise, oregano, thyme, salt, pepper, curry powder, garlic, and chopped green onions. After thoroughly combined, pour a spoonful of this dressing into the rice mixture and blend gently. The remaining dressing should be served in a separate bowl. (Make sure that both the rice salad and the dressing are chilled before serving.)

To prepare ahead of time: This can be prepared the day before or in the morning. Keep salad and dressing chilled separately.

Note: Other things can be added to this salad such as chopped celery and chopped green pepper. White or brown rice can be substituted for part of the wild rice.

CHICKEN SALAD WITH TOASTED ALMONDS

[serves 4 to 6]

3 cups diced, cooked chicken
3 hard-cooked eggs, diced
½ cup finely sliced celery
1 cucumber, peeled, seeded, and diced

¾ cup toasted almonds
½ cup sour cream
½ cup mayonnaise
salt and pepper
tomato wedges

Combine the chicken, eggs, celery, cucumber, ¼ cup of the almonds, and season lightly with salt and pepper. Mix the sour cream and mayonnaise together, then fold it into the chicken salad. Place this salad in a large bowl or on lettuce leaves on individual plates. Garnish with the remaining toasted almonds and with the tomato wedges.

To prepare ahead of time: All of the individual ingredients can be readied the day before. Combine them the day you are planning to serve the salad.

BEEF OR VEAL SALAD PARISIENNE [serves 4]

1 cup cooked string beans
¾ cup sliced cooked potatoes
½ cup diced red or green
    pepper

2 cups cooked beef (roasted
    or boiled) or veal, cut
    in strips (julienne)
sliced olives
salt and pepper to taste

For the dressing:

½ cup olive oil
1 generous teaspoon Dijon
    type mustard
½ teaspoon salt

½ teaspoon pepper
2 tablespoons red wine vinegar
1 tablespoon tarragon vinegar

For the garnish:

1 large tomato, cut in wedges
green or red pepper strips

2 hard-cooked eggs, cut in sixths
lettuce

Combine the string beans, potatoes, diced pepper, beef or veal, and sliced olives. Place in a large bowl. Season with salt and pepper.

Combine ingredients for the dressing and mix together thoroughly. Pour this dressing over the meat mixture and chill.

Place lettuce on a large platter. Toss the meat mixture and place it down the center, then garnish with the pepper strips, eggs and tomatoes.

To prepare ahead of time: The ingredients can be readied the day before, then they can be combined the following day. The dressing can be put on the meat mixture in the morning and kept chilled until ready to serve.

JERRY JERABEK'S PINEAPPLE PICKLES

1 No. 2½ can (about 1 lb.
    14 ozs.) pineapple
    chunks
1 cup cider vinegar

1 cup brown sugar (packed)
2 sticks cinnamon
20 whole cloves

Drain juice from the pineapple chunks and save it. To this juice add the remaining ingredients and bring this to a boil. Reduce heat and simmer uncovered for 10 minutes. Add the pineapple chunks, bring to a boil again, reduce heat, then simmer an additional 10 minutes. Seal in sterilized jars.

To prepare ahead of time: As stated above, these can be preserved in jars, however, it is comforting to know that if the thought of sterilizing jars, etc., is just too much, they can simply be placed in clean jars and kept for several months in the refrigerator.

Note: Jerry serves these always as part of the traditional Thanksgiving feast he prepares. They are superb, of course, with any kind of poultry.

VIRGINIA MORRIS' FAVORITE FRUIT SALAD

1 cup canned pineapple
    drained and cut in small
    pieces
1 cup Royal Ann cherries,
    pitted and drained

¼ pound (¾ cup) miniature
    marshmallows
¼ pound blanched and
    halved almonds

For the dressing:

4 egg yolks
4 tablespoons sugar
4 tablespoons tarragon vinegar

pinch of salt
1 cup whipping cream, whipped

Combine fruit, marshmallows, and almonds and set aside. Make the dressing: Beat the egg yolks, salt, sugar, and vinegar to a cream, then cook gently in a double boiler, stirring constantly until it thickens. Remove from heat and cool. Before serving, fold in the whipped cream.

Reserve a little of the dressing. Add the rest of it to the fruit mixture and chill thoroughly. Serve with a little of the dressing on the top.

To prepare ahead of time: This can be made the day before.

STUFFED PINEAPPLES

fresh pineapples
strawberries
cantaloupe
other fruit of your choice

chopped dates
toasted chopped walnuts
miniature scoops of fruit
sherbet or ice

Cut the pineapples in half lengthwise, leaving the green part on to serve as decoration. Remove the pineapple meat and dice it. Combine the diced pineapple with other fruit and chill.

Shortly before serving stuff the pineapple shells with the fruit. Sprinkle the chopped dates and walnuts over the top of the fruit. Top each stuffed pineapple with several miniature scoops of fruit sherbet or ice.

To prepare ahead of time: The pineapple can be cut the day before and some of the fruit that is non-perishable can also be readied. The pineapple halves can be stuffed several hours before serving, covered with plastic wrap, and kept refrigerated until ready to serve. Add the fruit sherbet at the last moment.

SKEWERED FRUIT TO ACCOMPANY POULTRY OR MEAT

large prunes soaked several
days in Port
preserved kumquats

watermelon pickles
small bamboo skewers

Pit the prunes. Place a prune, a watermelon pickle, and a kumquat on each skewer. Serve with broiled or roast chicken, or with roast beef.

To prepare ahead of time: By all means, do soak the prunes in Port at least several days ahead of time; they are even better if soaked for a week or two.

FRESH FRUIT SALAD EN BROCHETTE

large pineapple cubes
thick orange slices
thick banana chunks, dipped
in lemon juice

large cubes of cantaloupe
large cubes of honeydew melon
very large strawberries
fresh figs, peeled

Arrange the above fruit on long bamboo skewers in any order you prefer. Place on a large platter, cover with plastic wrap, and keep refrigerated until time to serve.

To prepare ahead of time: The skewers can be arranged in the morning, covered with the plastic wrap, and kept chilled until time to serve.

GRAPEFRUIT, AVOCADO, BANANA AND PIÑONS

[serves 4]

2 grapefruit, peeled and
then sectioned
1 large avocado, peeled
and sliced
1 large banana, cut in 4 chunks

2 tablespoons mayonnaise
piñons
paprika
lettuce leaves

Place lettuce leaves on individual plates. Arrange the avocado and grapefruit alternately on the lettuce. Roll the banana chunks in mayonnaise, then in the piñons. Place the bananas in the center of each salad. Spoon any remaining grapefruit juice on the avocado slices. Dip your fingers in some paprika, then put the paprika on the edges of the lettuce. Chill briefly, then serve.

To prepare ahead of time: The grapefruit can be sectioned the day before. The salads can be assembled several hours before serving. Keep tightly covered with plastic wrap in the refrigerator.

Yeast Breads, Quick Breads and Pancakes

Yeast Breads, Quick Breads and Pancakes

PROMETHEUS' WALNUT SECRET

1 package dry yeast	6 egg yolks
½ cup warm water	¾ cup milk, scalded and cooled
½ teaspoon salt	4 cups flour (1 pound)
1 tablespoon sugar	

For the filling:

¾ cup sugar	1 ¼ cups walnuts, finely chopped
¾ cup soft butter	1 teaspoon vanilla

For the glaze:

2 tablespoons sugar	1 or 2 teaspoons vanilla
⅓ cup milk	1 tablespoon butter

Dissolve yeast in the warm water, then stir in the salt, and sugar. Set aside while combining the other ingredients. In a mixing bowl, combine the egg yolks and the milk, then add the yeast mixture. Gradually beat in the flour either by hand (or with an electric dough hook), or knead until mixture is smooth. Place in a greased bowl, cover with a damp cloth, and let rise until doubled, about 1 to 1 ½ hours.

Prepare the filling: Cream together the sugar, butter and vanilla. Reserve chopped walnuts.

Roll dough out (or pat out) into a rectangle about 10″ by 16″. Spread with the filling, then sprinkle with the chopped walnuts. Roll up as for a jelly roll along the long side. Cut in pieces about 1 ½ inches wide. Place half of the pieces in the bottom of a well greased 10-inch tube pan with a tight-fitting bottom (or use a large Kouglof or bundt cake pan). Place them cut side up. Then make a second layer in the pan with the remaining pieces. Cover and let rise again until double in bulk, 30 to 45 minutes. Bake in a moderate oven for about 25 to 30 minutes (350°). While this is baking, prepare the glaze by warming the ingredients together and stirring until combined. Remove coffeecake from oven and pour the glaze gently over the top (or spoon it on). Return to the oven and bake another 20 to 30 minutes. Remove from oven and let it stand for a few minutes, then gently remove from pan and cool it on a rack.

To prepare ahead of time: This can be baked the day before or in the morning. If done the day before, wrap in foil and refrigerate. Reheat before serving.

To freeze: This freezes. Defrost, then reheat to serve.

KING'S KOUGLOF

2 cakes of fresh yeast	1 ½ teaspoons vanilla
⅔ cup flour	2 ¼ cups sifted flour (about
¾ cup lukewarm milk	9 ounces)
3 eggs	1 cup raisins
½ cup sugar	1 ½ cubes butter (6 ounces)
1 teaspoon salt	at room temperature
grated rind of 1 lemon	sliced almonds

Mix the yeast with the milk until dissolved, then stir in the ⅔ cup flour and set aside while mixing the other ingredients.

Put the eggs, sugar, salt, lemon rind, vanilla and flour in a mixing bowl and beat it either by hand or with an electric dough hook. Add the yeast mixture and continue to beat or knead the mixture in the bowl until the dough leaves the sides of the bowl. Beat in the softened butter bit by bit only until it has been incorporated. Beat in the raisins. Do not overbeat after the butter has been added. Cover and let rise until it has doubled in volume—about 1 ½ hours or so. Punch down and let rise again for 20 to 30 minutes. Then place the dough into a well greased mold which has been sprinkled with the sliced almonds. Let rise about 30 to 45 minutes (double in bulk), and bake at 375° for 30 to 40 minutes. Remove and invert to cool.

To prepare ahead of time: This can be baked the day before. Cool, wrap in foil, and refrigerate. Reheat the following day.

To freeze: This freezes very well.

A MERRY MONKEY BREAD

2 cakes of fresh yeast	1 cup lukewarm milk
2 tablespoons lukewarm water	1 teaspoon salt
	2 eggs, beaten
¼ cup sugar	4 cups sifted flour (1 pound)
¼ cup butter	¼ cup melted and cooled butter

Heat the milk, then add the sugar, butter and salt and stir. Crumble yeast into a large bowl and sprinkle the water on the yeast. Stir until it has dissolved. Add the milk mixture (which you are certain is cooled to lukewarm) and stir. Add the eggs. Add half the flour and beat very well. Add remaining flour and beat again until the dough is smooth. Cover and let rise until double in bulk (about 1½ hours).

Turn dough out onto a floured board and knead for a minute. Pat out and then cut into pieces about the size of 2-inch cubes. Dip each piece in the melted butter and place in an angel food cake pan (or a bundt cake pan). Press pieces down gently. Let rise until double (about 30 minutes or so), and then bake 30 to 40 minutes at 375°. Remove from oven and cool in the pan for about 5 minutes. Then carefully turn it out upside down and serve at once. Or cool on a cake rack and then later reheat to serve.

To prepare ahead of time: This can be baked the day before. After cooling cover with foil and refrigerate. Reheat in the foil before serving.

To freeze: Yes, this freezes.

BRIOCHE "BE-JAMMED" [makes 3 to 4 dozen]

2 cakes of fresh yeast
2 tablespoons lukewarm
   water
½ cup warm milk
1 cup melted butter
½ teaspoon salt
½ cup sugar
grated rind of one lemon

4 whole eggs
4 egg yolks
3 cups sifted cake flour
2 cups sifted all purpose flour
apricot and raspberry jam
melted butter
granulated sugar

Crumble yeast into a large bowl and sprinkle with the 2 tablespoons of lukewarm water. Stir to dissolve the yeast. Beat egg yolks and whole eggs until thick. Melt butter and combine with the milk, sugar and salt. Stir well. Combine with the beaten eggs. Test to see if it is lukewarm, then add to the dissolved yeast. Sift flours together and then add gradually to the egg mixture. Beat thoroughly. After all the flour has been added, beat again for about 3 minutes, or until dough is smooth. Cover with a damp towel and let rise for 1½ to 2 hours.

Place dough on a floured board and gently pat down. Cut off pieces about the size of a very large walnut or a very small egg. Place these pieces on greased baking pans and flatten each one. Let them rise about 15 minutes. Then, with a floured teaspoon, make a good-sized dent in the center of each and fill with either the apricot or the raspberry jam. Let rise about another 10 or 15 minutes. Then bake at 400° from 10 to 15 minutes. Remove from oven, brush with melted butter, and sprinkle with granulated sugar.

Serve with lots of fresh butter and additional jam.

To prepare ahead of time: These can be baked the day before. Cool, then wrap in foil and refrigerate. Reheat before serving.

To freeze: These freeze very nicely.

EASY BUT PLEASING RAISIN-NUT COFFEE CAKES

[makes about 3 dozen]

2 cakes of fresh yeast
2 tablespoons lukewarm
    water
1 cup warm milk
⅓ cup sugar

⅓ cup melted butter
1 teaspoon salt
2 eggs, well beaten
4 cups sifted flour (1 pound)

For the filling:

½ cup butter
½ cup milk
½ cup brown sugar
    (packed)

2 cups raisins or currants
3 teaspoons cinnamon
⅔ cup chopped nuts

Make the filling: Combine ingredients for the filling in a saucepan, stir over moderate heat until mixture comes to a boil. Remove from heat and cool.

Crumble yeast and sprinkle with the water. Stir to dissolve the yeast. Add butter, sugar and salt to the lukewarm milk, then add to the beaten eggs. Add this to the yeast after testing to make sure the mixture is not too hot. Gradually beat in the flour, beating until dough is smooth, Cover and let rise until double in bulk, about 1½ hours.

Turn dough out on a floured board and knead for half a minute. Divide dough into three portions. With each portion of the dough:

Roll out into an oblong about ¼ to ⅓ inch thick. Spread each portion of dough with ⅓ of the filling, then roll up tightly as a jelly roll. Cut into 1 or 1½ inch pieces and place them side by side in a greased pan (or pans). Let rise for 20 to 30 minutes. Bake at 400° for 12 to 15 minutes.

To prepare ahead of time: These can be baked the day before. Cool, then wrap in foil and refrigerate. Reheat before serving.

To freeze: These, like most coffee cakes freeze well.

MY FAVORITE WARM WATER FRENCH BREAD

2 packages dry yeast	2 cups warm water
⅔ cup warm water	7 to 8 cups all purpose flour
1 tablespoon sugar	(about 2 pounds)
1 tablespoon salt	cornmeal

For brushing the loaves:
   1 egg white mixed with a little cold
      water, then beaten lightly

Dissolve the yeast in the ⅔ cup warm water, then stir in the sugar and salt. Place this with the additional 2 cups of warm water in a large mixing bowl and gradually work in as much flour as is necessary to make a very stiff dough. Turn out and knead thoroughly on a floured board, adding more flour as needed. (This whole process can be done with an electric dough hook.) Place dough in a greased bowl, cover and let rise until almost double in bulk, about 40 to 45 minutes. Punch down and turn out on a floured board.

Divide the dough into 2 or 3 portions and then set them aside to relax for a few minutes, then shape them into either round or oblong loaves. Sprinkle baking pans heavily with corn meal and place the shaped loaves on top of the corn meal. Score the top of the loaves and then brush them with the egg white mixture. Let rise again for 15 or 20 minutes. Brush again with the egg white mixture.

Place the prepared loaves in a *cold* oven and set temperature at 400°. Bake for about 30 to 35 minutes, remove from oven, brush once again with the egg white mixture, and return to the oven having reduced the temperature to 300°, and bake about another 20 to 25 minutes. Remove and cool on racks.

To prepare ahead of time: These can be baked the day before. Cool, wrap in foil and refrigerate. Reheat before serving. This bread is delicious the next day served just as it is without reheating, and several days later it is equally excellent, toasted.

To freeze: This freezes magnificently. Defrost, then wrap in foil and heat until warm. Remove foil and complete heating unwrapped.

WHOLE WHEAT BREAD [makes 2 loaves]

2 packages dry yeast
½ cup warm water
1 cup water
¾ cup milk
1 cup All-Bran
3 tablespoons sugar
4 teaspoons salt

6 tablespoons butter or margarine (¾ of a stick)
⅓ cup molasses
3 cups unsifted whole wheat flour (12 ounces)
2 ¾ cups unsifted white flour (12 ounces)

Dissolve yeast in the warm water and set aside. Bring water and milk to a boil, then add the All-Bran, sugar, salt, butter, and molasses. Cool. Place this and the dissolved yeast in a large bowl and gradually beat in the two kinds of flour. If it is too difficult to beat by hand (this can be done with an electric dough hook if you have one), turn out on a floured board and gradually knead in the flour. Place in a greased bowl and let rise an hour or longer—until about doubled in bulk.

Punch dough down. Divide dough in half and shape into loaves. Place in greased pans about 3 by 5 by 8¾. Cover and let rise about 1 hour. Bake in a 400° oven for 30 to 35 minutes. Remove and let stand a minute or two, then gently remove from the pans and cool on racks.

To prepare ahead of time: This can be baked the day before. Keep tightly wrapped in foil overnight. Then slice and serve.

To freeze: This does freeze. Defrost, then use.

STONE GROUND WHOLE WHEAT BREAD
[makes 1 large or 2 small loaves]

1 ½ cakes fresh yeast
½ cup lukewarm water
1 cup milk, scalded and then cooled
⅓ cup honey

3 ⅓ cups stone ground whole wheat flour (can usually be obtained in health food stores)
2 eggs, beaten slightly
1 tablespoon salt
¼ cup melted butter

Crumble yeast in a large bowl and add the lukewarm water. Add the honey to the scalded milk and stir to dissolve honey. Add the milk and honey to the beaten eggs and then stir in the salt and melted butter. Test to make certain it is not too hot and then pour over the dissolved yeast. Add 2 cups of the flour and beat very well for about 4 minutes. Add remaining flour and beat until dough is very spongy. Cover and let rise for 2 to 2 ½ hours, or until double in bulk. Place in a greased loaf pan (or pans) and let rise again for 45 minutes to 1 hour. Bake in a 350° oven for 45 to 50 minutes, or until well browned and firm.

To prepare ahead of time: This can be baked the day before. Cool, wrap in foil and the next day slice and serve.

To freeze: This freezes without any problems.

100% RYE BREAD [makes 2 loaves]

2 packages dry yeast
½ cup warm water
2 cups milk, scalded and cooled
1 tablespoon salt

¼ cup brown sugar (packed)
⅓ cup molasses
¼ cup melted shortening or oil
½ cup cold water
2 pounds of rye flour (about)

Dissolve yeast in lukewarm water. Combine the scalded milk, salt, sugar, molasses, and the melted shortening or oil. Add the cold water and stir until lukewarm. Gradually beat in as much of the flour as possible, then knead in the rest of the flour. Place in a greased bowl, cover and let rise for about 1 hour—to a little less than double in bulk.

Punch down, divide dough into two portions and shape. Place in greased pans. Let rise 50 to 60 minutes. Bake at 400° for 10 minutes. Reduce heat to 350° and bake another 35 minutes. Remove from oven and from pans and cool on racks.

To prepare ahead of time: This can be baked one or two days ahead of time. Keep tightly wrapped in foil in the refrigerator. Slice very thin and serve with sweet butter.

To freeze: This freezes. Defrost, then slice and serve.

SOUR DOUGH CARAWAY RYE BREAD [makes 2 loaves]

2 packages dry yeast	2 tablespoons caraway seeds
¾ cup warm water	1 ½ cups sour milk
1 tablespoon sugar	1 cup whole wheat flour
1 cup white flour	3 cups unsifted rye flour (about)
1 tablespoon salt	

Dissolve the yeast in the warm water, then add the white flour and sugar and stir. Let this sponge rise about 15 or 20 minutes.

Combine the remaining ingredients and beat or knead, adding enough rye flour to make a very stiff dough. Let rise until double, about 1 to 1 ½ hours. Punch down and shape into two round loaves. Place them on greased baking sheets. Let rise again until double in bulk, about 30 to 45 minutes. Brush with cold water. Bake at 400° for 10 minutes. Reduce heat to 350° and bake about another 45 minutes to 1 hour.

To prepare ahead of time: This can be baked the day before. Keep tightly wrapped in foil.

To freeze: Yes, this freezes, as do most breads.

CRANBERRY BREAD [makes 1 loaf]

¼ cup shortening	1 cup raw cranberries,
1 cup sugar	chopped or ground
2 eggs	2 tablespoons water
2 cups sifted flour	grated rind of 1 orange
½ teaspoon salt	½ cup orange juice
½ teaspoon baking powder	½ cup walnuts, chopped
½ teaspoon baking soda	

Cream shortening, add sugar and beat until light and fluffy. Beat in eggs one at a time. Sift dry ingredients together and add alternately with the water and orange juice. Stir until blended but do not beat after adding the flour. Blend in the orange rind, cranberries, and chopped walnuts. Pour into a greased loaf pan (3 x 5 x 9) and bake about 1 hour or a little longer in a 350° oven.

To prepare ahead of time: This is even better if baked the day before. Wrap in foil and store in the refrigerator.

To freeze: Yes, this freezes.

A CONVENTIONAL BUT USEFUL BANANA BREAD
[makes 1 loaf]

⅓ cup shortening
⅔ cup sugar
2 eggs
1 ¾ cups sifted flour
½ teaspoon baking powder

½ teaspoon baking soda
¾ teaspoon salt
1 cup mashed ripe bananas
(about 2 or 3 bananas)

Cream shortening, add sugar gradually and beat until light and fluffy. Add eggs one at a time and beat again. Sift dry ingredients together, then add them alternately with the mashed bananas, stirring to combine well, but do not overbeat. Pour into a greased loaf pan (3x5x9) and bake at about 350° for approximately an hour. Remove from pan and cool on a rack.

To prepare ahead of time: I prefer this baked a day before. Cool, then wrap in foil. Store in or out of the refrigerator. Slice and serve cold or at room temperature.

To freeze: Yes, this does freeze. And furthermore, what a marvelous way to use up those ripe bananas.

A FOOLPROOF SPOON BREAD   [serves about 4 to 6]

1 teaspoon salt
1 cup white cornmeal
2 cups milk
1 cup milk (to be added later)

¼ cup butter
3 egg yolks
3 teaspoons baking powder
4 egg whites

Combine salt, cornmeal and the 2 cups of milk. Stir over low heat until thickened. Stir in the butter. Add the remaining 1 cup of milk and stir. Then beat in the egg yolks.

Just before baking, sprinkle the cornmeal mixture with the baking powder and stir very well. Beat egg whites until stiff, then fold them into the cornmeal mixture. Bake in a greased casserole for about 30 minutes at 375°.

To prepare ahead of time: The mixture up to the point of adding the baking powder and egg whites can be prepared in the morning. Place it in a large bowl and cover tightly. Leave at room temperature. Then shortly before baking time proceed with the rest of the recipe and serve very hot.

To freeze: If there is any leftover, do freeze it and use it to fill in at some family meal. Do not use freezing as a purposeful beforehand procedure, for it is at its prime prepared as directed above.

BUTTERMILK OR SOUR MILK DOUGHNUTS

[makes 8 to 12]

2 cups sifted flour
2 teaspoons baking powder
½ teaspoon baking soda
½ teaspoon salt
¼ teaspoon nutmeg
¼ teaspoon cinnamon
1 egg

½ cup sugar
2 tablespoons melted butter
½ cup buttermilk or sour milk
  (sour milk can be made by
  adding ½ teaspoon vinegar
  to ½ cup sweet milk)

Sift dry ingredients together, including the sugar. Beat the egg and combine it with the melted butter and the buttermilk or sour milk. Combine the two mixtures but do not beat.

Turn out on a floured surface and knead lightly. Pat or roll out the dough to about ⅓ inch thickness. Cut with a doughnut cutter and fry in hot deep fat (about 375°) for 2 to 3 minutes, turning doughnuts once or twice after they reach the top of the fat. Drain thoroughly on paper towels.

To prepare ahead of time: These can be made the day before. Refrigerate, then reheat before serving.

To freeze: These freeze. They can be reheated straight out of the freezer, or they can be reheated after defrosting.

NO SCUFFLE SCONES [makes 8 wedges]

1 cup sifted flour
¼ teaspoon salt
1 ½ teaspoons baking powder
¼ cup soft butter (scant)

1 egg (reserve a little of the
egg white for the topping)
3 tablespoons milk
granulated sugar

Sift dry ingredients together and place in a bowl. Cut in the butter, then add egg and milk and stir just until combined. Turn out on a floured surface and knead gently for a few seconds, then pat out ½ inch thick into a circle. Cut in 8 wedges, brush with a little egg white and sprinkle with sugar. Bake at 425° (after placing them on greased baking pans) for about 12 to 15 minutes. Serve hot with butter and jam.

To prepare ahead of time: These can be prepared in the morning and kept refrigerated until time to bake. Remove from refrigerator, then proceed as above.

To freeze: These can be baked and then frozen, however, I prefer eating them right after they come from the oven.

FRESH FABULOUS BLUEBERRY MUFFINS
[makes 1 dozen]

¼ cup softened butter
½ cup sugar
1 egg broken into a measuring
cup, then *milk* added to
measure 1 cup

1 ¾ cup sifted flour
2 ½ teaspoons baking powder
½ teaspoon salt
1 cup very fresh blueberries

Cream butter and sugar together until fluffy. Add the egg-milk mixture and beat. Sift dry ingredients together and add them, stirring only until all the flour is moistened. Do not beat. Stir blueberries carefully into the batter. Fill greased muffin tins about ⅔ full. Bake at 400° for 20 to 25 minutes.

To prepare ahead of time: These can be baked the day before. Wrap in foil and refrigerate. Reheat before serving.

To freeze: These can be frozen. Defrost, then reheat to serve.

QUICK COFFEE CAKE, NO. 1

⅓ cup butter
¾ cup sugar
1 egg
½ cup milk
1½ cups sifted flour

2 teaspoons baking powder
½ teaspoon salt
⅓ cup apricot jam
¼ cup currant jelly

For the topping:

¼ cup brown sugar
½ teaspoon cinnamon

3 tablespoons melted butter
½ cup chopped nuts

Prepare the topping: Blend all of the ingredients together and then set aside.

Cream butter and sugar together until light and fluffy. Beat in the egg. Sift dry ingredients together and then add to the mixture alternately with the milk, using only a few strokes to combine. Do not beat.

Pour batter into a greased and floured 8″ by 8″ pan. Dot surface with the apricot jam and currant jelly. Sprinkle with the topping previously prepared. Bake at 350° for 25 to 35 minutes. Serve warm.

To prepare ahead of time: This can be baked the day before or in the morning. Reheat before serving.

To freeze: This can be frozen. Heat before serving.

QUICK COFFEE CAKE, NO. 2

2 cups sifted flour
¾ cup sugar
½ teaspoon salt
2 teaspoons baking powder
½ cup softened butter

1 egg broken into a 1-cup
    measure, then *milk* added
    to the 1 cup mark
1 teaspoon vanilla

For the topping:

½ cup brown sugar,
    packed (generous)

cinnamon (3 to 5 teaspoons)
2 tablespoons butter

Sift flour, sugar, salt and baking powder together and then place in a mixing bowl. Cut in the softened butter either using a pastry blender, or just using your hands. Combine the egg-milk mixture with the vanilla and beat lightly. Add to the dry ingredients, stir until combined, but do not beat. Pour into a greased 9-inch square pan.

Sprinkle the top of the batter with the brown sugar, then with plenty of cinnamon, and then dot with the butter. Bake at 350° for about 25 to 30 minutes. Serve hot or warm.

To prepare ahead of time: This can be baked the day before. Cool, cover with foil and refrigerate. Reheat before serving.

To freeze: Yes, this freezes. Reheat before serving.

A MAGNETIC SOUR CREAM MARVEL

½ cup butter	1 teaspoon baking powder
1 cup sugar (generous)	1 teaspoon baking soda
3 eggs	¼ teaspoon salt
1 teaspoon vanilla	1 cup sour cream
2 cups sifted flour	

For the topping:

¾ cup brown sugar (packed)	3 tablespoons softened butter
1 tablespoon flour	1 cup walnuts, chopped
1 teaspoon cinnamon	

Prepare the topping: Combine the ingredients for the topping with your hands, blending them together thoroughly.

Cream butter and sugar, then beat in eggs one at a time. Add vanilla. Sift dry ingredients together, then add alternately with the sour cream.

Grease a large angel food cake pan. Pour in half the batter. Sprinkle with half the topping. Add remaining batter, then sprinkle with remaining topping. Bake at 350° for 45 minutes, reduce heat to 325° and bake about an additional 15 minutes, or until the coffee cake tests done. Serve warm.

To prepare ahead of time: This can be baked the day before. Wrap in foil and refrigerate. Serve at room temperature, or reheat and serve warm.

To freeze: This freezes beautifully.

DANIEL'S FAVORITE BANANA PANCAKES

3 eggs
1 cup sifted flour
1 mashed banana
½ teaspoon baking soda
pinch of salt

1 ¼ cups warm milk
¼ cup melted butter
additional butter for sautèing
the pancakes

Beat eggs, then add flour-alternately with the milk. Add soda, salt, mashed banana, and butter. Stir until well combined. Let stand at least 5 minutes. Add more milk if too thick.

Cook the pancakes in a skillet or on a griddle, using plenty of butter. I make them small, about 3 inches in diameter. Serve with maple or boysenberry syrup.

To prepare ahead of time: These can be cooked, stacked with melted butter, covered with foil, then later reheated in the oven. This can be done even the day before.

To freeze: Yes, these can be frozen. Brush with melted butter and then wrap in foil about 6 or 8 to a package. Defrost, then reheat in the oven.

SOUR CREAM PANCAKES

1 cup sour cream
2 eggs
½ teaspoon salt
½ teaspoon baking soda

1 cup flour
1 to 1 ½ cups milk
butter

Mix dry ingredients. Add milk and sour cream to the eggs. Combine mixtures and stir. Add additional milk if needed to make pancakes as thin as desired. Cook in a skillet or on a griddle using plenty of butter. Serve hot with syrup or jam or honey.

To prepare ahead of time: These can be cooked, brushed with melted butter, covered with foil and reheated later. If done the day before, refrigerate overnight.

To freeze: These can be frozen if brushed with melted butter and stacked about 8 or 10 to a package. Wrap in foil and freeze. Defrost, then heat in foil in the oven.

A LARGE APPLE PANCAKE FOR FOUR

3 eggs
⅔ cup sifted cake flour
¼ teaspoon salt
1 tablespoon sugar
1 teaspoon vanilla

½ cup milk
2 tablespoons melted butter
grated rind of 1 lemon
2 additional tablespoons butter

For the filling:

¼ cup butter
4 cooking apples, peeled,
cored and cut in
eighths

½ to 1 cup sugar
1½ teaspoons vanilla

Prepare the filling: Sauté the apples gently in the butter, simmering them with the sugar until just tender. Do not overcook them or they will be mushy. Stir in the vanilla. Keep warm.

Beat the eggs. Add the dry ingredients alternately with the milk. Stir in the vanilla, lemon rind, and the melted butter. Let this mixture stand about 1 hour if possible.

Heat a very large skillet (preferably a 16-inch one) in a 450° oven for 5 minutes. Remove from oven and add the butter. Now pour in the batter and bake at 450° for about 20 to 25 minutes. Remove from oven and slide the pancake on to a large platter which has been greased with a little butter. Fill with the apple mixture, roll up and slice into serving portions. Sprinkle with powdered sugar.

To prepare ahead of time: The apple filling can be cooked the day before or in the morning. Reheat gently before filling the pancake.

To freeze: The apple filling freezes. Defrost, then reheat before filling the pancake.

Cakes, Cookies and Pastries

Cakes, Cookies and Pastries

PAT ALTMAN'S TOSCA CAKE [serves about 8]

1 10-inch layer of sponge
   cake, or genoise, or plain
   butter cake
2 tablespoons flour
½ cup sugar

½ cup butter
2 tablespoons milk
¼ teaspoon vanilla
1 cup sliced blanched almonds

Mix sugar and flour together in a saucepan. Add butter, milk, vanilla and sliced almonds. Cook over low heat, stirring constantly until butter has melted and sugar is dissolved. Place cake on an ovenproof dish. Spread the almond glaze over top of cake leaving one inch unglazed around the edge. Place under broiler until glaze is golden brown. Watch carefully so it doesn't burn. Remove from oven and serve either hot or room temperature.

To prepare ahead of time: This can be done in the morning or the day before. To serve hot, reheat for a short time before serving.

To freeze: This can be frozen. Reheat before serving if you want to serve it hot or warm.

A FESTIVE WHITE CAKE WITH LEMON FILLING
[serves 12 to 16]

¾ cup shortening (butter or
   other)
1⅓ cups sugar
1½ teaspoons vanilla
2½ cups sifted cake flour
3 teaspoons baking powder
1 teaspoon salt

1 cup milk
6 egg whites
⅓ cup sugar
Lemon Filling (recipe follows)
Seven-Minute Frosting
   (recipe follows)

Cream shortening or butter, add sugar gradually and beat until fluffy, then add the vanilla. Sift flour, baking powder, and salt together 3 times, and then add to the creamed mixture alternately with the milk.

Beat egg whites until just barely stiff, then gradually beat in the remaining ⅓ cup sugar. Fold into the other mixture. Pour into two 9-inch layer cake pans which have been greased, bottoms lined with waxed paper, then greased again. Bake the cakes at 375° for 5 minutes, reduce heat to 350° and bake for about another 25 to 30 minutes. Remove from oven and cool for 5 minutes on cake racks, then turn out, remove paper, and return right side up to finish cooling.

Lemon Filling:

¾ cup sugar	⅓ cup lemon juice
2 tablespoons cornstarch	⅔ cup orange juice
3 tablespoons flour	⅓ cup water
⅛ teaspoon salt	3 egg yolks, slightly beaten
grated rind of 1 lemon	

Mix dry ingredients. Add rind, juices, and water; place in top of double boiler. Cook and stir until mixture thickens then beat it into the egg yolks. Return to double boiler and cook and stir until very thick. Chill thoroughly before using.

Seven-Minute Frosting:

2 egg whites	⅓ cup water
1½ cups sugar	⅛ teaspoon salt
2 tablespoons corn syrup	1 teaspoon vanilla

Combine everything but the vanilla and place in the top of a double boiler. Beat with an electric beater (or rotary hand beater) over boiling water until mixture forms stiff peaks—about 7 minutes. Remove from heat and add vanilla. Beat until of desired consistency.

To assemble: Slice each cake layer in half horizontally. Fill layers with the chilled lemon filling, then frost the whole outside of the cake with the seven-minute frosting. And then, if desired, cover the whole thing with plenty of shredded coconut.

To prepare ahead of time: This can be baked and filled and frosted the day before if you have room to store it in your refrigerator. If not, make the filling, the cakes, and then finish it off the following day.

To freeze: The cake layers freeze very well. The lemon filling can be frozen separately. However, the seven-minute frosting has a tendency to become granular, therefore, I do not recommend filling, frosting and freezing the whole thing.

ATHENA'S AGELESS CHOCOLATE CAKE [serves
WITH A TIMELESS CHOCOLATE FROSTING 12 to 16]

3 squares unsweetened
   chocolate
2 cups sifted cake flour
2 cups sugar
½ teaspoon baking powder
1 ½ teaspoons baking soda
1 teaspoon salt
½ cup butter (at room
   temperature)

¾ cup milk
3 eggs
½ cup milk
2 teaspoons vanilla
dark chocolate icing
   (recipe follows)
chopped pistachios for
   garnishing

First, be sure that all ingredients are at room temperature. Melt chocolate slowly and then let it cool. Sift all the dry ingredients together, including the sugar and place in a mixing bowl. Add the butter and ¾ cup milk and beat with an electric mixer on low speed for 1 minute. Add the melted and cooled chocolate and beat another minute. Add the remaining ½ cup milk, the eggs, and the vanilla and beat again at low speed for 1 or 2 minutes, scraping the sides occasionally. Be sure not to overbeat or the cake will be tough. Pour into three 9-inch layer cake pans which have been greased and floured. (Or grease the pans, line with waxed paper and grease the paper.) Bake at 350° for 30 to 35 minutes, or until cakes test done. Cool on racks for about 5 minutes, then invert to remove from pans, turn right side up and finish cooling.

Dark chocolate icing:

12 ounces dark
   SWEET chocolate

1 cup of very heavy cream
   (use whipping cream)

Melt the chocolate carefully in a large bowl over warm water, or in a barely warm oven. Heat the cream to the boiling point, then add it to the chocolate and beat vigorously, preferably with a whisk until chocolate is completely melted and somewhat cooled. (You can now flavor this if you want to with vanilla or rum.)

To assemble: Cut each of the three layers of chocolate cake in half horizontally. Fill and frost the cake with the already prepared dark chocolate icing. (Spread each layer with only a rather thin layer of the icing.) Sprinkle with the chopped pistachios.

To prepare ahead of time: This can be baked, filled and frosted several days ahead of time. Cover completely with foil or with plastic wrap and keep refrigerated. Bring to room temperature.

To freeze: Yes, this freezes perfectly. Just defrost in its foil wrapping, bring to room temperature and then serve.

LAVENDER AND LACE SPICE CAKE
WITH SEA FOAM ICING [serves 10 to 12]

½ cup butter
1 cup sugar
2 eggs
½ cup molasses
2 cups sifted cake flour
1 teaspoon cinnamon
½ teaspoon nutmeg
¼ teaspoon cloves

½ teaspoon salt
1 cup sour milk (or make it quickly by adding 1 teaspoon of lemon juice or vinegar to 1 cup milk)
1 teaspoon baking soda
1 teaspoon vanilla
Sea Foam Icing (recipe follows)

Cream butter and sugar together until light and fluffy. Beat in the eggs until very light. Add molasses and combine thoroughly. Sift flour, spices and salt together, and add alternately with the sour milk and soda. Stir in the vanilla. Pour into two greased and floured 9-inch cake pans and bake at 350° for about 35 minutes. Remove from oven and cool for 5 minutes. Remove cakes from pans and finish cooling cakes.

Sea Foam Icing:

¾ cup light brown sugar
   (firmly packed)
¼ cup light corn syrup
2 tablespoons water

¼ teaspoon salt
¼ teaspoon cream of tartar
½ teaspoon vanilla
2 egg whites, unbeaten

Combine all of these ingredients in the top of a double boiler and beat with a rotary beater, or with a portable electric beater, over boiling water. Remove from heat when frosting will hold its shape, about 5 to 7 minutes.

To assemble: Spread the icing between layers and then frost the top and sides. If desired you can decorate with chopped toasted almonds.

To prepare ahead of time: This can be baked, filled and frosted the day before. Refrigerate overnight, then bring to room temperature before serving.

To freeze: Only freeze the cakes. Defrost, then fill and frost.

DATE AND WALNUT CAKE [serves 8 to 10]

1 cup sugar	1 cup sifted cake flour
4 eggs	(3 ⅓ ounces)
¼ teaspoon salt	1 cup of dates, cut in small
1 teaspoon baking powder	pieces
	1 cup chopped walnuts

Set aside 2 tablespoons of the flour and mix with the chopped dates and walnuts. Beat eggs until very thick and light-colored, gradually beating in the sugar until mixture is almost as thick as cream after it has been whipped. Sift remaining flour together with the salt and baking powder, then fold into the egg mixture. Fold in the dates and nuts. Pour into a 9-inch spring form pan and bake at 325° for 45 minutes to 1 hour. Cool on a rack, then remove form. Serve plain with fruit compote, or with whipped and sweetened cream.

To prepare ahead of time: This can be baked the day before. Keep covered with foil overnight.

To freeze: Yes, this freezes. Just defrost and use.

GRAHAM CRACKER–COCONUT–NUT CAKE
[serves 12 to 16]

¾ pound (3 cubes) butter	½ cup milk
2 cups sugar	7 ounces flaked coconut (2 cans)
8 eggs	1 cup finely chopped pecans
3 ⅓ cups graham cracker	or walnuts
crumbs	1 teaspoon vanilla

Cream butter and sugar until light and fluffy. Beat in the eggs one at a time. Add graham cracker crumbs and milk alternately. Stir in the coconut, pecans and vanilla. Pour into a greased and floured angel food pan. Bake at 300° for about 1 hour and 15 minutes. Remove from oven. Let cake remain in pan for about 5 minutes, then invert on a rack and remove from pan.

To prepare ahead of time: By all means this can be baked one or more days ahead of time. Keep wrapped in foil. If kept in the refrigerator the cake will keep several weeks.

To freeze: Yes, this freezes.

Note: This is a very heavy textured cake, but excellent.

TWO LOAVES OF A TRADITIONAL HONEY CAKE

6 eggs
1 cup sugar
1 cup honey
2 tablespoons oil or melted
    shortening
3½ cups sifted flour
1½ teaspoons baking powder
1 teaspoon baking soda
¼ teaspoon salt

¼ teaspoon cloves
½ teaspoon allspice
½ teaspoon cinnamon
½ cup raisins
½ cup chopped nuts
½ cup finely chopped candied
    orange peel
2 tablespoons Brandy

Beat eggs, beating in the sugar gradually. Beat until light and very creamy. Stir in the honey and melted shortening or oil. Sift dry ingredients together and fold them into the egg mixture. Fold in the fruit and nuts, then lastly stir in the Brandy. Pour into 2 bread tins which have been greased, lined with waxed paper, then greased again. Bake at 300° to 325° for about 1 hour. Invert to cool. Remove pans while still warm and peel off the paper.

To prepare ahead of time: This can be baked the day before; keep wrapped in foil.

To freeze: Yes, these freeze.

CHOCOLATE ALMOND CAKE
WITH BING CHERRIES   [serves 12 to 16]

½ cup butter (room
    temperature)
¾ cup sugar
8 egg yolks
pinch of salt
1 teaspoon vanilla
½ pound dark sweet
    chocolate, melted

1 cup blanched almonds,
    measured and then ground
8 egg whites
¼ teaspoon cream of tartar
¼ cup sugar
2 cups pitted, sweetened bing
    cherries (can use the canned
    ones), well drained

Cream the butter and the ¾ cup sugar together until fluffy, then beat in the egg yolks, salt and vanilla. Stir in the melted chocolate and the ground almonds. Beat egg whites with the cream of tartar until they form soft peaks. Gradually beat in the ¼ cup sugar. Fold these into the chocolate mixture and pour into a large pan (9″ by 14″) which has been greased and floured. Place the pitted bing cherries on top (don't worry if they sink), and bake at 350° for 40 to 60 minutes, or until a toothpick after being inserted comes out dry. Cool, then cut in squares and serve plain or with whipped cream.

To prepare ahead of time: This can be baked the day before and kept refrigerated overnight.

To freeze: Yes, this can be frozen.

PAT ALTMAN'S MOTHER'S MACAROON TORTE
[serves 6 to 8]

4 eggs, separated	strawberry jam (enough for
½ cup sugar	a ¼ inch layer)
½ cup soda crackers	¼ pound almond macaroons
crushed coarsely	(or can substitute ⅓ of an
(about 10 squares)	8-ounce can of almond paste,
¼ teaspoon baking powder	cut into tiny bits)
pinch of salt	1 cup whipping cream
½ cup (scant) chopped	
walnuts	

Beat egg yolks very thoroughly with sugar. Add salt and baking powder, then fold in the crackers and walnuts. Beat egg whites until stiff, then fold them carefully in to the mixture.

Pour into a 10″ spring form pan and bake about 1 hour at 325°. Test with a toothpick. Let torte cool in the pan placed upside down on a cake rack. (Don't worry if it sinks a little in the middle.) When cool remove from pan.

Cover the top thickly with the jam. Break macaroons into quarters or pieces and sprinkle over the jam layer. Shortly before serving cover with slightly sweetened whipped cream.

To prepare ahead of time: This can be baked a day ahead of time. It can be filled with the jam and the macaroons in the morning, then add the whipped cream not more than on hour or so before serving.

Note: Pat occasionally adds a lovely garnish of fresh strawberries too.

OLD SOULS APPLESAUCE-DATE-NUT CAKE
[makes 2 loaves]

2 cups chopped nuts
2 cups raisins
1 cup chopped dates
3 cups sifted flour
2 teaspoons baking soda
¼ teaspoon salt
2 teaspoons cinnamon

1 ½ teaspoons cloves
½ cup butter
¾ cup firmly packed brown
    sugar
2 eggs
2 cups applesauce (canned
    is fine)

Sift dry ingredients together. Mix chopped nuts, raisins and chopped dates with half of the dry ingredients. Cream butter and sugar until fluffy. Add eggs one at a time and beat thoroughly after each addition. Add dry ingredients alternately with the applesauce, then stir in the floured fruit-nut mixture. Pour this batter into two well greased loaf pans (3x5x9) and bake at 350° for about 40 to 60 minutes.

To prepare ahead of time: These can easily be baked 4 or 5 days ahead of time, wrapped in foil and kept refrigerated. This cake will keep a long time in the refrigerator.

To freeze: This freezes.

NOT-SOON-FORGOTTEN FILBERT TORTE
[makes 2 10-inch cakes about 3 inches high]

12 egg yolks
1 cup sugar
¼ teaspoon salt
½ cup fine dry bread crumbs
½ teaspoon baking powder
1 pound filberts, ground
    (use blender)

grated rind of 1 orange
½ cup orange juice
12 egg whites
1 cup sugar
raspberry jelly or seedless
    raspberry jam

Beat egg yolks with 1 cup sugar and salt until pale yellow and thick. Slowly beat in the orange juice and orange rind. Mix baking powder, bread crumbs and ground filberts together, then fold into the egg yolk mixture. Beat egg whites until stiff, then gradually beat in the other 1 cup of sugar. Fold into the egg yolk-nut mixture. Divide batter into two greased 10-inch spring form pans. Bake at 325° for 45 minutes, or longer, or until cakes test done. Invert the cakes carefully on cake racks and leave them this way until completely cold, then remove forms.

Before serving glaze the cakes with raspberry jelly or seedless raspberry jam. If desired serve with sweetened whipped cream.

To prepare ahead of time: This can be done the day before. Keep tightly covered or wrapped.

To freeze: Yes this freezes. Freeze without the jelly or jam.

Note: This can, of course, be divided in half if only one torte is desired, that is, just half of each of the amounts given for the ingredients above.

LOKI'S LINZER TORTE   [serves 8 to 12]

¾ cup sweet butter (generous)
1 cup almond paste (8 ounces)
¼ cup powdered sugar
½ teaspoon cinnamon
2 eggs
1 cup sifted flour

⅛ teaspoon salt
½ teaspoon baking powder
1 cup raspberry jam
½ cup currant jelly
chopped pistachio nuts
whipped cream (optional)

Use an electric mixer if possible for this cake. Cream butter, almond paste and powdered sugar together until very light and fluffy. Beat in the cinnamon, then add one egg at a time, beating very well after each addition. Sift dry ingredients together and stir them into the batter.

Grease a 9-inch spring form pan and then dust with flour. Reserve 1 cup of the batter, then pour the remaining batter into the prepared pan. Spread the top with the raspberry jam. Put the reserved 1 cup of batter into a pastry bag using a no. 2 star tube, and pipe it on the cake in a lattice pattern. Bake at 350° for 40 to 45 minutes. Remove from oven and cool on a cake rack. When cool remove from the spring form.

Melt currant jelly. Drip it on the torte, especially on the latticed strips. Sprinkle with the chopped pistachio nuts.

Serve cold or at room temperature. Whipped cream can be added on top of the torte as a garnish or it can be served on the side in a separate bowl.

To prepare ahead of time: This can be baked in the morning or the day before. After cooling, cover and refrigerate.

To freeze: Yes, this does freeze.

RAVING RASPBERRY RUMBLE [serves about 12]

1 cup egg whites (about 8)
¾ cup sugar
1 teaspoon vanilla
1 cup sugar
2 tablespoons cake flour

3 cups macaroon coconut
(finely chopped, can be
purchased in all health
food stores)
3 boxes raspberries
3 cups whipping cream
sugar to taste

Beat egg whites until just stiff, then gradually add the ¾ cup sugar and the vanilla; continue beating until the mixture forms soft peaks. Meanwhile mix together the 1 cup of sugar, coconut, and cake flour. Fold this into the egg white mixture. Pour into three 9-inch layer cake pans which have been greased, lined with waxed paper, and greased heavily again. Bake for about 20 minutes at 350° or until lightly browned and firm to the touch. Cool on cake racks and remove paper.

Whip and sweeten cream. Sweeten raspberries. Combine the two. Place ⅓ of this mixture on each cake layer and then stack them. Decorate the top with a few additional raspberries. Chill until ready to serve.

To prepare ahead of time: The cakes can be baked the day before or in the morning. It is best to assemble the layers with the raspberry-cream no more than several hours before serving.

To freeze: The cakes freeze very well. Defrost, then fill as directed in the above recipe.

WALNUT-MERINGUE TORTE WITH A
STRAWBERRY-PINEAPPLE FILLING   [serves 10 to 12]

| 8 egg whites | 2 ½ cups ground walnuts |
| 1 cup sugar | |

For the filling:

2 cups whipping cream	½ cup diced canned pineapple
¼ cup sugar	1 teaspoon unflavored gelatin
1 teaspoon vanilla	2 tablespoons cold water
2 boxes strawberries, sweetened to taste	

Beat egg whites until just barely stiff, then gradually beat in sugar until stiff and glossy. Fold in the ground walnuts and pour into three 9-inch layer cake pans which have been greased, lined with waxed paper and greased again—then sprinkle with flour and toss out the excess. (If you have layer cake pans with removable bottoms, then use them.) Bake at 400° for about 15 to 20 minutes. Remove from oven, cool briefly, then remove from pans.

Make the filling: Dissolve gelatin in the 2 tablespoons of cold water, then place dish over a pan of simmering water and stir until gelatin has melted. Whip cream and flavor with the sugar and vanilla. Pour in the melted gelatin and whip again for a few seconds.

To assemble: Place first cake layer on a plate. Cover with ⅓ of the cream, then with half of the strawberries. Place a second layer of the cake on top of this, then next third of cream. Place pineapple on this. Finally add the third and last cake layer, then the last ⅓ of the cream, and then top with remaining berries. Chill until ready to serve.

To prepare ahead of time: The cakes can be baked the day before. It is best to assemble them the day this dessert is going to be served. It can be completed in the morning.

To freeze: The cakes can be frozen. The whole assembled dessert can also be frozen, however, the texture will be changed during the defrosting process, therefore, I do not advise doing so.

VERY PRETTY INDIVIDUAL CONFETTI FRUIT CAKES

3 cups Brazil nuts
1 cup pecans or walnuts
3 cups pitted dates
1 cup drained maraschino
    cherries, red and green
¾ cup sifted flour

½ teaspoon baking powder
½ teaspoon salt
3 eggs
¾ cup sugar
1 teaspoon vanilla

Place whole nuts, dates and cherries in a large bowl. Sift flour, baking powder and salt together, then sprinkle over the fruit and nuts and stir until thoroughly mixed and well coated. Beat eggs with the sugar until light and fluffy, that is, until a light lemon color. Add vanilla. Pour egg mixture over the fruit and stir again until well mixed.

Spoon batter into individual small muffin tins which have first been lined with waxed paper muffin tin liners. Bake at 350° for about 45 minutes or longer, depending upon the size of the individual muffin holders. Cool on racks and store in the refrigerator.

To prepare ahead of time: These can be baked several weeks ahead of time. Keep in the refrigerator, well wrapped.

To freeze: Yes, these do freeze. Just defrost, bring to room temperature and serve.

MABEL WEINER'S THIN BUTTER COOKIES

1 cup butter
1 ⅛ cups sugar
4 tablespoons cream (or milk)

2 ¼ cups flour (about 11 ounces)
1 teaspoon vanilla

Cream butter and sugar. Add cream (or milk), then stir in remaining ingredients. Combine and make into 2 rolls or 1 large one. Chill, then slice thinly and bake at 350°. (They can be sprinkled lightly with sugar before baked.)

To prepare ahead of time: These can be baked several days ahead of time and kept packed in airtight tins.

To freeze: These can be frozen. They can be frozen already baked, or they can be frozen after forming them into rolls.

POPPY SEED COOKIES

½ cup butter
¾ cup sugar
2 eggs
1 or 2 teaspoons lemon juice
½ teaspoon vanilla

2 ½ cups sifted flour
(10 ounces)
1 ½ teaspoons baking powder
1 teaspoon salt
½ cup poppy seeds

Cream butter and sugar. Add eggs, lemon juice and vanilla and beat until light. Sift flour, baking powder and salt together, then add to the egg mixture. Add poppy seeds. Chill several hours or overnight. Roll out, cut in shapes and bake at 350° for 12 to 15 minutes.

To prepare ahead of time: These can be baked a week or more ahead of time if they are kept packed between layers of waxed paper in air tight tins.

To freeze: Yes, of course these freeze.

BROWN SUGAR-RAISIN FORK COOKIES

1 cup butter
2 cups brown sugar
2 eggs
⅛ teaspoon salt
1 cup raisins

1 teaspoon vanilla
3 ½ cups flour
¼ teaspoon cream of tartar
½ teaspoon baking soda

Cream butter and sugar, add eggs and beat again until light and fluffy. Sift the flour, salt, cream of tartar and baking soda together and add to the batter with the raisins. Add vanilla. Stir only until all ingredients are well combined. Drop by teaspoonfuls on greased cookie sheets and flatten each with a floured fork. Bake at 400° until browned.

To prepare ahead of time: These can be baked several days ahead of time. Keep packed in airtight tins between layers of waxed paper.

To freeze: Yes, these freeze.

VANILLA SPRITZ COOKIES

1 cup butter	½ teaspoon salt
¾ cup sugar	1 egg
2 ¼ cups sifted flour	1 teaspoon vanilla
¼ teaspoon baking powder	

Cream butter and sugar. Beat in egg and vanilla, then stir in the flour, baking powder and salt. Put in a press and drop the cookies on lightly greased pans. Bake at 350° for about 10 to 12 minutes.

To prepare ahead of time: Yes, these can be baked several days ahead of time if they are kept in airtight containers, packed between layers of waxed paper.

To freeze: Yes, these freeze.

MEXICAN CINNAMON COOKIES

1 cup butter (room temperature)	¼ teaspoon salt
	1 teaspoon vanilla
½ cup powdered sugar (packed)	2 cups powdered sugar sifted with 1 teaspoon cinnamon
2 ½ cups sifted flour	to be used for rolling
½ teaspoon cinnamon	the cookies

Cream butter and sugar thoroughly, sift flour, cinnamon and salt together, then add to the first mixture. Stir until combined but do not beat hard. Add vanilla. Chill for an hour or so. Roll this batter into small balls about ¾ to 1 inch in diameter. Bake on a lightly greased pan at 400° for about 15 to 17 minutes. As soon as cookies have been removed from oven, roll them in the sugar-cinnamon mixture, then cool on a wire rack. Roll them once more in this mixture before storing them.

To prepare ahead of time: These can be baked at least a week ahead of time. Keep them in airtight containers in the refrigerator.

To freeze: Yes, these freeze. They can be served directly from the freezer.

CRISP AND EASY OATMEAL COOKIES

1 cup butter or shortening
1 cup brown sugar,
   firmly packed
1 cup white sugar
2 eggs
1½ teaspoons vanilla

1½ cups sifted flour
1 teaspoon salt
½ teaspoon baking soda
½ teaspoon baking powder
3 cups quick-cooking oats
½ cup nuts, chopped

Cream butter (or shortening) and sugar together until fluffy. Beat in eggs and vanilla. Sift flour, salt, baking soda and baking powder together and stir into the creamed mixture until blended. Do not overmix. Blend in the oats and nuts. Drop by spoonfuls on greased baking sheets. Bake at 350° or 375° for about 10 minutes.

To prepare ahead of time: These can be baked several days ahead of time. Keep them in airtight containers.

To freeze: Yes, these freeze.

SOFT MOLASSES DROPS WITH A GLAZE ICING

¾ cup butter or shortening
1 cup sugar
1 egg
1 cup dark molasses
2½ cups sifted flour
2 teaspoons baking soda

½ teaspoon salt
½ teaspoon cinnamon
¼ teaspoon cloves
½ teaspoon ginger
⅓ cup hot coffee

Cream shortening and sugar together until light and fluffy. Beat in the egg and molasses. Sift dry ingredients together, and then stir them in alternately with the coffee. Drop by teaspoonfuls on greased baking sheets. Bake at 350° for 10 to 15 minutes. Frost with the icing while they are still warm.

Glaze Icing:

1 cup powdered sugar, sifted
   or put through a sieve
1 teaspoon vanilla

pinch of salt
1 tablespoon of milk
   (or more if needed)

Combine the ingredients adding more sugar or milk until desired consistency is obtained.

To prepare ahead of time: These can be baked a day or two ahead of time. Keep them packed between layers of waxed paper in airtight containers.

To freeze: Yes, these can be frozen.

FLORENTINES

3 ounces candied orange peel, very finely chopped (about ¾ cup of the chopped peel)
3 tablespoons butter
½ cup whipping cream
½ cup sugar

¼ cup flour plus 1 tablespoon
⅛ teaspoon salt
1 cup almonds, ground (about 5 ounces)
8 ounces semi-sweet chocolate
1 teaspoon butter

Combine the butter, cream and sugar in a saucepan and stir over low heat until it comes to a boil. Cook gently for 1 minute, then remove from the heat. Stir in the ground almonds, flour, orange peel and salt.

Do a test: Drop a teaspoonful on a greased pan and bake at 375° for 10 to 15 minutes. The cookie should spread and flatten out. If the batter is too thick, add a little more cream. When of desired consistency, proceed with the baking of the cookies. Remove cookies from the pan immediately using a spatula. If they stick, reheat for a minute, then finish removing them. Cool.

Melt chocolate with the 1 teaspoon of butter over a pan of hot water. Cool slightly. After cookies are cold, ice the undersides of the cookies with the chocolate.

To prepare ahead of time: These can be baked and frosted several days ahead of time. Keep them in an airtight container between layers of waxed paper.

To freeze: Yes, these freeze. I prefer to freeze them without the chocolate, later frosting them as needed. However, they will keep quite well frosted for several weeks or a month in the freezer.

REASONABLE COOKIES

1 ½ cups butter (can use part
    margarine or shortening)
1 cup sugar
1 cup brown sugar
    (firmly packed)
2 eggs
1 teaspoon vanilla

2 cups flour
½ teaspoon baking soda
½ teaspoon baking powder
1 cup quick-cooking oats
3 cups cornflakes
1 cup coconut
½ to ¾ cup chopped walnuts

Cream butter and sugar together. Beat in eggs and vanilla. Sift dry ingredients together and add. Stir in remaining ingredients. Drop by spoonfuls on greased pans and bake at 350° for 10 to 15 minutes.

To prepare ahead of time: These can be baked ahead of time; keep in airtight containers.

To freeze: Yes, these freeze.

CRISP DARK CHOCOLATE COOKIES

12 ounces semi-sweet
    chocolate, melted and
    cooled
½ cup butter
1 cup sugar
2 teaspoons vanilla

2 eggs
2 cups sifted flour
1 teaspoon salt
2 teaspoons baking powder
1 cup quick-cooking oats

Cream butter and sugar. Beat in the vanilla and eggs. Sift flour, salt and baking powder together, then mix with the quick-cooking oats. Add melted chocolate to the butter-egg mixture, then stir in all of the dry ingredients. Form into two long rolls. Chill. Slice ⅛ inch thick and bake on ungreased pans for about 10 minutes at 375°. Watch so they do not burn.

To prepare ahead of time: These can be baked ahead of time. Keep them packed in airtight containers.

To freeze: These can be frozen before they are baked (in the rolls), or they can be frozen after they have been baked.

PERSIMMON-SPICE-RAISIN-NUT COOKIES

½ cup butter
1 cup sugar
1 egg
1 cup persimmon pulp
   (about 2 persimmons)
2 cups sifted flour
½ teaspoon salt
1 teaspoon baking soda

½ teaspoon baking powder
½ teaspoon cinnamon
½ teaspoon nutmeg
½ teaspoon ginger
¼ teaspoon cloves
1 cup chopped pecans
1 cup raisins

Cream butter and sugar. Beat in the egg, then add the persimmon pulp which you have mashed. Sift dry ingredients together and stir into the egg mixture. Stir in the chopped pecans and raisins. Drop cookies by spoonfuls on greased cookie sheets and bake at 375° for 12 minutes or so.

To prepare ahead of time: These can be baked several days ahead of time. Keep in airtight containers packed between layers of waxed paper.

To freeze: Yes, these do freeze.

SESAME SEED RING COOKIES

1 cup butter (½ pound)
½ cup sugar
½ cup milk
1 teaspoon baking powder
¼ teaspoon salt

½ teaspoon cinnamon
4 cups sifted flour
1 egg beaten with
   1 tablespoon water
sesame seeds

Cream butter and sugar. Sift flour, baking powder, salt and cinnamon together and add alternately with the milk. Chill the dough for several hours or overnight.

Shape dough with floured hands into small rings. Dip the top of each ring into the egg mixture, then into sesame seeds. Place rings on greased cookie sheets and bake at 350° for about 15 to 20 minutes, or until golden brown.

To prepare ahead of time: These can be baked several days ahead of time. Keep in airtight containers.

To freeze: Yes, these freeze.

GLORY OF FRANCE COOKIES FILLED WITH
CHOCOLATE ICING OR WITH RASPBERRY JAM

¾ cup blanched almonds,
   toasted, then ground
½ cup filberts, toasted and
   skinned, then ground
¼ cup sugar

4 egg whites
⅛ teaspoon cream of tartar
⅛ teaspoon salt
½ cup sugar
raspberry jam

For chocolate icing:

6 ounces dark sweet
   chocolate

½ cup heavy cream (must use
   whipping cream)
1 teaspoon vanilla

Mix ground almonds and filberts with the ¼ cup sugar and set aside. Beat egg whites, cream of tartar and salt until just stiff, then gradually beat in the ½ cup of sugar. Fold these beaten egg whites into the ground nut mixture.

Using a pastry bag with a No. 6 round tube, press out cookies on to a greased and floured baking pan (or on to silicone non-stick baking paper)—making them about 1 inch in diameter. If you are not able to use a pastry bag, then drop by spoonfuls instead. Bake at 300° for about 10 to 15 minutes or until crusty on top but still soft. Cool a few minutes, then remove from pans with a sharp knife or spatula.

For the chocolate icing: Melt chocolate over very low heat, heat whipping cream to boiling point, then whip the two together and flavor with vanilla. This is best made ahead of time so that it has a chance to cool and thicken.

To assemble: Place 2 cookies together either with the chocolate icing, or with the raspberry jam.

To prepare ahead of time: These can be baked several days ahead of time and kept packed in airtight tins. I like to fill them the day I plan to serve them.

To freeze: Freeze these unfilled for the best possible taste. However, they are still excellent when filled and frozen.

COCONUT MACAROON CUP CAKES

1 cup egg whites (about
   8 egg whites)
¾ cup sugar
1 teaspoon vanilla
1 cup sugar

3 cups macaroon coconut
   (finely chopped coconut
   available in health food
   stores)
2 tablespoons cake flour

Beat egg whites until just stiff, then add gradually the ¾ cup sugar and the vanilla and continue beating until the mixture forms soft peaks. Meanwhile mix together the 1 cup sugar, coconut and cake flour. Fold this into the egg white mixture.

Place paper baking cups in muffin tins and fill ⅔ to ¾ full. Bake at 350° for about 20 minutes or until golden brown on top.

To prepare ahead of time: These can be baked the day before. Keep tightly covered, preferably in airtight containers in the refrigerator. (These can even be baked several days ahead of time.)

To freeze: These freeze beautifully.

Note: Make these in the tiny muffin cups if you have them. They will then be available (if frozen) on a moment's notice.

CHEESECAKE COOKIES

⅓ cup melted butter
⅓ cup brown sugar, packed
1 cup flour
½ cup walnuts, chopped
1 8-ounce package cream
   cheese

¼ cup sugar
1 egg
1 tablespoon lemon juice
2 tablespoons cream or milk
1 teaspoon vanilla

Mix brown sugar, chopped nuts and flour together in a large bowl. Stir in the melted butter and mix until light and crumbly with one's hands. Remove 1 cup of the mixture to be used later as a topping. Place remainder in an 8-inch square pan and press firmly. Bake at 350° for about 12 or 15 minutes.

Beat cream cheese until smooth with the ¼ cup of sugar. Beat in the egg, lemon juice, milk and vanilla. Pour this on to the baked crust.

Top with the reserved crumbs. Return to a 350° oven and bake for about 25 minutes. Cool thoroughly, then cut into squares.

To prepare ahead of time: These can be baked the day before. Cover with plastic wrap and keep refrigerated.

To freeze: Yes, these can be frozen.

ITALIAN STYLE SLICED AND TOASTED COOKIES

¼ cup butter	½ teaspoon salt
2 cups sugar	3 teaspoons baking powder
1 ¼ teaspoons anise extract	1 cup finely chopped
6 eggs	candied cherries
6 cups sifted flour	1 cup piñon nuts
(about 24 ounces)	

Cream butter and sugar, then beat in the anise extract and the eggs. Combine the flour, salt and baking powder and then add gradually to the mixture. Chill the dough at least 30 minutes, or longer if time permits.

Divide dough into 4 parts. Roll each into a rectangle about 8 by 12 inches and spread each with ¼ cup of the cherries and ¼ cup of the piñons. (All piñons can be used in place of the cherries.) Roll up each rectangle tightly, starting from the long side and place on greased cookie sheets. (I put two rolls on each cookie sheet.) Bake at 350° for about 20 to 30 minutes, or until lightly browned.

Remove from oven and cool for a few minutes, then slice diagonally into ½ inch slices. Place slices cut side down, close together on the cookie sheets and return to a 375° oven until lightly toasted, about 10 minutes.

To prepare ahead of time: These can be baked a week or more ahead of time. They can be kept at room temperature if packed in an airtight container.

To freeze: Yes, these freeze.

ORANGE MARMALADE BARS WITH
ORANGE MARMALADE FROSTING

First layer:

1 cup butter	1 teaspoon baking powder
1 cup sugar	⅛ teaspoon salt
1 egg yolk	2 cups sifted flour
1 teaspoon vanilla	

Cream butter and sugar together until fluffy. Add egg yolk and vanilla. Sift dry ingredients together and add them to the butter mixture. Spread this batter in a pan about 9" by 14" and bake at 350° for 20 minutes. Remove from oven and cover with the second layer mixture:

Second layer:

1 egg white (left from above egg yolk)	1 teaspoon baking powder
	2 cups coconut
3 eggs	1 cup walnuts, finely chopped
½ cup sugar	1 cup orange marmalade
¼ cup flour	

Beat eggs until light, then gradually beat in the sugar, flour, and baking powder. Stir in the remaining ingredients and after spreading on the baked first layer, bake again in a 325° oven for about 30 to 35 minutes. Remove and cool on a cake rack, then spread with the orange marmalade frosting:

Orange marmalade frosting:

2 tablespoons softened butter	¼ cup orange marmalade
2 cups powdered sugar	1 teaspoon orange extract

Beat the ingredients together until of spreading consistency. Spread on the cooled cookies. Cut into diamond shaped bars.

To prepare ahead of time: These can be baked a day or so ahead of time. Keep refrigerated in an airtight container.

To freeze: Yes, these can be frozen.

BUTTERSCOTCH DATE BARS

½ cup butter
2 cups brown sugar (packed)
2 eggs
2 teaspoons vanilla
1 cup sifted flour

2 teaspoons baking powder
½ teaspoon salt
2 cups chopped dates (or 1 ½
   cups chopped dates plus
   1 cup chopped walnuts)

Melt butter in a sauce pan, then stir in the brown sugar over low heat, until somewhat dissolved, about a minute or two. Remove from heat. Beat in the eggs, one at a time. Add the vanilla. Sift dry ingredients together and mix them into the above mixture. Stir in the dates (and nuts if preferred). Spoon this batter into an oblong pan (about 9″ by 14″) which has been greased and floured. Bake at 350° for about 30 minutes. Cool and then cut into bars.

To prepare ahead of time: These can be baked a day or so ahead of time. Keep packed in an airtight container between layers of waxed paper.

To freeze: Yes, these freeze.

FOREVER LASTING LECKERLI

½ cup honey
1 cup sugar
¾ cup finely chopped
   orange peel
grated rind of one lemon
1 cup blanched, sliced almonds
¼ cup water

2 ¼ cups sifted flour (9 ounces)
1 teaspoon nutmeg
1 teaspoon cinnamon
½ teaspoon cloves
¼ teaspoon salt
1 teaspoon baking soda
1 teaspoon vanilla

For the glaze:

½ cup sifted powdered sugar   2 to 4 tablespoons warm water

Heat honey, stir in the 1 cup sugar, then add the orange peel, lemon rind, almonds and water. Add vanilla. Combine the flour, nutmeg, cinnamon, cloves, salt and baking soda, and mix thoroughly. Add the orange mixture and stir until blended. Place dough in a bowl and cover with a plate or with plastic wrap and leave at room temperature for 1 or 2 days.

Divide dough in half and roll out each portion ¼ inch thick. Cut into bars and place on greased cookie sheets. Bake at 325° for about 20 to 25 minutes or until lightly browned.

Remove cookies from oven and brush on the glaze which is made by combining the sugar and water until a thin consistency is obtained. When cookies are completely cooled, pack in tins.

To prepare ahead of time: These can be made weeks ahead of time. Keep them packed between layers of waxed paper in airtight tins.

To freeze: Yes, these can be frozen.

JOANNE WEINER'S REMARKABLE PASTRIES

Pastry:

2 cups flour (½ pound)   ½ pint sour cream
½ pound butter

Cut butter into the flour, then mix in the sour cream. Divide into 5 portions and chill them overnight.

For the filling:

marmalade, jelly or jam   dark and light raisins
cinnamon   coconut
chopped nuts   sugar

To assemble: Roll out each pastry portion into a rectangle about 6 by 8 inches wide and about 12 inches or more long. Spread with the marmalade, jelly or jam, then sprinkle with cinnamon, sugar, chopped nuts, raisins, and with coconut if desired. Roll up along the long side and seal to close (use water or egg to make the pastry stick). Score at the top of the rolls at about ¾ inch intervals. Bake at 350° for 30 minutes or more, or until pastry is golden brown. Remove the rolls from the oven and slice them immediately, using the score lines as guides.

To prepare ahead of time: These can be baked ahead of time and kept refrigerated for a day or two. Best if they are kept tightly covered in an airtight container.

To freeze: Yes, these freeze. Freeze them after they have been baked.

MY VERSION OF BAKLAVA

1½ to 2 pounds Fillo pastry sheets (purchased usually in a Greek market or delicatessen)

3 cups blanched almonds, roasted, then ground in a blender

2 cups walnuts, chopped

1 pound (or more) of melted butter

2 cups honey

1 cup sugar

1 cup water

1 tablespoon grated orange rind

1 teaspoon cinnamon

Mix the nuts together and set aside. Combine the honey, sugar, water, orange rind and cinnamon and stir over low heat until it comes to a boil, reduce heat and simmer for about 10 minutes. Set aside.

Grease a 9″ by 14″ by 2″ baking pan. Place about 8 of the pastry sheets in it, brushing each one generously with butter. Sprinkle with ¼ of the nuts. Sprinkle them with some of the melted butter and with a couple of spoonfuls of the syrup. Cover this with 4 pastry sheets, brushing each with butter, then with another ¼ of the nuts, then with the sprinkling of melted butter and syrup. Repeat this procedure another two times. After covering the last layer of nuts with the butter and syrup, top with about 8 layers of pastry, brushing each with butter. Press down firmly, trim if necessary and cover top generously with butter. Score the pastry into pieces about 1½″ by 3″ (either in diamond shapes or in rectangles). Bake in a preheated 325° oven for about 35 minutes. Reduce temperature to 300° and bake another 45 minutes to an hour. (Don't burn it. If necessary reduce the oven temperature a little more, but make sure it is very well baked through. It may take a little longer than mentioned.)

Remove from oven and place on a rack to cool for about 20 minutes. Cut scored pieces all of the way through. Heat syrup until it is warm, then pour over the baklava. Let it stand at room temperature for several hours before serving. It is really best to make this the day before serving.

To prepare ahead of time: This can be prepared as much as several days ahead of time. Keep covered in the refrigerator.

To freeze: Yes, this can be frozen.

Note: The number of pastry sheets depends upon size of pan and size of sheets. Be sure to use the trimmings too if necessary after cutting them to fit the pan.

LOUISE YORK'S FRENCH APPLE PIE [serves about 6]

Rich pastry: (Use this recipe or any of your preference.)

Note: This makes enough for 2 9-inch or 10-inch shells, or enough for one pie with a top and bottom crust. (Save other half of pastry in the freezer.)

2 cups flour	1 egg
¾ cup shortening	2 tablespoons lemon juice
(can use part butter)	2 tablespoons ice water
½ teaspoon salt	

Mix flour and salt together, then cut in the shortening. Combine the egg, lemon juice and ice water and beat slightly. Pour over the flour-shortening and cut in with a knife until all of the dry ingredients are absorbed. Turn out and knead gently only 2 or 3 times. Chill at least 30 minutes, but overnight is best. (Pastry dough can be cut in half and chilled in two portions, ready to roll out.)

For the pie:

1 9-inch or 10-inch unbaked	½ cup sugar
pie shell	¾ teaspoon cinnamon
4 cups peeled and thinly	⅛ teaspoon salt
sliced apples	

For the topping:

¾ cup brown sugar	whipped cream or vanilla
¾ cup flour	ice cream (to gild the lily)
⅓ cup softened butter	

Mix the apples with the ½ cup sugar, cinnamon and salt and place them in the pie shell. Mix the topping ingredients together with a pastry blender or with the hands until crumbly, then place on top of the apples. Bake at 400° for about 35 minutes, or until the apples are done. Serve warm with whipped cream or ice cream.

To prepare ahead of time: This can be baked the day before or in the morning, and served cold, or reheated.

To freeze: Yes, this freezes.

RICH COCONUT PIE [serves about 6]

Rich pastry for a bottom crust only, 9-inch size (use half the recipe on p. 216)

4 cups fresh grated coconut (or use canned and reduce amount of sugar by ½ cup)	1 ½ cups sugar
	½ cup butter
	3 eggs
¼ cup water	1 teaspoon vanilla

Roll pastry out and fit into a 9-inch pie pan. Cook the grated coconut, water and sugar together slowly for about 20 minutes, stirring occasionally so that the mixture doesn't burn. Stir in the butter and cook an additional 5 minutes. Remove from heat and cool briefly.

Beat eggs with vanilla and then combine with the coconut mixture. Pour all into the pastry and bake at 450° for 10 minutes. Reduce temperature to 375° and bake an additional 15 minutes. Serve warm or at room temperature.

To prepare ahead of time: This can be baked the day before or in the morning. (Refrigerate overnight.) Reheat, if desired, before serving.

To freeze: Yes, this freezes. Reheat before serving.

FRESH PEACH PIE [serves about 6]

Rich pie pastry for a 10-inch pie, top and bottom crust (see recipe on p. 216)

8 cups sliced fresh peaches	6 tablespoons flour
1 tablespoon lemon juice	½ teaspoon cinnamon
1 ¼ cups sugar	pinch of salt

Roll out half of the pastry and fit into a 10-inch pie pan. Combine the sugar, flour, cinnamon and salt and blend thoroughly. Combine peaches and lemon juice. Mix the two mixtures together and then spoon into the pastry lined pan. Cover with a top pastry and slash the top with some kind of an attractive design. Seal the edges. Bake at 400° for 45 to 50 minutes.

To prepare ahead of time: This can be baked the day before or in the morning. If baking it the day before, refrigerate overnight and plan to serve the pie either cold, or hot (having reheated it).

To freeze: Freeze after baking. Defrost, then reheat before serving.

BANANA CREAM TARTLETS [makes 12 to 16]

12 to 16 baked tartlet shells (see recipe for rich pastry on p. 216)

¾ cup sugar	5 egg yolks
3 tablespoons cornstarch	1 teaspoon vanilla
3 tablespoons flour	1 cup whipping cream, whipped
¼ teaspoon salt	and sweetened slightly
2½ cups milk	sliced bananas
¼ cup butter	a little lemon juice

Mix sugar, cornstarch, flour and salt in the top part of a double boiler, then stir in the milk. Add the butter. Cook and stir until very thick. Beat egg yolks in a separate bowl and gradually add hot mixture stirring all the time. Return to double boiler and cook until very thick, stirring constantly. Remove from heat and cool over ice, stirring to prevent a skin from forming. Stir in the vanilla. Chill.

Place a layer of sliced bananas in the bottom of each of the baked shells, then some of the cream filling. Place sliced bananas on top of the filling (having dipped these first in some lemon juice to prevent discoloration). Decorate the edges of the top of each tartlet with the whipped cream. Chill until ready to serve.

To prepare ahead of time: The shells can be baked the day before and the cream filling can be prepared the day before and kept refrigerated overnight. Do not fill the shells until the day you are planning to serve these.

To freeze: The pastry tartlet shells can be baked and frozen.

PECAN PIE [serves about 6]

1 9-inch unbaked pie shell (use half the recipe for pastry on p. 216)

3 eggs
1 cup brown sugar (packed)
¾ cup dark corn syrup
¼ teaspoon salt
1 teaspoon vanilla

4 tablespoons melted butter
1 cup pecan halves (toasted in a 300° oven for 5 or 10 minutes)

Beat eggs. Add sugar, syrup, salt, vanilla and butter and beat again.

Scatter the pecans in the pie shell. Pour egg mixture over the pecans. Bake at 400° for 10 minutes. Reduce to 325° and bake for another 40 to 45 minutes.

To prepare ahead of time: This can be baked the day before. Refrigerate overnight. Reheat before serving.

To freeze: This freezes. Defrost, reheat and then serve, either warm or at room temperature.

AS EASY AS APPLE PIE [serves 6 to 8]

1 recipe of rich pie crust for a 10-inch pie, top and bottom needed (see recipe on p. 216)

6 large green apples (need 6 plus cups sliced apples)
1 ¼ cups sugar (or a little more)
3 tablespoons flour
½ teaspoon salt

¼ teaspoon nutmeg
1 teaspoon cinnamon
3 tablespoons butter
1 or 2 teaspoons lemon juice if apples are not tart

Core, peel and thinly slice the apples. In a separate bowl mix the sugar, flour, salt, nutmeg, and cinnamon together.

Roll out half of the pastry and line a 10-inch pan. Place half of the flour-sugar mixture on top of this pastry. Next fill with the sliced apples, then cover with the remaining flour-sugar mixture. Sprinkle with the lemon juice if needed, and dot with the butter. Roll out other half of pastry and cover the apples. Press the two crusts together firmly, using cold water to seal them well. Prick top crust (or cut a design) and then bake at 425° for 50 to 60 minutes—until the juices begin to bubble and the pie is brown. (If pie pastry browns too rapidly, reduce oven temperature somewhat.)

To prepare ahead of time: This can be baked the day before. Keep refrigerated. Serve cold, or reheat and serve hot.

To freeze: This freezes. Defrost, then reheat before serving.

DAVID'S BLUEBERRY PIE [serves about 6]

Rich pie pastry for the top and bottom crust of a 9-inch pie (see recipe on p. 216)

2 cups canned bluberries (juice and all)—try to get the little ones—called wild blueberries	¾ cup sugar 2 ½ tablespoons cornstarch 1 tablespoon lemon juice 2 tablespoons butter

Roll out half of the pastry and line the pie pan. Mix the sugar and cornstarch together. Add the blueberries and juice and stir until dissolved. Add lemon juice. Cook this mixture over moderate heat, stirring, until it boils. Remove from heat and cool. Pour into pastry lined pan, dot with butter, and cover with the rolled out other half of the pastry. Seal edges and cut a design in the top pastry. Bake at 425° for about 35 to 40 minutes.

To prepare ahead of time: This can be baked the day before and served cold the following day, but I prefer it baked and served the same day.

To freeze: This can be frozen. Reheat after defrosting before serving.

BILLY BOY CHERRY PIE [serves 6 to 8]

rich pastry for a top and bottom crust for a 10-inch pie
(see recipe on p. 216)

2 cans red tart cherries, drain
and reserve the juice (this is
about 3 to 3½ cups of
drained cherries)
5 tablespoons cornstarch

1 tablespoon lemon juice
1½ cups sugar (or more if
desired)
2 tablespoons butter

Mix sugar and cornstarch together in a saucepan, then stir in the
reserved cherry juice. Add lemon juice and cook, stirring constantly, until it comes to a boil. Remove from heat and stir in the
cherries. Set aside to cool slightly. Roll out bottom crust and line the
pan. Pour in the cherry mixture and dot with butter. Cover the top
crust and seal the edges. Cut a design in the top crust. Bake at 400°
to 425° for 45 minutes or longer, or until pastry is well browned and
you can see the filling bubbling.

To prepare ahead of time: This can be baked the day before. Refrigerate overnight, then reheat before serving.

To freeze: This freezes. Defrost, then reheat before serving.

Desserts

Desserts

BAROQUE BANANA SHORTCAKE WITH RUM-EGGNOG SAUCE [serves about 16]

1 layer of genoise cake
  (11" by 17" by 1")—
  (recipe follows)
Rum-eggnog sauce—
  recipe follows)
8 to 10 bananas

1½ quarts whipping cream
  (6 cups)
1 tablespoon gelatin
¼ cup cold water
2 or 3 teaspoons vanilla
½ cup sugar

Genoise cake:

4 eggs
1 cup sugar
1 cup sifted cake flour
1 teaspoon baking powder

¼ teaspoon salt
3 tablespoons butter
  (melted and cooled)

Sift flour, baking powder and salt together three times, then leave in the sifter. Beat the eggs with an electric mixer until light and thick, then gradually beat in the sugar, continuing to beat until mixture is a light lemon color and is quite thick. This takes 10 minutes or more of beating. Sift flour mixture onto this gradually, folding it in with as few strokes as possible. Pour and cut in the melted butter, using just a few strokes. Pour into an oblong pan (11" by 17" by 1") which has been greased, lined with waxed paper, then greased again. Bake in a 350° oven for about 15 to 20 minutes. Remove from oven and cool for only a few minutes, then turn upside down, remove paper carefully, and turn right side up to finish cooling.

Rum-eggnog sauce:

3 egg yolks
1 cup powdered sugar
  (packed)
¼ cup of light rum
  (or a little more)

1 cup whipping cream, whipped
a drop of yellow food coloring
  (optional)

225

Beat egg yolks with the powdered sugar until very thick, then beat in the rum. Fold in the whipped cream and then add the yellow coloring, if wanted. Place in a serving bowl and refrigerate until time to serve.

To assemble: Whip the cream until stiff, then beat in the vanilla and sugar. Soak the gelatin in the ¼ cup cold water for about 5 minutes, then dissolve it over simmering water. Add melted gelatin all at once to the whipped cream and beat at the same time.

Note: This amount of gelatin is necessary to give the whipped cream a little stability for this dessert.

Cut the genoise cake into three equal lengthwise sections. Place one of these on a very long board or platter and cover it with sliced bananas and some of the whipped cream. Place a second layer of cake on top of this. Again cover with sliced bananas and some of the whipped cream. Place third layer of cake on top of this. Cover thinly with sliced bananas, then coat the top and the sides with the remaining whipped cream mixture, putting some of it on fancily with the aid of a pastry tube—if possible. Chill for a few hours.

Serve in slices giving each portion a spoonful of the Rum-eggnog sauce.

To prepare ahead of time: The cake can be baked the day before. Keep it tightly covered with foil or plastic wrap. The entire dessert can be assembled in the morning and kept refrigerated until time to serve.

To freeze: The cake can be frozen. Defrost it, then proceed as in the above recipe. While I do not recommend freezing the assembled dessert as a "party procedure," by all means do put any leftovers in the freezer for family use later.

CHAFING DISH PEACHES TO MYSTIFY GUESTS

[serves 12]

12 servings of vanilla ice cream (have ready in large individual bowls in the freezer)

Assembled on tray or trays:

12 peach halves (fresh or canned)	⅔ cup heavy cream
1 cup butter, sliced	2 to 3 teaspoons ground nutmeg (use a generous amount)
2⅔ cups brown sugar (packed for measurement)	½ cup Cognac or Brandy

Melt butter in the blazer of a large chafing dish. Let it sizzle. Add peach halves and heat gently for several minutes. Spoon on the brown sugar and continue to cook, stirring occasionally. Sprinkle the nutmeg on and pour in the cream. Stir and cook. The syrup must ultimately simmer and thicken some. After the sauce begins to simmer, baste peaches with it for about 5 minutes or so. Warm the Cognac, then add it to the peaches and ignite it. Continue to spoon sauce over the peaches.

Serve half a peach on each portion of ice cream, and plenty of the sauce. The ice cream should be very cold, and the sauce should be bubbling hot.

To prepare ahead of time: All of the ingredients can be assembled in bowls on trays in the morning.

To freeze: Ice cream can (and should) be ready in dishes in the freezer.

Note: Allow plenty of time to prepare this dessert leisurely in front of your guests—it cannot be hurried. For some households this is too many to prepare for. Don't hesitate to cut this recipe in half and serve it to six.

EXULTATION CRÊPE SUZETTE TORTE   [serves 12]

Need:

30 to 35 French pancakes made in a 9-inch skillet	Suzette Filling (Prepare this first!)
	Suzette Sauce

French pancakes:

12 eggs	1 cup melted butter
4 cups milk	additional butter for
3 cups flour	cooking the pancakes
½ teaspoon salt	

Beat the eggs, then add the flour and milk alternately to the beaten eggs. Add salt and melted butter and let the batter stand at least an hour. (This can be prepared the night before, covered, then left overnight in the refrigerator.)

Check the batter before using it to see that it is the consistency of heavy cream, then cook the pancakes. Heat a 9-inch skillet and add just a very little butter, then enough batter to make a very thin pancake. Continue to cook pancakes and as each one is cooked stack them on a heatproof round dish with a tablespoon of the Suzette Filling between each pancake. (See recipe below, which you have previously prepared.) If pancakes seem to be too thick add more milk to the batter.

Suzette Filling:

1½ cups sugar	2 tablespoons cornstarch dissolved in ¼ cup cold water
grated rind of one orange	
grated rind of one lemon	
2 cups orange juice	1 cup butter
juice of half a lemon	¼ cup Curaçao (or Cointreau or Grand Marnier)

Place the first six ingredients in a sauce pan and stir over heat until mixture comes to a boil. Reduce heat and simmer for 5 to 10 minutes. Stir in the butter and after it has melted, remove from heat and add the Curaçao. Set aside to cool.

Suzette Sauce:

grated rind of 1 orange	⅓ cup Grand Marnier
1 cup orange juice	(Cointreau or Curaçao
¾ cup sugar	can be used)
½ cup sweet butter	

Place first three ingredients in a sauce pan and stir until mixtures comes to a boil. Simmer for about 5 minutes. Add butter and stir until melted. Remove from heat and add the Grand Marnier.

To assemble: Each pancake should be cooked and spread with some of the Suzette Filling as directed above. They should be placed on a plate that can ultimately go into the oven—a heavy ovenproof dish of stoneware or some such thing is just right, or stainless steel, etc. You will end up with a somewhat tall cake-like-looking dessert. Cover this completely with foil and set aside until ready to heat and serve.

When almost ready to serve, place in a 350° oven, still covered with the foil, and heat until piping hot. (This will, of course, depend upon the temperature of the "torte" before putting it in the oven—anywhere from 20 minutes to an hour or more if it has been frozen and defrosted.)

Bring to the table with the Suzette Sauce in a separate bowl at the side. Cut in wedges and serve with a spoonful of the Suzette Sauce for each portion.

To prepare ahead of time: This can be prepared the day before and kept refrigerated overnight. Remove torte from refrigerator several hours before time to heat. Reheat Suzette Sauce before serving.

To freeze: One of the real glories of this dessert is that it freezes. Freeze the Suzette Sauce separately without the Grand Marnier, adding it before serving. Start defrosting the "torte" early in the morning of the day you are planning to serve it, then proceed with the heating as directed above.

Note: This "torte" can also be flambéed at the table. Pour a few ounces of heated Cognac over it (or easier, just use 151 proof Rum), ignite, let flames burn out, then serve.

CHOCOLATE-ORANGE FLAMING FOLLY [serves 4 to 6]

Dark, rich, hot fudge sauce
(recipe follows)
⅓ cup chopped toasted
almonds
1 generous tablespoon
grated orange rind

2 ounces 151 proof, Demerara
Rum (fool-proof for
flaming)
4 or 6 portions of vanilla ice
cream in individual bowls

Dark, rich, hot fudge sauce:

2 squares (2 ounces)
unsweetened chocolate
1 tablespoon butter

⅓ cup boiling water
1 cup sugar
2 tablespoons light corn syrup

later: 1 tablespoon butter
1 teaspoon vanilla

Melt chocolate and the 1 tablespoon butter over very low heat and stir. Add boiling water and blend, then stir in the sugar and syrup. Stir over low heat until mixture begins to boil, then cook over moderate heat without stirring for about 3 or 4 minutes. Remove from heat and add butter and vanilla.

To assemble: Place the hot fudge sauce in the blazer of a chafing dish and add the toasted almonds and grated orange rind. Bring this to the table and heat and stir the mixture before your guests, and when hot and bubbling, add the Rum and flame. Spoon sauce over the vanilla ice cream and serve.

To prepare ahead of time: The hot fudge sauce can be prepared a day or two ahead of time and kept refrigerated, just reheat before using.

To freeze: The vanilla ice cream should be dished up beforehand and kept ready in the freezer—if possible.

BAKED ALASKA WITH RASPBERRY SAUCE   [serves 8]

one 9-inch layer of genoise
   cake (recipe on p. 225
   makes 2 9-inch layers)
½ quart vanilla ice cream
½ quart strawberry ice cream

1 quart peach ice cream
6 egg whites
1 cup sugar
1 package frozen raspberries
¾ cup currant jelly

Raspberry sauce: Defrost raspberries, spin in a blender, then strain through a sieve. Melt currant jelly, then combine with the raspberry purée. Chill in refrigerator until time to serve.

Meringue: Beat egg whites until very stiff. Add sugar gradually and beat constantly until mixture is very stiff and glossy.

To assemble: Place the cake on a foil or heavy paper-covered wooden board. Place the ice cream in layers on the layer of cake, gradually shaping it into a mound and leaving 1 inch all along the outer edge of the cake free of ice cream. (If necessary, place this in the freezer for a while to harden thoroughly.)

Cover the cake and ice cream with the prepared meringue, being certain that all of the ice cream is completely covered and sealed with the meringue. Again, if possible, return to the freezer until ready to bake.

When ready to bake, place the "Alaska" in a preheated 450° oven and bake for about 3 to 5 minutes, just until meringue has browned. Serve at the table and pass the Raspberry Sauce in a separate bowl.

To prepare ahead of time: The cake can be baked the day before.

To freeze: This is the ultimate in simplicity if you use your freezer. Assemble the whole thing, meringue included, several days ahead of time, then shortly before serving place in the preheated oven as directed above. The "Alaska" should not be kept frozen much more than 3 or 4 days as the meringue begins to deteriorate after that time.

PREDICTABLE CHOCOLATE SOUFFLÉ [serves 4 or 5]

2 squares unsweetened
  chocolate (2 ounces)
¼ cup butter
¼ cup flour
¼ teaspoon salt
1 ¼ cups milk

5 egg yolks
1 teaspoon vanilla
1 tablespoon Brandy
⅔ cup sugar
6 egg whites

To accompany the soufflé:

sweetened whipped cream and
  hot fudge sauce or softened
  vanilla ice cream

Melt chocolate and set aside. Melt butter in a sauce pan and stir in the flour. Add milk and stir constantly until mixture comes to a boil. Stir in the salt. Beat the egg yolks lightly in a separate bowl with the vanilla and Brandy, then gradually beat in the hot cream sauce. Add the melted chocolate and beat again. (A wire whisk is particularly handy for this.) THE SOUFFLÉ CAN BE PREPARED AHEAD OF TIME UP TO THIS POINT, JUST COVER BOWL WITH A PLATE OR WITH PLASTIC WRAP AND SET ASIDE AT ROOM TEMPERATURE.

Before baking, beat egg whites until just barely stiff, then gradually beat in the sugar. Do not overbeat. Stir a large spoonful of the egg white mixture into the chocolate-egg yolk base and combine thoroughly (this is to soften it). Now fold the remaining egg white mixture into the chocolate mixture, using a gentle motion and as few strokes as possible. (Don't worry if some of the egg white still shows.)

Pour into a graesed 1 ½ quart casserole (or preferably a soufflé dish) which has a greased waxed paper collar tied around the outside of the top of the dish. Bake in a 375° oven for about 45 minutes. Serve at once with sweetened whipped cream and hot fudge sauce, or with softened vanilla ice cream.

To prepare ahead of time: The base for the soufflé can be prepared in the morning (as directed above), and the soufflé dish and its collar can also be prepared in the morning. Then all that is left to do is to beat the egg whites, fold them in, and bake.

Note: Always arrange to make the soufflé so that your guests are kept waiting some—not the soufflé waiting for the guests. During this waiting period you can bring in the dessert plates, the sauce and whipped cream, etc. The wait will only heighten the drama when you bring in this best of all possible desserts.

I often make two of these to serve 8 or 10 guests. This is better than trying to make one large one.

SOUFFLÉ GRAND MARNIER (OR KIRSCH)

[serves 4 or 5]

¼ cup butter	10 lady fingers soaked in
¼ cup flour	Grand Marnier (or Kirsch)
1 cup milk	4 egg yolks
⅓ cup Grand Marnier	⅓ cup sugar
(or Kirsch)	6 egg whites
¼ teaspoon salt	

To accompany the soufflé:
sliced strawberries or fresh raspberries or sliced peaches sweetened and marinated in either Grand Marnier or Kirsch

Place ladyfingers on a flat plate and soak them in some Grand Marnier (or Kirsch).

Melt butter in a saucepan and stir in the flour. Add milk and stir constantly until mixture comes to a boil. Add the Grand Marnier (or Kirsch) and the salt. Beat the egg yolks lightly in a separate bowl, then gradually beat in the hot cream sauce. THE SOUFFLÉ CAN BE PREPARED AHEAD OF TIME UP TO THIS POINT, JUST COVER BOWL WITH A PLATE OR WITH PLASTIC WRAP AND SET ASIDE AT ROOM TEMPERATURE.

Just before time to bake the soufflé, beat the egg whites until just barely stiff, then gradually beat in the sugar. Do not overbeat. Stir a large spoonful of the egg white mixture into the egg yolk base and combine thoroughly to soften the base. Now fold the remaining egg white mixture into the rest of it, using as few strokes as possible. Don't worry if some of the egg white still shows.

Pour half of this mixture into a greased 1½ quart soufflé dish (or casserole) which has a greased waxed paper collar tied around the outside of the top of the dish. Place the soaked ladyfingers on top of this. Next, cover with the remaining soufflé mixture. Bake in a 375° oven for 30 to 40 minutes. Serve at once with the fresh fruit marinated in one of the liqueurs as a sauce.

To prepare ahead of time: The base of the soufflé can be prepared ahead in the morning (as directed above), and the soufflé dish and its collar can also be prepared in the morning. Finish it by beating the egg whites and sugar and folding them in, and bake as directed in the recipe.

Note: Time your soufflé so that your guests are kept waiting rather than the soufflé.

CARAMEL AND BANANA SURPRISE SOUFFLÉ (MARGARET HALL'S)   [serves 4 to 5]

2 small bananas (or one large banana)
a special caramel (see recipe below)

Vanilla Soufflé (see recipe below)

Special caramel:

Simmer an unopened can of sweetened condensed milk in boiling water (can must be covered with water) for 2½ to 3 hours. Remove from water, cool slightly, open can and then use as directed.

Vanilla Soufflé:

¼ cup butter
¼ cup flour
¼ teaspoon salt
1⅓ cups milk
1 teaspoon vanilla

4 egg yolks
⅓ to ½ cup sugar
(depending upon taste)
6 egg whites

Melt butter, stir in flour, then gradually add milk and stir constantly until mixture comes to a boil. Beat egg yolks in a separate bowl with the salt and vanilla, then gradually beat in the hot cream sauce. THE SOUFFLÉ CAN BE PREPARED AHEAD OF TIME UP TO

234

THIS POINT, JUST COVER BOWL WITH A PLATE OR WITH PLASTIC WRAP AND SET ASIDE AT ROOM TEMPERATURE.

Shortly before baking the soufflé, beat the egg whites until just barely stiff, then gradually beat in the sugar. Do not overbeat. Stir a large spoonful of the egg white mixture into the egg yolk base, then fold in the rest, using as few strokes as possible. Don't worry if some of the egg white still shows.

Place the previously prepared caramel in the bottom of a greased 1½ quart soufflé dish (or casserole) which has a greased waxed paper collar tied around the outside rim of the dish. Place the sliced bananas on top of the caramel. Pour in the prepared vanilla soufflé and bake in a 375° oven for 30 to 40 minutes. Serve at once—be sure to give each guest some of the bananas and caramel at the bottom of the dish.

To prepare ahead of time: The caramel can be prepared several days ahead of time and kept refrigerated. The base of the soufflé can be prepared in the morning as directed in the recipe, then proceed with the egg whites as in the above directions.

A VERSION OF VALTESSE SOUFFLÉ   [serves 4 or 5]

3 tablespoons praline powder (see recipe below)	1 teaspoon vanilla
2 tablespoons flour	1 ounce melted semi-sweet chocolate
2 tablespoons butter	6 egg whites
1 cup milk	¼ cup sugar
¼ teaspoon salt	5 ladyfingers soaked in
¼ cup sugar	5 tablespoons Maraschino
3 egg yolks	

To accompany the soufflé:
whipped cream, sweetened, then flavored with Maraschino

Praline powder:

¾ cup sugar	¾ cup blanched almonds

Melt the sugar with the almonds in a heavy skillet over a moderate heat, stirring occasionally. When sugar has caramelized, turn out into a greased metal pan and let it cool. When hard, break into pieces, then whirl in the blender, doing about ⅓ of this amount at a time. Keep this powder in a tightly sealed jar in the refrigerator—it will keep for months this way.

To make the soufflé:
Melt butter, stir in flour. Add milk and stir constantly until mixture comes to a boil. Add the salt and the ¼ cup of sugar. Beat egg yolks in a separate bowl, then gradually beat in the hot cream sauce. Add the vanilla and the praline powder and divide this mixture into two bowls. Add the melted chocolate to one of them. THE SOUFFLÉ CAN BE PREPARED AHEAD OF TIME UP TO THIS POINT, JUST COVER THE BOWLS WITH PLASTIC WRAP AND SET ASIDE AT ROOM TEMPERATURE.

Shortly before baking the soufflé, beat the egg whites until barely stiff, then gradually beat in the remaining ¼ cup sugar. Fold half of this into the chocolate mixture and the other half into the vanilla mixture. Grease a 1 ½ quart soufflé dish and tie a greased waxed paper collar around the edge of the dish. Place the soaked ladyfingers in the bottom of the dish, then put some of the chocolate mixture in the center and the vanilla around it, then more chocolate in the center, then more vanilla around, gradually building it until completely filled. Bake at 375° for 30 to 40 minutes. Serve at once with the sweetened and Maraschino-flavored whipped cream as a sauce.

To prepare ahead of time: The vanilla and chocolate base of the soufflé can be prepared in the morning and left as directed in the above recipe. (The praline powder can be made weeks ahead of time.) The flavored whipped cream can also be prepared in the morning and kept refrigerated.

Note: If building a two-colored, two-flavored soufflé seems too complicated, just dispense with this procedure and make it all one flavor—either vanilla or chocolate. It is delicious, that way, too.

LEMON SOUFFLÉ WITH RASPBERRY SAUCE

[serves 4 or 5]

¼ cup butter
¼ cup flour
pinch of salt
1 cup milk
grated rind of one lemon

¼ cup lemon juice
4 egg yolks
½ cup sugar
6 egg whites

For the sauce:

1 package of just barely defrosted raspberries combined with 1½
cups softened vanilla ice cream

Melt the butter, stir in flour and salt. Add milk and stir constantly
until mixture comes to a boil. Beat in the lemon rind and lemon juice.
Beat egg yolks slightly in a separate bowl, then beat in the hot cream
sauce. THE SOUFFLÉ CAN BE PREPARED AHEAD OF
TIME UP TO THIS POINT, JUST COVER BOWL WITH A
PLATE OR WITH PLASTIC WRAP AND SET ASIDE AT
ROOM TEMPERATURE.

Shortly before baking the soufflé, beat the egg whites until just
barely stiff, then gradually beat in the sugar. Do not overbeat. Stir a
large spoonful of the egg whites into the lemon base, then fold in the
rest with as few strokes as possible. Don't worry if some of the egg
white still shows.

Pour into a greased 1½ quart soufflé dish (or casserole) which has
a greased waxed paper collar tied around the top edge of the dish.
Bake at 375° for about 35 minutes. Serve at once with the sauce.

To prepare ahead of time: The base for the soufflé can be prepared
in the morning as directed in the above recipe. You can also prepare
the soufflé dish and its collar. The raspberry-ice cream sauce can be
combined several hours ahead of time and kept in the refrigerator
until ready to serve.

PEGGY LECKY'S BAKED AND CHILLED
APRICOT SOUFFLÉ WITH CUSTARD SAUCE   [serves 6]

1 cup dried apricots	8 egg whites (1 cup)
1 cup water	½ cup sugar
½ cup sugar	

Boil apricots with the water until tender (covered). Purée them in a blender, then add the ½ cup sugar. Beat egg whites until almost stiff. Add remaining ½ cup sugar gradually and continue beating until stiff. Fold into the apricot mixture, pour into a large greased casserole (about 2 quart size), place in a pan of hot water and bake at 350° for approximately 40 minutes. Remove and chill. Serve cold with custard sauce.

Custard Sauce:

2 eggs or 4 egg yolks	2 cups scalded milk
⅓ cup sugar	1 teaspoon vanilla
⅛ teaspoon salt	

Beat eggs (or egg yolks), sugar and salt together. Add scalded milk gradually and stir. Place in top of a double boiler and stir constantly over medium heat until mixture thickens. Remove from heat and add the vanilla. Chill before serving.

To prepare ahead of time: Both the apricot soufflé and the custard sauce can be made the day before and kept refrigerated until time to serve.

Note: The apricot soufflé can be baked in individual casseroles—for about 25 minutes instead of the longer baking time.

CRÊPES WITH FRESH BING CHERRIES   [serves 6 to 8]

12 to 18 French pancakes (about 5 or 6 inches in diameter), see recipe on p. 242	1 cup sugar
	⅓ cup Kirsch
	2 tablespoons cornstarch
	¼ cup cold water
2 pounds fresh bing cherries, pitted (about 4 cups)	

Marinate the pitted cherries in the sugar and Kirsch for several days —1 week or 2 weeks are even better. (Keep them refrigerated.) Stir every few days.

Drain cherries but save the juice Dissolve the cornstarch in ¼ cup cold water. Bring dissolved cornstarch and cherry juice to a boil, stirring constantly, and cook until thickened and clear. Pour this over the cherries and stir, but do not cook the cherries. Cool.

Fill each of the pancakes with about 5 of the cherries and with some of the thickened sauce. Place the filled pancakes in a shallow casserole (or casseroles), and pour the remaining juice over all. Decorate tops of the pancakes with some of the cherries. Just before serving, place in a 350° oven until very hot, then serve 2 or 3 per guest on warm plates.

To prepare ahead of time: The pancakes can be cooked the day before and filled. Keep refrigerated overnight. Remove from refrigerator several hours before serving, then proceed with the heating as directed above.

To freeze: The pancakes can be frozen separately. (See directions on p. 241. The pancakes can also be frozen filled, but if using fresh cherries, they will lose some of their firm texture.

CRÊPES WITH APPLES, SUGAR AND RUM

[serves about 6]

12 French pancakes (about 7 or 8 inches in diameter), see recipe on p. 242
6 cooking apples, peeled, cored and sliced (medium size)
¼ cup butter

2 teaspoons lemon juice (if apples are not tart enough)
½ to 1 cup sugar (depending upon apples)
1½ teaspoons vanilla
melted butter
brown sugar
151 proof Rum

Sauté the sliced apples in the ¼ cup butter for a few minutes, add sugar to taste, cover and simmer only until tender. Don't overcook. Remove from heat and stir in the vanilla. Set aside until ready to fill the pancakes.

Place a generous tablespoon of the cooked apples on each pancake, roll up and place in a shallow casserole (or casseroles). Do not make more than one layer. Sprinkle each rolled pancake with some melted butter. Cover with foil. Heat in a 375° oven long enough to get them thoroughly hot. (This will depend upon how warm the pancakes and apples are when you begin.) Remove from oven, sprinkle top of each rolled pancake with brown sugar. Place under broiler only until sugar begins to caramelize. Watch! It can burn easily. Bring apple-filled pancakes to the table. Pour on some of the 151 proof Rum, flame, then serve.

To prepare ahead of time: These can be completely assembled with the apples and refrigerated until time to heat, either the day before or in the morning.

To freeze: The pancakes can be filled with the apples and frozen very successfully. Defrost, then proceed with the heating as in the above recipe.

CRÊPES WITH PRALINE-CREAM AND A
RASPBERRY-STRAWBERRY SAUCE [serves 6]

12 French pancakes (about 6 inches in diameter), see recipe on p. 242

2 or 3 cups fresh strawberries (about 2 baskets)
¼ cup Kirsch
¼ cup 151 proof Rum

For the Praline-cream filling:

3 egg yolks
⅓ cup sugar
2½ tablespoons cornstarch
pinch of salt
1 cup milk
2 tablespoons Kirsch

¾ cup whipping cream plus some sugar to sweeten
1 teaspoon vanilla
⅓ cup toasted filberts, measured then ground in a blender
⅓ cup diced toasted almonds

For the Raspberry-strawberry sauce:

1 10-ounce package frozen raspberries
1 10-ounce package frozen strawberries

¼ cup sugar
1 teaspoon cornstarch dissolved in 1 tablespoon cold water

240

Make the Praline-cream filling: Beat egg yolks with sugar and salt in the top of a double boiler, then beat in the cornstarch. Heat milk in a separate saucepan to boiling, then add to the egg yolks, beating while doing so. Place over boiling water and stir constantly until the mixture thickens. When very thick, remove from heat and cool quickly over ice, adding the Kirsch. Chill thoroughly.

Whip the cream and sweeten it. Flavor with vanilla. Fold the cream into the chilled custard, then fold in the nuts. Taste and add more sugar if needed. Chill.

Make the Raspberry-strawberry sauce: Defrost berries and purée them in a blender, then strain through a fine sieve. Add sugar and then heat to the boiling point. Quickly stir in the dissolved cornstarch, stir until mixture boils, then remove from heat. Set aside to be reheated before serving.

To serve: Fill each pancake with a generous tablespoon of the filling and roll up. Arrange rolls on a very large lightly buttered platter and cover with plastic wrap. When ready to serve bring platter to dining room. Place sauce in chafing dish and heat to simmering point. Add the strawberries to the sauce, stir for a few seconds, then add the Kirsch and the Rum and flame. Give each guest 2 crêpes, some of the sauce, and some of the strawberries.

To prepare ahead of time: The pancakes can be cooked the day before, stacked with melted butter in between them, wrapped in foil and kept refrigerated. Be sure they have reached room temperature before you try to fill and roll them. The filling and the sauce can both be prepared the day before and kept refrigerated overnight.

To freeze: The pancakes can be cooked and frozen. Freeze them in foil packages, about 6 or so to a package, with melted butter between each pancake.

Note: If the pancakes after refrigerating or defrosting seem to be too stiff to roll, place them in their foil package in a very low heat oven just until they become pliable.

CRÊPES SUZETTE CHEZ NOUS [serves about 6]

French pancakes:

3 eggs	4 tablespoons melted butter
1 tablespoon sugar	⅛ teaspoon salt
(optional)	additional butter for cooking
1 cup milk	pancakes
¾ cup flour	

Beat eggs with sugar and salt, add flour and milk alternately. Add melted butter. Let stand for 1 hour or longer. Batter should be the consistency of heavy cream. Add more milk if necessary.

Cook pancakes with a little additional butter in a small skillet (5 or 6 inches in diameter), stacking them after they have been cooked with melted butter in between; this keeps them moist. Pancakes can be cooled, wrapped in foil packages—about six to a package—and frozen at this point.

Suzette Sauce:

¾ cup sugar	3 tablespoons of Curaçao or
grated rind of one orange	Cointreau or Grand Marnier
grated rind of one lemon	2 tablespoons of Cognac or
1 tablespoon lemon juice	Brandy
1 cup orange juice	2 tablespoons of 151 proof Rum
½ cup sweet butter	(for insurance)

Combine rinds, sugar and juices and cook slowly, stirring until mixture comes to a boil. Cook slowly for about 3 minutes. Add butter and stir until it melts. Remove from the heat. Add the orange liqueur, Cognac or Brandy, and stir. (Save Rum for later.)

To serve: Place sauce in the chafing dish and bring to a simmer. Fold pancakes in half, then in half again and place in the simmering sauce. Add the 151 proof rum, flame it, spoon it while it is flaming over the pancakes, then serve.

To prepare ahead of time: The pancakes can be cooked the day before, stacked with melted butter in between and kept refrigerated until the following day. Reheat them wrapped in foil in a slow oven, then proceed with the above recipe.

To freeze: The sauce can be frozen, but do so without the addition of the liqueurs. The pancakes can be frozen, see recipe above. Reheat them after defrosting in a slow oven, wrapped in foil.

RUTH SCHIRESON'S APRICOT CRÊPES   [serves about 6]

For the crêpes:

1 cup flour	2 cups milk
1 tablespoon sugar	3 tablespoons melted butter
pinch of salt	2 tablespoons lemon juice
2 whole eggs	1 teaspoon finely grated
2 egg yolks	orange rind

For the filling:

8 ounces dried apricots	2 tablespoons Cointreau
⅓ cup apricot jam	

For the topping:

½ pint whipping cream,	sifted brown sugar
whipped	toasted slivered almonds

Combine ingredients for the crêpes, then make very thin crêpes in a 6- or 7-inch pan. (If a teflon pan is used, no additional butter is required.) Cook until lightly browned on the underside, then turn and cook for a minute or less. Stack on a flat plate.

Cook apricots in water to cover until soft and almost dry. Mash well, then combine with the jam and Cointreau. Cool to room temperature.

Spread about one tablespoon of filling on each crêpe, then roll and place close together in a heat-proof shallow serving dish, with edges of pancakes underneath. Heat in a 350° oven long enough to heat thoroughly. Remove from oven, spread with whipped cream and sprinkle lightly with brown sugar. (Sifting sugar through a small strainer helps distribute the sugar evenly.) Place under broiler and watch! Broil until top is bubbly. Sprinkle with slivered toasted almonds. Serve about three to each guest.

To prepare ahead of time: The apricot purée can be made days ahead of time and kept refrigerated. The pancakes can be cooked and filled early in the day, up to the point where the topping is added. Proceed with the heating before serving as directed.

To freeze: The pancakes can be frozen, with melted butter between each. Defrost completely, then fill. The apricot filling can be frozen too.

Note: Ruth Schireson suggests that Cointreau may be passed to your guests, and a little poured on each serving.

243

RASPBERRY ICE CREAM [serves about 6]

1 cup sweetened raspberry
purée (use frozen berries,
purée in blender, then
strain through a fine
sieve)

½ cup whipped cream
sugar to taste
1 teaspoon vanilla

For the pastry cream:

3 egg yolks
⅓ cup sugar
2 tablespoons cornstarch

pinch of salt
1 cup milk
1 or 2 tablespoons Kirsch

Make the pastry cream: Beat the egg yolks with the sugar in the top of a double boiler. Add the salt and cornstarch and beat again. Heat milk in a separate saucepan to boiling, then add it to the egg yolk mixture, beating all the while. Place all over boiling water and cook, stirring constantly, until very thick. Remove from heat and cool quickly over ice, stirring occasionally. Add the Kirsch and chill.

Whip the cream, sweeten to taste and add the vanilla. Sweeten the raspberry purée to taste. Fold these two into the chilled custard. Spoon into individual dessert dishes or small crocks, cover tightly with plastic wrap and with foil and freeze until ready to serve.

To prepare ahead of time: Yes, of course, if you can keep it in a freezer.

To freeze: The only way.

LEMON ICE CREAM [serves about 6]

1 cup milk
1 cup cream
1 cup sugar

grated rind of 2 lemons
½ cup lemon juice

Combine milk, cream and sugar and heat over low heat, stirring until sugar is dissolved. Cool slightly, then combine with the lemon rind and lemon juice. Freeze to a mush. Whip with an electric beater, then freeze again. Cover tightly and store until ready to serve.

To prepare ahead of time: This should be done ahead of time.

To freeze: Yes.

ICIEST LEMON ICE

2 cups sugar	1 cup lemon juice
4 cups water	1 tablespoon grated lemon rind

Cook water and sugar together for about 5 minutes. Cool. After cooling, stir in the lemon juice and grated lemon rind. Freeze to a mush. Beat with an electric beater, then freeze again. Cover tightly and serve when needed.

To prepare ahead of time: Yes, by all means.

To freeze: Yes.

Note: This is delicious served on fresh fruit salad instead of the more usual scoop of cottage cheese.

MAGICAL MEXICAN BANANA SHERBET

1 ½ cups crushed ripe bananas	⅓ cup orange juice
(do not mash too much)	⅓ cup lemon juice
½ cup sugar	1 large can evaporated milk
⅔ cup light corn syrup	(the 2 cup size)

Combine first 5 ingredients and marinate until sugar has dissolved. Add milk. Freeze. Cover and store until needed.

To prepare ahead of time: Yes.

To freeze: Yes.

Note: This is a marvelous and practical way to use up those bananas which are getting a little too ripe. Most of the ingredients you would probably always have on hand.

FIESTA CRANBERRY SHERBET

4 cups fresh cranberries	1 cup orange juice
3 cups water	⅓ cup lemon juice
2 ¼ cups sugar	

Cook cranberries in the water until soft. Press through a sieve or food mill and combine with the sugar. Heat and stir until the sugar dissolves. Remove from heat and stir in the juices. Cool thoroughly. Freeze until almost firm, then whip with an electric beater and return to freezer. Cover tightly and store until ready to serve.

To prepare ahead of time: Yes.

To freeze: The perfect way to prepare your holiday dessert weeks ahead of time and a pleasant change from the more usual "pie."

BURNT ALMOND MOUSSE

⅔ cup blanched almonds	½ cup sugar
3 egg yolks, slightly beaten	¼ cup water
½ cup real maple syrup	½ teaspoon vanilla
pinch of salt	2 cups whipping cream

Toast almonds slowly in a 300° oven. Remove from oven and cool. Put through a grinder or whirl in the blender.

Melt the ½ cup sugar in a large skillet over moderate heat. When melted and caramel color, add the ¼ cup water and stir over low heat until caramel has dissolved. Combine this with the egg yolks, maple syrup and salt and cook over low heat, stirring constantly until thickened somewhat. Cool.

Whip cream, add vanilla, and add egg yolk mixture. Fold in the ground almonds. Freeze in small dessert dishes or in individual molds. If frozen in molds, unmold before serving.

To prepare ahead of time: Yes.

To freeze: Yes.

FANCIED FRESH FIGS AND PEACHES WITH
ICE CREAM AND A RUM-CUSTARD SAUCE [serves 12]

2 dozen very small fresh figs,
   peeled (or half that number if they are large)
12 fresh peach halves (or
   canned if you are
   desperate)
⅔ cup sugar

1 cup water
½ teaspoon vanilla
1 teaspoon grated orange rind
1 teapsoon grated lemon rind
¼ cup heavy rum
1 quart vanilla ice cream
½ quart coffee ice cream

For the rum-custard sauce:

¼ cup sugar
1½ cups milk
1 tablespoon cornstarch
½ cup juices from the marinade
   for the figs

4 egg yolks
pinch of salt
2 teaspoons rum

Cut 1 dozen of the figs in half (or 6 large ones in quarters) and leave the other dozen whole (or leave the other 6 large ones cut in half). Combine the sugar, water, vanilla, and the grated rinds in a saucepan and stir over low heat until it boils. Reduce heat and simmer for 3 or 4 minutes. Add the ¼ cup rum. Pour this over the figs and let them marinate in this syrup in the refrigerator for 1 to 2 hours, then prepare the rum-custard sauce.

Rum-custard sauce: Dissolve the cornstarch in ¼ cup of the cold milk. Add this to the egg yolks and beat lightly. Heat the remaining 1¼ cups milk, sugar and salt in the top of a double boiler and when warm, pour over the egg yolks and beat. Return all to double boiler. Add the ½ cup of the fig marinade and cook over boiling water until it thickens. Remove from heat and cool. Add rum and chill.

To assemble: Place 1 scoop of vanilla ice cream and ½ scoop of coffee ice cream in each desert bowl or large dessert glass. Place half a fig (or if the large ones, ¼ a fig) and some of the marinade over the ice cream. Add half a peach. Pour a good spoonful of the Rum-custard sauce over all and top this with a whole fig (or half a fig if the large ones) as decoration.

To prepare ahead of time: The rum-custard sauce and the figs in their marinade can be done the day before.

To freeze: The ice cream can be dished up the day before and left in the individual bowls in the freezer until shortly before serving.

CHOCOLATE ICE CREAM TRUFFLES   [serves about 6]

1 quart chocolate ice cream   ½ pound dark sweet chocolate
⅛ pound candied cherries

Chop the chocolate coarsely; it should be in pieces about the size of very small peas.

Form the ice cream into 6 balls, each with two of the candied cherries in the center. Freeze for a short time.

Roll the ice cream balls in the coarsely chopped dark chocolate and freeze until ready to use.

To prepare ahead of time: Yes, of course.

To freeze: Yes, these freeze, but do keep them wrapped in plastic wrap if you are planning to leave them there more than a day.

Note: Chocolate addicts particularly appreciate this dessert.

MERITORIOUS MELANGE OF FRUIT
ON STRAWBERRY ICE CREAM

fresh seedless grapes   sliced bananas
sliced fresh peaches   fresh orange juice
pitted bing cherries,   some Kirsch
    sweetened and   scoops of strawberry
    soaked in Brandy   ice cream

Combine all of the fruit with the orange juice and the Kirsch and the Brandy and marinate for a few hours. If you are going to marinate the fruit longer than that, do not add the bananas until shortly before serving.

Place scoops of the strawberry ice cream in attractive bowls or glasses and spoon on the melange.

To prepare ahead of time: The fruit can be marinated the day before, with the exception of the bananas. Add those shortly before serving.

To freeze: To save time, scoop ice cream into dessert dishes and leave in the freezer until time to serve.

CHOCOLATE CUPS FILLED WITH LIME OR RASPBERRY ICE

½ pound dark sweet
    chocolate
3 tablespoons butter
paper baking cups and
    muffin pans

lime ice or raspberry ice
thin, long mint sticks
    (the crisp colored kind)

Heat chocolate and butter together over warm water. Remove from heat and stir until blended. Cool for a few minutes.

Place paper baking cups inside metal muffin pans, the standard size. With a teaspoon, swirl chocolate mixture around the sides and bottoms of the cups, covering them completely with a thin layer of chocolate. Place pans in the refrigerator and chill. Later peel off paper and return chocolate cups to refrigerator until ready to use.

To serve: Fill chocolate cups with the ice and then place a mint stick in each one. This should be done with an eye to color.

To prepare ahead of time: The chocolate cups can be made the day before and kept refrigerated.

To freeze: The chocolate cups can be frozen either filled or unfilled. Keep them covered with plastic wrap so that they do not absorb freezer odors and so that crystals do not form.

AMBER COFFEE PECAN FROZEN FANTASY (ALICE PARRISH'S)   [serves 8 to 10]

1 quart coffee ice cream
Amber sauce (recipe follows)

1 cup pecans
2 tablespoons butter

Amber sauce:

1 cup brown sugar (packed
    for measurement)
½ cup light corn syrup

½ cup heavy cream
¼ cup butter
½ teaspoon vanilla

Combine all of the ingredients except the vanilla and cook over low heat, stirring constantly, for about 5 minutes. Remove from heat and add the vanilla. Cool.

To prepare: Sauté the pecans in the butter until lightly browned. Remove from heat and cool.

Place a few pecans in the bottom of small individual dessert dishes, or in demitasse cups, then add a spoonful or so of the sauce. Next add a scoop of the coffee ice cream, then top with a spoonful of sauce and then a few more pecans. Cover with foil or plastic wrap and keep in freezer until ready to serve.

To prepare ahead of time: The sauce can be prepared the day before.

To freeze: Yes!

Note: This is a perfect from the freezer to the table dessert.

RUM WHIMSY   [serves 6]

1 quart of vanilla ice cream	12 ladyfingers
2 bananas	1 box strawberries
¾ cup shredded coconut	

For the rum syrup:

½ cup sugar	juice of half a lemon
¼ cup water	½ cup Jamaican rum

Make the rum syrup: Cook sugar, water and lemon juice together until sugar is dissolved, then add the rum. Cool.

Line large individual dessert glasses with a layer of vanilla ice cream. Add a layer of sliced bananas. Dip ladyfingers in the prepared rum syrup, then add 2 each to the top of the bananas. Sprinkle next with coconut. Add more vanilla ice cream, then more coconut. Place in deep freeze and keep frozen until 5 or 10 minutes before serving. Remove from freezer, then place a ring of strawberries on top and serve.

To prepare ahead of time: If you have no freezer, prepare the rum syrup the day before and chill overnight, then assemble the desserts and serve.

To freeze: These are to be frozen ahead of time with the exception of the strawberries.

GLORIA NIMMER'S FRUITS AUX MACARONS

[serves 12]

4 packages almond macaroons
(13 ounces each)
1 can of apricots (1 lb.,
13 ounces)
1 can of peaches (1 lb.,
13 ounces)
1 can of pears (1 lb.,
13 ounces)

1 can of plums (1 lb.,
13 ounces)
1 can of pitted bing cherries
(1 lb., 13 ounces)
½ cup Sherry (sweet) or
more if desired
whipped cream (optional)

Roll 2 of the packages of the macaroons into fine crumbs. Spread over bottom and partially up the sides of a shallow, lightly buttered baking dish suitable for serving. (Gloria uses a round dish about 11 inches in diameter and about 1½ inches deep.)

Drain all of the fruit very thoroughly. Arrange the apricots, peaches, pears and plums in the lined dish. Crumble the other 2 packages of macaroons very coarsely—leaving some largish pieces—generously over the fruit. Then arrange the cherries on top of this. Sprinkle the Sherry over the top.

Bake at 350° for about 45 minutes, or until well heated and browned.

Serve hot with icy cold whipped cream.

To prepare ahead of time: This can be prepared, covered, and refrigerated overnight (up to 1 or 2 days). Bake it the following day.

To freeze: This can be frozen either before or after baking, however, Gloria believes it best unfrozen.

Note: This is absolutely glorious served as a kind of special fruit dish with meat or poultry! As a matter of fact, that is the way we first encountered it at the Nimmers. It is then, of course, served without the whipped cream.

WHOLE FRESH PEACHES WITH KIRSCH SAUCE

[serves 8]

8 large perfect fresh peaches
1½ cups sugar
3 cups water
1 teaspoon vanilla
lemon rind of a whole lemon,
    removed with a potato
    peeler

1 teaspoon lemon juice
piñon nuts or chopped pistachios
    for garnishing

For the Kirsch sauce:

3 egg yolks
1 cup powdered sugar
¼ cup Kirsch

1 cup whipping cream,
    whipped

Prepare a syrup of the water, 1½ cups sugar, lemon rind, lemon juice, and vanilla by bringing these ingredients to a boil. Boil for several minutes, then cover and simmer for 5 to 10 minutes. Place the peaches with their skins still on in the syrup, cover and simmer slowly for about 10 minutes or less. Remove from heat, cool peaches in syrup. Remove skins of the peaches, then return peaches to the syrup and chill.

Prepare the Kirsch sauce: Beat egg yolks until they are thick, then gradually beat in the powdered sugar and the Kirsch. Beat until very thick. Fold in the whipped cream and chill.

To serve: Place a whole peach on each individual dessert plate, or in large dessert bowls, and pour some of the Kirsch sauce over each peach. Sprinkle the top of each peach either with the piñon nuts or with some chopped pistachios.

To prepare ahead of time: Peaches can be poached the day before and kept in their syrup in the refrigerator. The Kirsch sauce can be made the day before and kept in the refrigerator overnight—be sure to stir it before serving.

CHARLESTON AMBROSIA

[serves 12 to 18]

2 very fresh, very ripe
   pineapples
6 large navel oranges
1 cup orange juice
sugar

1 cup (or more) of sweetened
   grated coconut
Curaçao, Cointreau or
   Grand Marnier

Peel and then dice or shred the pineapples. Peel the oranges and then section them, removing all of the white membrane. Place pineapple and orange pieces in a large bowl and add the orange juice and enough sugar to sweeten to taste. Add some orange liqueur, cover and marinate in the refrigerator for several hours. Shortly before serving sprinkle the coconut over the fruit.

To prepare ahead of time: This can be done the day before and kept covered overnight in the refrigerator.

Note: Sliced bananas can be added to this delicious and refreshing dessert, however, they should not be added until shortly before serving, that is, an hour or so before.

RASPBERRIES, CHOCOLATE AND CREAM [serves 6 to 8]

4 cups fresh raspberries,
   sweetened to taste
2 cups whipping cream
sugar

1 teaspoon vanilla
½ cup dark sweet chocolate
   shavings (can do this
   with a potato peeler)

Sweeten raspberries to taste. Whip the cream and add a little sugar and the vanilla. Set aside a little of the whipped cream for topping. Set aside a little of the chocolate shavings for later decoration. (If you like more chocolate, just shave a little more with the potato peeler.)

Fold remaining whipped cream into the sweetened raspberries and add the chocolate. Place this mixture in individual dessert dishes. Decorate with the reserved whipped cream and chocolate shavings. Chill until ready to serve.

To prepare ahead of time: This can be done in the morning, covered and refrigerated until time to serve.

ORANGES GRENADINE [serves 8]

8 oranges
3 cups sugar
3 cups water
½ lemon

2 tablespoons grenadine
¼ cup Curaçao or Cointreau
or Grand Marnier

Coarsely grate the peel from 4 of the oranges. Combine this grated peel with the 3 cups of sugar, 3 cups of water, the juice and skin of the half a lemon and the grenadine syrup. Bring slowly to a boil, stirring until mixture boils. Cook, uncovered, over high heat for 30 to 40 minutes.

Peel all of the oranges, removing all of the white membrane but leaving the oranges whole. Place them in a large bowl and pour the prepared orange syrup over them while the syrup is boiling hot. Discard the lemon. Stir in the orange liqueur, cover and refrigerate all day or overnight. (Turn and stir the oranges occasionally, or weight them down into the syrup with a plate.) Serve very cold.

To prepare ahead of time: These are best prepared the day before.

PARTHIAN PRUNES WITH CREAM AND CHOCOLATE
[serves about 8]

18 very large dried prunes
(more or less)
1 cup almond paste (the
canned is very good)

1 cup whipping cream, whipped
4 ounces dark sweet chocolate,
grated
½ cup granulated sugar

Soak the prunes in water to cover for about 2 or 3 days. Do not cook them. Remove pits and replace with a piece of the almond paste.

Place 2 or 3 of the stuffed prunes on each small dessert dish. Chill them. Top each prune with some of the whipped cream. Combine the grated chocolate with the sugar. Sprinkle a teaspoonful of this chocolate-sugar mixture over each serving of whipped cream.

To prepare ahead of time: The prunes can be stuffed the day before and kept refrigerated. Do not add the whipped cream and chocolate topping until several hours before serving.

STRAWBERRIES HURRAH [serves 10 to 12]

3 boxes fresh
  strawberries
¾ cup orange juice
scant ½ cup sugar
¼ cup orange liqueur
  (Curaçao or Cointreau or
  Grand Marnier)
2 packages (10-ounce size)
  frozen raspberries

2 cups whipping cream
1 teaspoon gelatin soaked in
  2 tablespoons cold water
16 almond macaroons,
  crumbled
10 or 12 large strawberries,
  for decoration

Clean the strawberries, then place in a bowl and cover with the orange juice and the scant ½ cup sugar. Add the orange liqueur. Cover and chill.

Puré the raspberries in a blender, then strain through a sieve. Whip the cream. Melt the soaked gelatin over simmering water and when melted, whip it into the cream—that is, add it all at once to the cream, beating all the while. Combine half of the cream with the raspberry purée and reserve the other half for decorating.

To assemble: Arrange this dessert either in individual glass bowls or large glasses. First place a layer of strawberries and juice in the bottom. Next, sprinkle with the crumbled macaroons, then spoon on the raspberry-cream mixture. Decorate the top of each with some of the reserved whipped cream and with the large strawberries.

To prepare ahead of time: This can be done in the morning, covered and refrigerated until time to serve.

CHOCOLATE POTS DE CRÈME [serves 6 to 8]

2 cups heavy cream
¼ cup sugar
6 egg yolks

8 ounces dark sweet chocolate
1 teaspoon vanilla

Heat cream and sugar over very low heat (or use a double boiler) and stir to dissolve sugar. Melt chocolate over hot water, stirring while it melts, then remove from heat. Combine cream and melted chocolate.

Beat egg yolks in a bowl and gradually pour in the hot mixture, beating all the while. Return all to the top of a double boiler and cook, stirring constantly, over hot simmering water until mixture thickens (can take from 10 to 20 minutes). Remove from heat and add vanilla. Pour into pots de crème or into demitasse cups or into small custard dishes. Chill thoroughly.

To prepare ahead of time: This can be prepared the day before and kept refrigerated until time to serve.

Note: This is a very rich and "chocolaty" crème. If a less potent chocolate flavor is desired, reduce the amount of chocolate by 2 or 3 ounces; we like it with the 8.

CRÈME RENVERSÉE   [serves 5 or 6]

¾ cup sugar	⅓ cup sugar
5 tablespoons water	1 cup milk
2 whole eggs	1 cup cream
2 egg yolks	1 teaspoon vanilla

Make the caramel: Heat the ¾ cup of sugar in a heavy skillet and cook over low heat, stirring constantly, until sugar melts and turns a caramel color, a golden brown. Remove from heat and add the water, then return to low heat and continue stirring until the syrup simmers and the whole thing is dissolved. Pour this caramel into 5 or 6 small baking molds or cups or French baking crocks. Turn the molds or crocks so that the sides as well as the bottoms get a coating of the caramel.

Make the custard: Beat the whole eggs and egg yolks together. Heat the milk, sugar and cream together and stir to dissolve the sugar. Add this to the eggs and stir, then add the vanilla.

Pour the custard into the containers which have been caramelized. Place these in a shallow baking pan in which there is about ½ inch of hot water. Bake at 325° for about 40 to 60 minutes. (Custard is done when knife inserted in center comes out clean.) Chill for half a day, or preferably overnight. Turn upside down to serve by running a knife around the sides to loosen the custard.

To prepare ahead of time: By all means, do make these the day before you plan to serve them.

Note: When these are not turned upside down they are known as crème caramel. Delicious either right side up or upside down—probably my favorite dessert!

CHEESE CAKE RICH AND DEVASTATING

[serves about 16 to 20]

Crust:

1½ cups graham cracker crumbs	6 tablespoons melted butter
¼ cup sugar	¾ teaspoon cinnamon

Mix crumbs, sugar and cinnamon together. Pour melted butter over and mix thoroughly. Press this mixture on the bottom and sides of a 10-inch spring form pan, reserving a small spoonful of the crumbs for a later topping.

Cheese Filling:

2 pounds cream cheese	1½ tablespoons lemon juice
⅛ teaspoon salt	2 cups sour cream
1 cup sugar	¼ cup sugar
4 eggs	1 teaspoon vanilla

Cream the cheese until fluffy, then add the 1 cup of sugar and gradually add the eggs and beat thoroughly. Add lemon juice and salt. Spoon mixture into crust. Bake at 350° for about 40 minutes. Blend sour cream, sugar and vanilla. Spread over the partially baked cake, sprinkle with the reserved crumbs and bake at 475° for an additional 10 minutes. Remove and cool on a cake rack, then chill for several hours. Remove from refrigerator about an hour before serving and remove the sides of the spring form pan.

To prepare ahead of time: This can be prepared the day before.

To freeze: Yes, this can be frozen. Be sure to give it enough time to defrost thoroughly.

Note: This is attractive served on a large platter, garnished with small bunches of grapes.

CHEESE CAKE LIGHT AND DELICATE [serves 12 to 16]

Crust:

> 1½ cups zweibach crumbs   ⅓ cup sugar
> ⅓ cup melted butter

Mix together. Press on bottom and sides of a 10-inch spring form pan. Chill.

Filling:

> 1½ pounds cream cheese   2 to 2½ tablespoons lemon juice
> ½ teaspoon salt   6 egg yolks
> ½ cup sugar   1 cup sour cream
> ¼ cup sifted flour   6 egg whites
> 1½ teaspoons vanilla   ¾ cup sugar

Combine the cream cheese, salt and the ½ cup sugar and cream thoroughly. Add the lemon juice, vanilla, flour and egg yolks and beat again very thoroughly. Stir in the sour cream. Beat the egg whites until barely stiff, then gradually beat in the remaining ¾ cup sugar and beat until stiff. Fold into the cheese mixture.

Pour into chilled crust and bake at 325° for about 1¼ to 1½ hours. Turn off oven and leave cake for another hour. Remove to a cake rack until completely cooled, then chill. But do remove cheese cake from refrigerator about an hour before serving. It is best when not too cold.

To prepare ahead of time: This can be baked the day before and kept refrigerated overnight.

To freeze: Yes, this can be frozen. Be sure to give it ample time to defrost.

CHOCOLATE LOVERS' CHOCOLATE ROLL
WITH CHOCOLATE RUM SAUCE [serves 8 to 10]

5 eggs, separated
1 cup powdered sugar
¼ cup granulated sugar
4 tablespoons cocoa

2 tablespoons flour
1 quart ice cream, either coffee,
   vanilla, or burnt-almond

Grease a shallow baking pan (about 11" by 17") and line it with waxed paper. Then grease the waxed paper.

Sift sugars, cocoa and flour together. Beat egg yolks until very light and very thick, then gradually add the sugar-cocoa mixture and beat again until all is smooth and thick. Beat egg whites until stiff but not dry. Fold them into the egg yolk mixture. Pour into the prepared pan and bake at 350° for about 15 or 20 minutes. Do not overbake.

Turn cake out onto a damp towel. Remove waxed paper and cut off the crisp edges. Lift towel to help cake form a roll. Let the roll cool, then place it on some waxed paper which has first been sprinkled with powdered sugar. Leave it rolled up until time to fill.

Chocolate rum sauce:

¾ pound dark sweet
   chocolate
½ cup strong coffee

3 tablespoons butter
2 or 3 tablespoons rum

Melt chocolate in the coffee over very low heat. Add butter and rum and stir until smooth. Serve either hot or cold.

To serve: Carefully open up the chocolate roll. Cover with a layer of the ice cream about 1 inch thick. Roll up and if you have a freezer, place there for a short time. Cut in diagonal slices about ¾ inch thick and serve with the chocolate rum sauce.

To prepare ahead of time: It is best to do this the day you plan to serve it, unless you have a freezer.

To freeze: This can be baked, filled, sliced and frozen. Keep it well covered in the freezer. (Or you can slice it just before serving.)

Note: Real chocolate lovers occasionally even want the ice cream filling, chocolate!

CHOCOLATE MOUSSE WITH TOASTED ALMONDS AND WHIPPED CREAM [serves 8]

5 tablespoons cold water
8 ounces dark sweet chocolate
5 egg yolks
5 egg whites

1 tablespoon dark rum
toasted blanched almonds
whipping cream, whipped and
　sweetened

Melt chocolate in the top of a double boiler with the cold water, stirring while it melts. Cool slightly. Beat egg yolks until very light in color and very thick. Gradually beat in the melted chocolate. Beat in the rum. Beat egg whites until stiff and fold them into the egg yolk mixture. Pour into small cups or dishes. Place the toasted almonds on top of each mousse in a pretty pattern and chill for 4 hours or overnight. Before serving, garnish each mousse with some of the sweetened whipped cream.

To prepare ahead of time: This can be prepared the day before.

APHRODITE'S APPLES [serves about 6]

6 cups peeled, sliced
　green apples
1 ¼ cups brown sugar
　(packed)
⅓ cup butter
⅛ teaspoon salt

½ teaspoon cinnamon
1 cup sifted flour
1 cup pecan halves
whipped cream or vanilla
　ice cream

Place sliced apples in an attractive shallow casserole. Cover with half of the sugar. Combine remaining sugar, butter, salt, cinnamon and flour and mix thoroughly; use hands or a pastry blender. Pat this mixture on top of the apples, covering them completely. Bake for about 35 minutes in a 350° oven. Now, cover the top of the casserole with the pecan halves, pressing them down very well. Return to oven and bake an additional 20 to 25 minutes.

Serve hot with whipped cream or with vanilla ice cream.

To prepare ahead of time: This can be baked the day before and reheated before serving. It is also very good served cold.

To freeze: Yes, this freezes. Defrost, then reheat before serving.

MARGARET VIDALES' MAGIC MANGO DESSERT

[serves 5 or 6]

1 1-pound can of sliced
   mangoes, drained
1 15-ounce can of sweetened
   condensed milk
juice of one lemon

fresh fruit, sliced and
   marinated in a little
   orange juice
piñon nuts

Place the drained mangoes, sweetened condensed milk and lemon juice in a blender and whirl until smooth. Place this mixture in 5 or 6 small dessert dishes or cups. Chill for several hours.

Before serving top with the fresh fruit and a teaspoon or so of orange juice. (Use something like sliced fresh peaches or fresh strawberries—or even fresh orange segments which have had all of the white skin and pulp removed.) Garnish with a few of the piñons.

To prepare ahead of time: This can be prepared the day before and kept refrigerated.

Note: This is not only very simple to prepare but it is unbelievably delectable!

A HOT OR COLD LEMON LYRIC

[serves about 6]

1 cup sugar
4 tablespoons flour
⅛ teaspoon salt
2 tablespoons melted butter
5 tablespoons lemon juice

grated rind of 1 lemon
3 egg yolks, well beaten
½ cup milk
3 egg whites

Mix together thoroughly: the sugar, flour, salt, butter, lemon juice, lemon rind, egg yolks, and milk. Beat egg whites until stiff but not dry. Fold them into the egg yolk mixture. Pour into a greased 1 quart baking casserole. Place casserole in a pan of hot water and bake at 300° or 325° for about 45 minutes or longer, or when firm to the touch and browned on top.

To prepare ahead of time: Since this is good either hot or cold, this can be done the day before; in that case, serve it cold.

Note: The top of this dessert will be like sponge cake and the bottom like a lemon custard.

261

FOAM OF THE SEA MERMAID TORTE [serves about 10]

lady fingers, about 1 dozen	3 boxes of fresh strawberries,
7 egg whites	lightly sugared
pinch of salt	2 cups whipping cream, whipped
2 ¼ cups sugar	and flavored with vanilla
2 teaspoons vanilla	and a little sugar
1 teaspoon vinegar	

Line bottom and sides of a lightly greased 10-inch spring form pan with split ladyfingers, crust side to the outside.

Beat egg whites with salt until just stiff. Gradually beat in about 1 ½ cups of the sugar, folding in the rest. (The beating is most easily done with an electric mixer.) Beat in the vanilla and vinegar. Spoon this all into the lined pan and bake at 275° for about 1 hour. Turn off oven and leave the torte in for another 10 or 15 minutes. Remove from oven and cool, then remove the spring form.

Serve the mermaid torte with the strawberries and whipped cream.

To prepare ahead of time: The torte can be baked the day before. Leave at room temperature covered with waxed paper. Freshen the torte in the oven (275°) for about 10 or 15 minutes the day you are planning to serve it.

To freeze: Only freeze the leftovers for the family. It is still very good, but not a preferred procedure for a party.

Note: This is equally good served with sliced sweetened peaches or with fresh raspberries—or when fresh fruit is difficult to come by, try it with diced canned pineapple and sliced bananas.

The ladyfingers can be eliminated if desired. Just grease the spring form pan and dust it lightly with flour.

HAPPY WINTER DAY TORTE [serves 8 to 10]

¼ cup flour
1 teaspoon baking powder
½ teaspoon salt
1 cup sugar
3 eggs, well beaten
1 cup chopped walnuts
1 cup chopped dates
3 oranges, segmented or sliced

3 large bananas, sliced
½ cup sugar
2 tablespoons Grand Marnier
1 cup whipping cream, whipped
1 cup drained and pitted bing
   cherries (the canned ones
   are fine)

Combine the flour, baking powder, salt and the 1 cup of sugar and mix thoroughly. Beat the eggs, then add the dry ingredients. Stir in the dates and walnuts. Pour into a greased and floured 8-inch square pan and bake at 275° for about 1 hour. Cool. Pull the cake into pieces with your fingers and place these pieces in a large bowl.

Combine the oranges, bananas, ½ cup sugar and the Grand Marnier and chill thoroughly. (This can be done while the cake is baking.) Whip the cream.

To serve: Fold the marinated fruit into the cake pieces—do so, oh so gently! Pile this mixture on the center of an attractive platter. Place the whipped cream on top of this, but leave an inch or two showing around the edges. Place the pitted cherries in the whipped cream, pressing them only enough to stay in place, but still visible.

To prepare ahead of time: The cake can be baked the day before. The dessert should be assembled not more than an hour or so before serving. (It is good the next day too, but different.)

To freeze: This can be frozen, BUT, it is something completely different—more like a frozen pudding.

Index